Accounting Standards in Depth
Volume 2:
Solutions

4th edition

R J Kirk

The Chartered Institute of Management Accountants
26 Chapter Street
London SW1P 4NP

Copyright © CIMA 1994–2002

First published in 1994, revised 1995, 1998 and 2002 by:

The Chartered Institute of Management Accountants

ISBN 1 85971 539 7

Contents

The Author

Robert Kirk BSc (Econ) FCA CPA qualified as a chartered accountant in 1976. He trained in Belfast with Price Waterhouse & Co., and subsequently spent two years in industry in a subsidiary of Shell (UK) and four further years in practice. In 1980 he was appointed a director of a private teaching college in Dublin where he specialised in the teaching of professional accounting subjects. He later moved into the university sector, and is currently Professor of Financial Reporting in the School of Accounting at the University of Ulster.

He has been lecturing on the CIMA Mastercourses presentations *Recent Accounting Standards* and *Accounting Standards in Depth* since 1985. He has also presented continuing professional education courses for the Institute of Chartered Accountants in Ireland over the same period.

His publications to date, in addition to numerous professional journal articles, include two books on company law in Northern Ireland, co-authorship with University College Dublin of the first Survey of Irish Published Accounts, a joint publication with Coopers & Lybrand on the legislation enacting the 7th European Directive into UK legislation and two Financial Reporting publications for the CIMA Study Packs.

Introduction

This text contains solutions to the examination questions included in the companion text, *Accounting Standards in Depth*. The questions therein have been carefully selected from the major accounting bodies – CIMA, ACCA, ICAEW, ICAI and CPAI.

The questions in that book are reproduced as they were originally set in the professional examination. The solutions included here, however, are based on the most recent legislation and accounting standards which may not have been in existence at the time of devising of the question.

The intention of *Accounting Standards in Depth* is that the reader will be tested on numerical application, on an understanding of the underlying theory and on presentation of financial statements under the current regulatory framework. The questions have also been carefully chosen to test the reader's ability to write good practical reports, perform calculations and present both extracts and full sets of financial statements.

The Regulatory Framework and the Standard-setting Process

Solution 1 – Consensus standards

(a) Analyse and compare Gaaps as applied in the UK

At present the only 'officially recognised' generally accepted accounting principles (Gaaps) in the UK are those contained within the Companies Act 1985, Schedule 1. They are derived from the principles in the EC 4th Directive (1978).

The five principles enunciated are similar to SSAP 2:

(1) The going concern concept.
(2) The consistency concept, i.e. from one year to the next.
(3) The prudence concept, i.e. the amount of any item shall be determined on a prudent basis and in particular (a) only profits realised at the balance sheet date shall be included in the profit and loss account, and (b) all liabilities and losses which have arisen or are likely to arise in respect of the financial year shall be taken into account, including those which become approved between the year end and the date of signature of the accounts by the directors.
(4) The accruals concept, i.e. all income/charges should be accounted for regardless of their date of receipt/payment.
(5) The concept of aggregation, i.e. that all individual assets/liabilities should be separately determined.

The first four are almost identical to SSAP 2 and the fifth derives from the Continental principle of 'aggregation' and the more legalistic view this takes of financial statements.

As well as the EC Directive, the IASC has produced a Principles Standard IAS 1 *Disclosure of Accounting Policies* (1998). This retains the going concern, consistency and accruals principles but instead of prudence it introduces two new concepts, i.e. materiality and substance over form. In addition the 'aggregation' concept does not appear in IAS 1.

Taking all three documents together (SSAP 2, IAS 1 and the 4th Directive) there can be said to be three concepts which have general consensus, i.e. going concern, consistency and accruals. Interestingly, although prudence is included in both IAS 1 and SSAP 2 it has in recent years come under a fair degree of criticism in the UK. In SSAP 4 (revised) 1990 it was clearly regarded as a secondary concept to accruals and should only play a part when the going concern concept is in any doubt, and under the new FRS 18 it is really only adopted in evaluating assets.

None of the three authorities has attempted to pretend that the principles are an all-embracing theory of accounting or a partial conceptual framework. SSAP 2 regarded its four concepts merely as 'broad basic assumptions which underlie the periodic financial accounts of business enterprises'. In a note it considered it 'expedient to recognise [the concepts] as working assumptions having general acceptance at the present time'. IAS 1 merely says that the 'fundamental accounting assumptions' underlie the preparation of financial statements, but are usually not specifically stated because their acceptance is assumed. The Companies Act 1985 simply enacts its principles but does not justify them as part of some greater conceptual framework.

The IASC/IASB has developed its own conceptual framework, *Framework for the Preparation and Presentation of Financial Statements* (1989), in which it details the objectives of financial statements, the underlying assumptions (accruals and going concern), the qualitative characteristics of financial statements, the elements of financial statements and recognition and measurement criteria. Interestingly, both the prudence and economic substance concepts are treated as qualitative characteristics and not assumptions.

The ASB has recently embarked on a similar course and has developed a new *Statement of Principles*, the eight chapters of which are largely similar to those of the IASC.

At present there are no equivalent developments within the EC.

(b) *The case for and against the assertion that before developing a standard, a logical and coherent framework should be derived*

From (a) it is clear that accounting standards, both ASC/ASB and IASC, are not based on firm theoretical foundations from which they can be logically derived. As a result the stability of accounting standards is in doubt as the foundations are built on sand and the 'house' is liable to fall down. The ASC made a serious error in not attempting to derive a conceptual framework first before embarking on the construction of standards or at least devising a set of basic principles.

However, the reality was very different as the ASC was set up in defence of the accounting profession and most of its standards have been developed on an *ad hoc* basis. It was formed when the accountancy profession was under attack in the UK and there was fear of government interference. Financial scandals such as the Pergamon/Leasco and AEI/GEC affairs had undermined investor confidence in financial reporting and exposed the widely arbitrary and variety of accounting options available in practice. They also revealed the lack of comparability between financial statements of different companies or even of the same company at different times. The ASC had to act quickly and decisively to bring some fast rules into place so as to re-establish the credibility of the profession. With hindsight, this was a mistake because industry has still produced some glaring scandals in recent years, e.g. Polly Peck, Maxwell Communications plc, BCCI etc., some of which could be said to be partially hidden by weak standards.

Certainly the order of priority was haphazard, starting with associated company treatment per SSAP 1 rather than tackling the more basic and fundamental standard, SSAP 2 *Disclosure of Accounting Policies*. At no time were basic ideas of what might constitute an asset, liability, expense or income ever formulated.

One could also argue that the early SSAPs (e.g. SSAPs 4, 6 and 8) did not tackle the real controversial issues and when the ASC attempted to tackle the more complex problems it came across a strong lobbying process from bodies such as the CBI and the One Hundred Group and even specific sectors of industry itself (e.g. property investment companies changing SSAP 12 into SSAP 19 to enable non-depreciation of investment properties).

Up to the death of the ASC, only 22 extant SSAPs were still in existence, an average of only 1.5 per annum, which is insignificant compared with the output in the USA. There have certainly been spectacular failures, notably in the field of inflation accounting.

In conclusion, the failure of the ASC and the lack of a consistent conceptual framework have resulted in weak standards and a lack of confidence in the ASC. This is the result of having no strong theoretical and objective backcloth against which its standards could be set. A set of standards is better than nothing but it is not a long-term solution to the problem. A firm, agreed set of principles needed to be set up by the ASB, and this has now been achieved.

Solution 2 – SOP 2001

(a) SSAP 2 *Disclosure of Accounting Policies* was published almost thirty years ago and, until the publication of the Statement of Principles in December 1996, it was the only conceptual document published by either the Accounting Standards Committee or the Accounting Standards Board.

At the time of its publication SSAP 2 identified four fundamental concepts as having a critical effect on financial reporting. These were the accruals, going concern, consistency and prudence concepts. They were recognised as only a partial attempt to identify the conceptual underpinnings of the subject and there were several other concepts that could just as easily be incorporated as being fundamental. These would include the business entity, money measurement, substance over form and double entry concepts, etc. However, the 'Fab Four' have served accounting practice well over the past thirty years.

The accruals concept (sometimes known as the matching principle) ensures that revenues are matched to their related expenditures as far as their relationship can be determined and that this will not necessarily coincide with the actual cash receipts and payments. It forms the basis for ensuring that any goods not sold are carried forward as closing stock on the balance sheet and that any unpaid expenditure, such as electricity consumption, is accrued as a liability and included within current expenditure.

The prudence concept takes a pessimistic view of financial reporting by only including revenues if they are almost certain to be received in cash and accruing any possible losses as soon as they are recognisable. This tends to result in a deliberate understatement of profitability but this reflects the conservative attitude to financial reporting that accountants in the past have felt comfortable with.

The going concern concept assumes that the reporting entity will still be in operational existence for the foreseeable future. This means that assets can be recorded at cost or valuation but not at the prices that they would fetch if forced into a break-up situation, which would tend to understate their true value.

The consistency concept requires reporting entities to adopt the same accounting policies from year to year and to treat like items in the same period in a similar manner. If this is not carried out it would be impossible to identify trends in financial performance.

(b) *Impact of Statement of Principles on current financial reporting*

The Statement of Principles has fundamentally changed the conceptual basis behind the preparation of financial statements. It was developed largely from the work carried out in the United States by the Financial Accounting Standards Board (FASB) in the development of their conceptual framework in the 1980s. As such it reflects the underlying culture in that environment, particularly the idea that it is more important to get the balance sheet right first before examining the matching of revenues and expenditures in the performance statements.

The main changes to SSAP 2 are that the concepts will be removed from the accounting standard and instead are included within the more conceptual Statement of Principles. The latter is merely a statement of best practice.

FRS 18 *Accounting Policies* will still require reporting entities to disclose their material accounting policies but in addition they will be required to disclose any material estimation techniques adopted in applying those policies.

The Statement of Principles still includes all four fundamental concepts within the eight chapters of the document but their character has changed. The accruals concept is incorporated in Chapter 5 and still requires revenues to be matched to their related expenditures. However, before any expenditure can be carried forward as an asset to be matched against a future revenue, it must pass the definition of an asset (in Chapter 4) and also pass the recognition criteria (in Chapter 5) of the Statement. The accruals concept is now secondary to the need to properly record assets and liabilities on balance sheet.

The prudence concept has been clearly downgraded in the new Statement. It is briefly mentioned in Chapter 6. The intent is clearly to restrict the use of the concept in creating liabilities, some of which had clearly no substance. On the other hand, it is clear that prudence should be applied in assessing the value of assets, and assets must be written down if their value has fallen below their recoverable amount.

The consistency concept has not really changed and is incorporated as part of the qualitative characteristic of comparability. However, its intent is the same as in SSAP 2.

The going concern concept remains unchanged and is clearly restated as part of the Measurement chapter.

Examples of financial reporting standards affected by the Statement of Principles

FRS 5 Reporting the Substance of Transactions

This standard was introduced in 1994 to ensure that the substance of transactions is reported over their legal form. This was the first standard to put priority on getting assets and liabilities right first before recording gains and losses. FRS 5 is really the practical application of the Statement of Principles.

FRS 12 Provisions, Contingent Liabilities and Contingent Assets

The downgrading of the prudence concept now means that it is much more difficult to create provisions. Unless they meet the definition of a liability (i.e. there is clearly a legal or constructive obligation) and pass the recognition tests (i.e. there is sufficient evidence of future cash outflows and they can be reliably measured), provisions may not be created. As a result former 'big bath' provisions have had to be removed from balance sheets. These include provisions for major overhauls, restructuring unless communicated to those affected and foreseeable losses.

FRS 19 Deferred Tax

It is almost certain that deferred tax will have to be provided in full under *FRS* 19, in order to fully record liabilities on the balance sheet. Strangely, this will also accord with the accruals concept as the previous standard was an *ad hoc* approach to deliberately reduce the deferred tax balance to a more acceptable level.

FRS 17 Retirement Benefits

Under the present SSAP 24 *Accounting for Pension Costs* the key concept adopted is the accruals concept. It requires entities to match the cost of employing their workforce (including pensions) against the revenue the entity receives from selling its goods and services.

However, in defined benefit schemes, a surplus/deficit will be spread over the average remaining service lifetime of the employees in the scheme. As a result, however, it creates artificial assets and liabilities on the balance sheet. After the Statement of Principles was published it was clear that the emphasis had to be turned towards getting the assets and liabilities right first before trying to match revenues and expenses. This is being put into action in FRS 17.

There are other topics that have still to be investigated. SSAP 13 *Accounting for Research and Development* will probably need to be revised with an outcome that development costs are unlikely to be carried forward as an asset and will probably have to be written off as an expense in the future. The leasing standard SSAP 21 will also likely be changed to ensure that all liabilities are recorded on the balance sheet and the distinction between an operating and a finance lease will be abolished.

In summary, the advent of the Statement of Principles and its subsequent impact on the four fundamental concepts has already resulted in major changes in existing standards and other standards will be substantially altered in the near future.

Solution 3 – Immateriality

(a) *Definition of immateriality*

The concept of materiality has never been defined in any UK accounting standard. Nevertheless, there is an assumption in financial reporting that only material items should be reported and disclosed in the profit and loss account and balance sheet of an entity.

Materiality is defined in the IASC's *Framework for the Preparation and Presentation of Financial Statements* as one of the main qualitative characteristics in financial reporting. According to the IASC statement (paragraph 30):

> 'information is material if its omission or misstatement could influence the economic decisions of users taken on the basis of the financial statements. Materiality depends on the size of the item or error judged in the particular circumstances of its omission or misstatement. Thus, materiality provides a threshold or cut-off point rather than being a primary qualitative characteristic which information must have if it is to be useful.'

Essentially there is a subjective judgement to be taken as to whether or not an item should be judged material. The interpretation of what constitutes a material item is therefore left largely to the accountant's professional expertise. When considering this point the accountant must consider an item in relation to the overall view of the financial statements, the individual total to which it belongs, any associated matters and the corresponding amounts in previous years.

In some instances, however, the concept of materiality may be overridden by statutory requirements. For example, even small amounts of directors' remuneration must be disclosed in order to comply with the Companies Act 1985.

(b) *Action required if the directors decide to depart from an SSAP's requirements*

Normally all financial statements are required to comply with current accounting standards if they are to show a true and fair view of the entity's financial position. However, if the directors decide that they do not wish to comply with a particular standard then they are obliged to state that fact in the financial statements and to justify their stance. This might be the case where the directors want to use the true and fair override, i.e. that in order for the company to show a true and fair view it is essential to depart from the rigidity of the standard to achieve this. This, of course, can only be justified in very exceptional circumstances.

The directors would have to ensure that the notes to the financial statements fully explained the departure from the SSAP/FRS, and any financial effect should also be quantified in the note. This justification is essential because under the Companies Act 1989 large companies and plcs must now state in the notes whether or not the financial statements have been prepared in accordance with accounting standards. In July 1991 the newly constituted Financial Reporting Review Panel wrote to 240 plcs asking them why they were not complying with this legislation.

Under the changes introduced by the Companies Act 1989 there are now statutory procedures in place to enable financial statements to be revised if they are felt to be unsatisfactory. The Financial Reporting Review Panel has publicly reprimanded a number of prominent companies for failing to comply with accounting standards, and all have agreed to alter their accounts to comply in future years. However, no company has yet forced a particular issue to court but this may reflect the fact that most of the items reviewed to date have not been controversial.

In addition to the above the auditors of a company should qualify their report if the accounts fail to comply with accounting standards, unless they agree with the directors' departure from the standard.

Solution 4 – IASC and EC influence on British published financial statements

The UK standard-setting procedures cannot operate in isolation in a world in which multinational companies trade and their shareholders are located in countries across the world. In addition, the fact that the European Community (EC) is progressing towards a single market and single currency will mean that the ASB must monitor carefully any directives from the EC.

The IASC influences the UK process because the ASB is a member of the IASC. As such it is obliged to incorporate international standards within the UK's SSAP/FRS framework and must attempt to:

(1) ensure that published financial statements comply with international standards and that the auditors are satisfied that such compliance exists; and

(2) persuade government and standard-setters that financial statements should comply with international standards.

Strictly speaking, the directors of limited companies should incorporate international standards when preparing their financial statements. However, this is generally only achieved when the ASC/ASB incorporates them in an SSAP/FRS noting (usually in the last few paragraphs) that the standard complies with IASs or indicating in which specific areas it fails to comply.

A recent development of the IASB has been an attempt to harmonise accounting principles on a worldwide basis. It is proposed that many of the former options in the IASs should be removed. An example of this is the insistence by the IASC that goodwill is an asset and must therefore initially be capitalised and subsequently amortised through the profit and loss account. This, of course, should help to put companies on a 'level playing field' footing in terms of the accounting effects of acquisitions.

The influence of the EC is slightly different. At present it is encapsulated in the directives issued by legislative process, usually as part of the EC's attempt to harmonise company law within the Community. To date the directives which have had most influence on standard setters have been the 4th and 7th, now incorporated in the Companies Act 1985. The 4th Directive concentrated on standard formats for both the profit and loss account and the balance sheet and was largely influenced by French and German models. The 7th Directive, on the other hand, was influenced mainly by the true and fair view concept but particularly by the need to emphasise economic substance/commercial reality so that entities which are controlled by a parent are in fact consolidated. It had, therefore, more of an Anglo-Saxon influence. As a direct result of this particular directive, SSAPs 1, 14 and 23 became obsolete. Clearly the legislation is less detailed than that provided by an SSAP/FRS. The ASB has tried to put the 'flesh' on the basic structure provided by the Act/Directive. Most of this is now in place in FRS 2 *Accounting for Subsidiary Undertakings*, FRS 6 *Acquisitions and Mergers*, FRS 7 *Fair Values in Acquisition Accounting*, FRS 9 *Associates and Joint Ventures* and FRS 10 *Goodwill and Intangible Assets*.

The Treaty of Rome means that the UK is obliged to enact the directives once they have been adopted by the Council of Ministers, but there is always an opportunity to delay enactment for a couple of years.

The European influence is unlikely to increase in the future, as it has agreed to put its weight behind the development of world accounting standards via the IASB, particularly with its decision in June 2000 that all listed companies in the EC be forced to comply with IASs in full by 2005.

Solution 5 – Beak plc

(a) The following are possible reasons why companies may wish to omit assets and liabilities from the balance sheet:

(i) Companies are concerned to maintain low *gearing* ratios. The reasons for this are that it is felt that brokers and analysts favour companies with relatively low levels of gearing. Off balance sheet finance schemes have been designed to conceal information about the amount of debt finance raised by a company.

Off balance sheet finance schemes can increase the borrowing capacity of a company either by avoiding debt covenants or by misleading investors about the true level of gearing.

(ii) Accounting ratios such as *return on capital employed* can be *improved* if certain assets in their development stage can be kept off the balance sheet until they produce a higher level of profit. Once the development stage is complete, the assets and related borrowings can then be brought onto the balance sheet.

(iii) It has been argued that stock market perceptions of the likelihood of a rights issue can be affected by the level of borrowing of a company. If a listed company has high levels of borrowing, then the likelihood of finance being raised by a rights issue is perceived to be lower and this is said to adversely affect the share price. Off balance sheet transactions can lower the stated level of borrowing and the expectations of a rights issue.

(iv) Companies have sometimes used 'quasi-subsidiaries' whereby assets and liabilities are acquired in an entity that is in effect controlled by the reporting company but does not meet the legal definition of a subsidiary. A reason why a company may choose to do this is because the subsidiary is loss making and these losses would probably have to be reported as post-acquisition losses in the group accounts.

(v) Many off balance sheet finance schemes are entered into for genuine commercial reasons. For example it may be a means of sharing the risk in a joint venture between a merchant bank and a company. The merchant bank may bear most of the financing risk and the company may bear most of the operating risk. Financial markets now allow companies to protect themselves from certain risks, and such transactions are not undertaken to mislead users of financial statements but because they are judged to be in the best interests of the company.

(b) The financial statements were 'being economical' with the truth in that assets over which entities had control and which generated benefits were not on the balance sheet and similarly related borrowings were not disclosed on the balance sheet either. This destroyed the 'true and fair view'. It is important that entities report the commercial reality of their transactions otherwise readers would be misled as to their 'true' performance/position.

These developments raised fundamental questions about the nature of assets and liabilities and when they should be included in the balance sheet. As a result the ASB became concerned about these practices for the following reasons:

(i) Such practices conflicted with the fundamental aims and objectives of financial statements. Users of financial statements were not always able to appreciate the full effect of such transactions on the financial affairs of the company because often there was insufficient information about these transactions.

(ii) There had been significant press comment about the use of such arrangements and the credibility of standard setters had been brought into question.

(iii) The fundamental concepts of comparability, consistency and truth and fairness of financial statements was brought into question by such schemes. If financial statements and related notes did not allow proper assessment of a company's results, then the financial statements could not achieve their objective of helping users assess the financial performance of an entity for both stewardship and decision-making purposes.

(c) (i) *Sale and possible repurchase*

Beak plc has the option of buying the land back at any time in the next five years but is not compelled to do so, and therefore is protected from any collapse in the value of the land below £20 million. This risk has therefore been transferred to Wings plc in return for the commission of 1 per cent above the current bank base rate. However, Beak plc has retained the benefits of ownership and can also benefit from any increase in the value of the land by exercising its option. At the time of the agreement, both parties must have anticipated that the option would be exercised. Beak plc would presumably not sell the land at below the current market price. Wings plc must have anticipated that any profit from the contract would be derived from the receipt of the 'commission' payment from Beak plc. It is unlikely that the land value would fall below one-third of its present value and therefore the degree of risk transferred to Wings plc is quite minimal. The essence of the contract is effectively a loan of £20 million secured on the land held by Beak plc. Accounting practice would dictate that the commercial reality of the transaction reflected a financing deal rather than the legal form of a sale.

	DR	Bank	£20m	
	CR	Loan		£20m
Not	DR	Bank	£20m	
	CR	Disposal of land		£20m

(ii) *Consignment stock*

The main problem surrounding this example is the determination of the substance of the agreement. The accountant has to determine whether Sparks Ltd has bought the cars or whether they are on loan from Gocar plc.

There are certain factors which point toward the treatment of the cars as stock of Sparks Ltd. Sparks Ltd has to pay a monthly rental fee of £100 per car and after four months has to pay for the cars if they are unsold. This could be regarded as a financing agreement as Sparks Ltd is effectively being charged interest by Gocar plc which is varying with the length of time for which Sparks Ltd hold the stock. Sparks Ltd is also bearing any risk of slow movement of the cars. The purchase price of the car is fixed at the price when the car was first supplied. Thus any price increases in the product are avoided by Sparks Ltd which would indicate that there is a contract for the sale of goods. Sparks Ltd has to insure the cars and is partially suffering some of the risks of ownership of the vehicles.

Gocar Ltd cannot demand the return of cars from Sparks and therefore has no control over the assets.

A fixed penalty charge of 10 per cent of the cost of the car is chargeable to Sparks if cars remain unsold; therefore the risks of ownership are with Sparks. The double entry should therefore be:

DR	Stocks	£xxx	
CR	Loan		£xxx

Solution 6 – Timber Products plc

(a) (i) The objective (FRS 5, para 1) of the FRS *Reporting the Substance of Transactions* is to ensure that the substance of an entity's transactions is reported in its financial statements. The commercial effect of the entity's transactions, and any resulting assets, liabilities, gains or losses, should be faithfully represented in its financial statements. This will affect the accounting for any arrangement the effect of which is to inappropriately omit assets and liabilities from the balance sheet. It achieves this by requiring financial statements to be prepared reporting the substance rather than the legal form of transactions. It is applicable to all transactions but is particularly pertinent when complex arrangements are incorporated into agreements which effectively divorce 'legal form' from 'substance'.

(ii) The FRS recognises two types of transaction where an asset might cease to be recognised:

The first is where all significant benefits and risks relating to an asset are transferred. An example is where a car manufacturer supplies parts at listed trade price to a service station customer.

The second is where not all significant benefits and risks relating to an asset are transferred, but it is necessary to change the description or monetary amount of the original asset or to record a new liability for any obligation assumed. An example is where a company sells its debts to a factor but the factor only pays up 80 per cent of the monies due as a non-returnable proceed, the balance only being paid if the factor can collect the full debts. There is effectively a sharing of risks and thus the asset or debt should initially be recorded gross but with a reduction on the face of the balance sheet for the proceeds received.

(b) (i) *Disclosure using linked presentation*

The transaction appears to satisfy the criteria set out in FRS 5 for linked presentation in that the finance will be repaid only from the proceeds generated by the specific item it finances and there is no possibility of any claim on the entity being established other than against funds generated by that item and there is no provision whereby the entity may either keep the item on repayment of the finance or reacquire it at any time.

The accounting treatment for linked presentation is as follows:

	£m	£m
Current assets		
Receivables subject to financing arrangements		
Gross receivables		
(after providing £600,000 for bad debts)	14.40	
Less: non-returnable proceeds		
90% of net debtors £14.4m	(12.96)	1.44
Current asset: Cash		12.96

(ii) *Sale and repurchase of stock*

Under FRS 5 the transaction would be regarded as a financing transaction in that Timber Products plc has not transferred the risks and rewards of ownership of the timber. It has in fact borrowed money on the security of the timber. The timber will therefore appear as stock in the balance sheet and the loan will appear as a creditor. Each year there will be an interest element charged to the profit and loss account and added to the liability. The interest charged should represent a constant rate of return on the outstanding liability.

The balance sheet as at 31 October 2001 will show:

	£m
Stock	40.0
Loan payable after more than one year	42.8

Note: The loan is secured by stock of £40m at cost

The profit and loss account will show:

	£m
Interest payable (7% × £40m)	2.80

Calculation of underlying finance cost

	£m
Cost borrowed	40.0
Repayment	56.1
Finance cost	16.1

$$\text{Annuity} = \frac{56.1m}{40.0m} = 1.4025: \text{ five years' time} = 7\%$$

(iii) *Consignment stock*

The interest may not be added to the value of stock as there is no creative activity occurring. It is not an essential cost in getting the stock to its exact location and condition.

The problem in this transaction is to determine the substance of the transaction, i.e. whether or not the 'outstanding' stock of £4m at selling price (£3m cost price) has been sold. If it has, this would mean that the stock appears in the balance sheet of the retailers at £4m.

Possibly the principal point that would support recognition of a sale and derecognition of the stock in the balance sheet of Timber Products plc is the fact that the retailers are able to purchase at the trade price as at the date of delivery. If they were required to pay the trade price as at the end of the six-month display period then the substance would be that the rewards remained with Timber Products plc and the stock would continue to be recognised by their balance sheet at cost of £3m, or net realisable value if lower.

Thus, the more prudent view treats the transaction as a genuine sale or return, with the manufacturer holding the price for six months.

There is a further point, which is that the retailers could take the opportunity immediately prior to the end of the six months to return all unsold consignment stock. This would support the view that the risks and rewards remained with Timber Products plc.

The decision in this case has to be taken on balance, i.e. giving weight to those matters that are likely to have a commercial effect in practice. There is no absolute answer. The persuasive factor is probably the date of fixing the price which would support treating the item as sold and therefore derecognised from the Timber Products plc balance sheet.

The accounting entries on that basis would be:

Profit and loss account for the year ended 31 October 2001

Sales	£10m
Cost of sales	£7.5m
Other income	£50,000
Insurance costs	£15,000
Carriage costs	£10,000
Balance sheet as at 31 October 2001	
Debtors	£4m

A provision for returns should be made based on past experience.

(iv) *Quasi-subsidiary*

The arrangement with Inter plc has been structured so that it does not meet the legal definition of a subsidiary within the provisions of FRS 2, para 14. However, the commercial effect is no different from that which would result were Inter plc to be a subsidiary of Timber Products plc and under FRS 5 it falls to be treated as a quasi-subsidiary. As Sir David Tweedie stated on the introduction of FRS 5: 'if it looks like a duck, talks and waddles like a duck, then duck account it!'

Under FRS 5, the factory will appear as an asset in the Timber Products consolidated accounts. Its value will be reduced to £8.5m being its cost to the group and the profit on disposal will be cancelled out; the fee will be cancelled as an intra-group transaction; the loan interest will appear as £1.5m in the consolidated profit and loss account; the loan of £10m will appear as a creditor in the consolidated balance sheet.

(c) 'State what further information you would seek in order to determine the substance of the transaction':

The question to be answered is what risks has Timber Products plc borne in this transaction.

It clearly bears the operating risk in the form of maintenance and insurance costs. It needs to be determined whether it has also borne the charge for covering the finance cost of the equipment during construction. Further information is required in considering this transaction to assess whether Extractor-Plus plc is in effect receiving a lender's return. If that were the case, the equipment would appear as an asset in the balance sheet and an amount equal to the cost of the asset as a loan secured on the asset.

More information is necessary to establish whether there has been an attempt to word the agreement so that it falls outside the SSAP 21 definition of a finance lease. The additional information would include matters such as the cost of the equipment, the length of the contract, and any minimum lease payments particularly in the event of low hourly usage. However, FRS 5 with its substance approach, might influence the accounting treatment and the standard should be used, in conjunction with and as a complementary tool, to finally decide on the 'correct' accounting treatment.

Solution 7 – D Ltd

To: Managing director of D Ltd   Date
From: Management accountant
Subject: Explanation of how FRS 5 affects the accounting treatment of assets and liabilities

(a) FRS 5 *Reporting the Substance of Transactions* seeks to clarify the way in which a company reports transactions in its Corporate Report. The substance of a transaction is to be determined by the effect it has on the assets and liabilities of the business. FRS 5 insists that the substance of a transaction take precedence over its legal form.

The definition of an asset concerns the control of success to future economic benefits – usually by a legal right. Control in this sense is affected by ensuring that the benefits concerned accrue to the business, and should not be confused with 'management' of an asset. Control means the ability to determine the ultimate destination of benefits from a transaction, or to restrict others from directing major policies. The business that stands to lose or gain from the risk inherent in the economic operation of an item is deemed to own that item as an asset under FRS 5 and the Statement of Principles (Chapter 4). The existence of the asset must be supported by sufficient evidence that the benefits will actually flow to the entity.

Liabilities, on the other hand, are obligations to transfer future economic benefits as a result of a past transaction or event. The term 'obligation' implies that the business is unable to avoid this outflow of resources. It may either be a 'legal' or a 'contractual' obligation. If a liability is contingent on the occurrence of uncertain future events, the recognition of that liability in a financial statement is dependent on the contingency rules in SSAP 18 and only probable losses may be accrued on the balance sheet.

Before it can be recognised in the accounts, an asset must be capable of measurement to produce an amount which is 'sufficiently' reliable. Evidence of future inflows or outflows of benefits must be adequately substantiated. The prudence concept encourages an element of reasonableness to be injected into the estimate of a liability. But prudence is not regarded with the same weight as SSAP 2. A liability, for example, may only be recorded if there is no realistic chance of its being avoided. A mere intention to expend money is not sufficient by itself.

Once an asset or liability is recognised, subsequent transactions may cause a change to its status if it affects say the right to the benefit, or the risk inherent in earning that benefit. A transaction to finance an asset will not affect the right to benefits or the risk inherent in the use of the asset, but may create an associated liability to repay. If a transaction transfers to others all significant rights to benefits and significant exposure to the risks of an asset, that asset should cease to be recognised.

An asset has now been defined as a transaction in which a reporting entity 'has access to the future economic benefits controlled by the entity as a result of a past transaction or event'.

An asset/liability may not necessarily be 'kicked off' balance sheet immediately if a transfer of risks and benefits occurs. If there is a genuine sharing of risks then the asset/liability may have to be restated using the linked presentation approach whereby all non-returnable proceeds to date are deducted from the asset on the face of the balance sheet. This ensures that both the potential risk on the full amount of the asset and the maximum rewards based on the net amount are disclosed on balance sheet. It is used particularly in limited recourse situations such as factoring of debts.

(b) *Motor vehicles on consignment*

Your suggestion is to treat this transaction as a consignment stock of the motor cars, held by D Ltd (the dealer), but legally owned by E plc (the manufacturer), until legal title passes and liability to pay is created. Under FRS 5, the stock should be treated as an asset by the dealer, if the dealer has access to benefits from the stock, or is exposed to risks inherent in those benefits. The terms of our trade with E plc are that:

(i) D Ltd is charged a penalty for return of the stock which increases as the holding period is extended – a risk.

(ii) D Ltd is insulated from normal price increases by E plc – a benefit.

(iii) The transfer price rises by 1 per cent per stockholding month. This is really a finance charge for delaying payment to the manufacturer – a risk.

(iv) D Ltd, the dealer, bears the risk of obsolescence and must pay for unsold stock six months after delivery.

(v) E plc cannot demand the return of the stock under normal trading conditions – a benefit to D Ltd.

In this case, the commercial substance of the transaction suggests that the stock must be treated as an asset by D Ltd, with an associated liability to E plc – a short-term loan bearing an interest charge.

Under FRS 5, therefore, an additional liability must be shown on D Ltd's balance sheet which will have a detrimental impact on our gearing ratio and borrowing limitations. Unfortunately the new accounting treatment insists that the commercial reality of a transaction be disclosed, and not its legal form, in order to provide a true and fair view.

(vi) Legally the property remains with E plc – benefit.

Signed: Management accountant

Solution 8 – S Ltd

Internal memorandum

To: Board of Directors, S Ltd
From: Management Accountant
Re: Application of the Principles in FRS 5 to Factoring of Debts
Date: 30 June 2001

(a) How the principles set out in FRS 5 should be applied

FRS 5 *Reporting the Substance of Transactions* was published in 1994 to ensure that the substance of all transactions are recorded on the balance sheet. It applies the principles, in practice, set out in the Statement of Principles (December 1999).

In particular, an asset or liability may only be recorded on balance sheet if it meets the definition of an asset/liability (i.e. it has rights or other access to future economic benefits controlled by the entity as a result of a past transaction or event or it has an obligation to transfer economic benefits as a result of a past transaction or event respectively).

In addition, an asset or liability may only be recognised if there is:

(i)   sufficient evidence of the asset or liability; and
(ii) the asset/liability can be reliably measured.

One specific feature of FRS 5 in making the decision as to who controls an asset is the allocation of risk. Whoever bears the risks and ultimately the rewards is a significant indicator of which party should record the asset on the balance sheet.

Effectively FRS 5 requires the preparer to 'lift the legal veil' and get back to the commercial reality of the transaction. Subsequently a follow-up transaction will result in the removal of an asset off balance sheet if the reporting entity can no longer control the asset and has passed the risks of ownership on to a third party. However, it is possible that only part of the risk may be transferred, in which case a linked presentation may be appropriate, provided that certain criteria are met.

(b) How the debt factoring arrangement can be accounted for

The principles set out in FRS 5 should be applied to the arrangement and thus it is important to identify the party that bears the risks of a transaction. Each aspect of the contract should be investigated.

Taking each aspect of the agreement in turn:

1.   Transfer of debt to F plc, subject to credit approval – possibility of risks attaching to F plc.

2.   Receipt of 70 per cent of gross debts – is it non-returnable? – if so, could be a linked presentation.

3.   F plc collects the debts – possible transfer.

4.&5.   F plc credits cash to factoring account of F plc and handles all aspects of cash collection.

6.   F plc has full recovery of bad debts even though only receivable from debts outstanding – evidence of a full recourse agreement.

On the balance of the terms of the agreement it would appear that the original selling company has full recourse for all bad debts and therefore still retains the risks over the debts. Legal title may have passed to F plc but the economic control over the asset still rests with S Ltd. As such the debtors should remain on the balance sheet and the finance received treated as a loan until such time as the debtors are cleared by F plc.

Solution 9 – Tree plc

(a)   Evaluation of the extent to which advice given to the managing director is in accordance with generally accepted accounting principles

Financial statements of an entity should reflect the substance of its transactions

The statement is perfectly correct. Since the publication of FRS 5 *Reporting the Substance of Transactions* in April 1994, accountants must always reflect the substance or commercial reality of all transactions in preference to their legal form. In order to achieve that objective, accountants must decide whether or not a transaction results in the creation or change to its assets and liabilities. Assets are defined as 'rights or other access to future economic benefits controlled by the entity' whereas liabilities are defined as 'obligations (legal or constructive) that transfer economic benefits to another party as a result of past transactions or events'.

The way to determine substance is to consider its effect on the assets and liabilities of the entity carrying out the transaction

It is not enough merely to pass the definition of an asset or liability. In addition, FRS 5 requires two recognition tests to be passed – is there sufficient evidence of the future economic benefits or transfer and can they be reliably measured? If the answer to either question is in the negative then neither an asset nor a liability may be created on the entity's balance sheet. Often a transaction might look like an asset, e.g. advertising expenditure, but it fails the first recognition test and must be written off as expenses. These are referred to as revenue investments and can include training and maintenance expenditure. Similarly, a home-grown brand may well result in substantial benefits being received in the future but they are very difficult to reliably measure and thus should not be reported on balance sheet. On the other hand, a price was paid for a purchased brand and it should be capitalised.

Assets and liabilities that do pass the tests do not remain indefinitely on balance sheet. If either of the tests are failed in the future then they must be removed immediately from the balance sheet. They are effectively derecognised. However, their legal form or transfer has no impact at all on their accounting treatment.

(b)   Explanation how individual transactions should be accounted for in the books of Tree plc

Transaction 1

The legal position of the transaction is that Tree plc has sold the property to a bank for £5m. The substance is very different as Tree plc has the right to repurchase the property between March 2001 and September 2006. The property is expected to rise by around 5 per cent over the next few years so its value in 2006 is projected to be £13.4m. In the meantime the company is only paying out £600,000 per annum over a period of six years, giving a total interest payment of £3.6m. As can be seen from the figures below, it is almost certain that the repurchase of property will take place. FRS 5 requires the accountants to investigate the series of transactions as a whole and it is clear that in this particular case the substance of the arrangement is that of a loan, and not a sale. The probability of Tree plc repurchasing the property is very high so it has not really relinquished the risks and rewards of ownership to the bank. Although the property is rent-free, the bank is effectively getting a return of £600,000 per annum, payable at the date of repurchase, but this should be charged on an annual basis to the profit and loss in order to reflect the substance of the arrangement. The double entry bookkeeping should therefore read as follows:

Dr	Bank	£5,000,000		On
Cr	Loan		£5,000,000	Initial receipt
Dr	Profit and loss (Interest)	600,000		Annually
Cr	Loan		600,000	
Dr	Loan	8,600,000		Assuming final
Cr	Bank	8,600,000		repurchase in 2006

Workings

	£	£
Repurchase price		5,000,000
Interest		3,600,000
Total payments		8,600,000
Total receipts	5,000,000	
Final sale	13,400,000	
		18,400,000
Overall gain if repurchase		9,800,000

Transaction 2

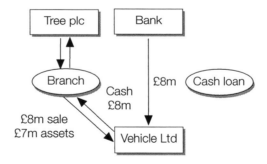

The legal position is clear – the branch has been sold to Vehicle Ltd, a subsidiary of the bank. However, the substance of the arrangement is that the bank has deliberately set up a 'special purpose vehicle' as a legal subsidiary and transferred £8m funds to that vehicle. That money has then gone directly into the coffers of Tree plc, similar to a situation if Tree plc itself had borrowed monies directly from the bank, using the property as collateral. It is clear from the arrangements that Tree plc effectively controls the day-to-day operations of Vehicle, presumably by way of separate contracts. Effectively this means that Vehicle is really a 'quasi-subsidiary' of Tree plc and should be consolidated in the financial statements of the Tree Group. It appears that the arrangement was a deliberate attempt to avoid borrowings being recorded on the balance sheet and there is no real substance to the creation of a subsidiary by the bank. In order to comply with FRS 5, therefore, the operating profit of £2m in Vehicle should be recorded within the group's operating profits but the profit on sale of £8m – £7m should be removed. The original net assets of £7m plus the growth during the year should be added to total group assets. As the company does not own any of the shares, the minority interest must be credited with the full value of the net assets.

Dr	Net assets	£7m	
	Profit on disposal of branch	1m	
Cr	Minority interest		£8m

The interest payable by Vehicle Ltd would be cancelled as part of the consolidation exercise as follows:

Dr	Bank	£1.2m	
	Interest payable	0.8m	
Cr	Operating profits		£2m

Solution 10 – BLFB plc

(a) Memorandum

To: Assistant Financial Controller
From: Management Accountant
Date: 23 January 2001

Re: *Implementation of FRS 5* Reporting the Substance of Transactions

(i) *Meaning of substance and how substance should be determined*

Substance is often described as reflecting the commercial reality of a transaction rather than necessarily its legal form. Accountants have a major role in ensuring that the financial statements reflect a true and fair view of its transactions. Only if the commercial reality of transactions are reflected will this be achieved.

In order to ensure that substance is recorded, a transaction or series of transactions must give rise to the creation of a new asset/(s) or liability/(ies) or alternatively the transaction/(s) has resulted in a change in existing assets/liabilities.

Provided that the answer to either of the above is positive then an asset/liability may be recorded or altered as long as certain recognition tests are also passed:

(1) Is there sufficient evidence of the existence of the asset or liability; and

(2) Is the asset/liability capable of being reliably measured in monetary terms?

(ii) *Why does FRS 5 require transactions to be accounted for in accordance with their substance?*

During the 1980s there were many creative accounting techniques set up based on the idea that companies wanted to take borrowings 'off balance sheet' in order to improve their gearing ratios and returns on capital employed. It was said by some commentators that financial statements were only 'being economical with the truth'.

Generally, most transactions undertaken by companies ensure that both the legal form and the commercial reality of a transaction are identical. However, in many more complex cases, in order to achieve off balance sheet financing, the legal profession has introduced additional clauses into contracts that deliberately attempt to divorce their commercial reality or substance from their legal form. The job of the accountant is always to ensure a true and fair view of the financial statements. This is unlikely to occur in these circumstances.

In addition FRS 5 has been published with the task of improving the relevance and usefulness of financial reports in accordance with the qualitative characteristics which are set out in Chapter 3 of the Statement of Principles.

(b) (i) and (ii) Accounting treatment of sale of timber from BLFB plc to Southland Bank plc

The commercial substance of this transaction is a secured loan from Southland Bank plc, using the stock of maturing timber as security. It is incorrect to treat the transaction as a genuine sale, even though the legal title has passed to the bank. Clearly, the substance of the transaction is that the risks and rewards attached to the ultimate sale of the maturing timber rest with BLFB plc and not Southland Bank. These include the security and maintenance of the stock under controlled conditions over the full five years of the maturity period. If the price of timber were to fall, the bank would not lose but BLFB plc would. The double option (whereby BLFB plc must repurchase the stock and similarly Southland Bank have a legal obligation to sell the timber) means that effectively the sale has not taken place in reality.

The journal entries required to implement FRS 5 and to correct the original entries are as follows:

		Dr	Cr
1 July 1999	Sales	£45m	
	Stock of maturing timber	40m	
	Creditor – Southland Bank plc		£45m
	Cost of sales		40m

Being the reversal of the sale of timber and the restatement of the timber as stocks, while at the same time recording a liability of a recognition of a secured loan on balance sheet.

30 June 2000	Interest expense		
	(8% x £45m)	3.6m	
	Creditor – Southland Bank plc		3.6m

Being the accrual required to record the interest incurred for the year based on the difference between the selling price of £45m and the repurchase price of £66.12m.

Workings

Amount borrowed	1 July 1999	£45.00m
Amount to be repaid	30 June 2004	66.12m
Total interest payable		£21.12m

Amount borrowed £45m ÷ £66.12m   Amount repaid = 0.681
From discount tables this represents 8% over the five-year period

Initial borrowing	£45.00m	Interest 8% 2002	4.20m
Interest 8% 2000	3.60m		56.69m
	48.60m	Interest 8% 2003	4.54m
Interest 8% 2001	3.89m		61.23m
	52.49m	Interest 8% 2004	4.89m
			66.12m

2

Asset Valuation: Accounting for Tangible Fixed Assets

Solution 1 – Capital-based grants

(a) SSAP 4 was originally issued in April 1984 and concentrated on the typical type of grant available at that time, i.e. the standard capital-based grant. During recent years this automatic right to receive a grant, provided that the company could claim it was in a qualifying business and was using the plant/building for a qualifying purpose, has been replaced by the adoption of discretionary grants. Prospective grantees now have to plead their case with the respective grant-awarding agency.

These new awards are generally a hybrid of both a revenue (job creation) and a capital nature. As a result the SSAP was amended in July 1990 and now takes a fairly flexible approach to the decision as to how to account for these new awards.

Essentially the treatment revolves around the concept of accruals or matching, i.e. to ensure that the grant is matched against the expenditure to which it relates. Only if the going concern assumption is in doubt should the prudence concept be taken into account. The new standard applies equally to all grants including any from quasi-government agencies.

As a result grants which relate specifically to fixed assets should be credited to revenue over the expected useful life of those assets. In SSAP 4 (original) two methods of accounting were permitted as follows:

(1) *The cost of the purchased asset is reduced by the capital grant*
This 'net cost' will result in a smaller depreciation charge than would otherwise be the case. Therefore the grant is automatically released via a lower depreciation charge to the profit and loss account over the useful economic life of the asset.

(2) *The grant is credited to a deferred capital grants reserve*
The gross cost of the fixed asset will be depreciated in the normal manner. In addition to a depreciation charge, a release of the capital grants reserve will be credited to the profit and loss account over the same period. The two combined will result in the same net charge to profit and loss as in method (1).

Considerable doubt was expressed on the legality of method (1). As a result the ASC sought a legal opinion as to whether or not the netting off of the grant against cost was in fact in contravention of companies legislation whereby a liability could not be offset against an asset. Counsel stated that in their opinion the approach was in fact breaking the law and that companies should be given a 'health warning' not to adopt that particular policy. However, both methods are still retained in SSAP 4 for organisations which are not limited companies.

(b) Both methods achieve the same objective of matching the benefit of the grant against the spreading of the expenditure over the asset's useful life. Other proposed methods, for example an immediate credit direct to profit and loss or to reserves, fail to comply with either the fundamental accruals or the prudence accounting concepts.

The advantage of method (1) is its simplicity and the fact that it records the true net cost of acquiring the asset.

Method (2) has the additional advantage of recording the fixed asset at its full normal cost, which facilitates a comparison with assets acquired without grants and from other locations. In addition, capital allowances are based on gross cost and therefore there is no need to adjust the depreciation charge when calculating deferred taxation. It also avoids the danger of accidentally releasing grants to shareholders' funds on the revaluation of the fixed assets, as the following example shows:

	Net cost		Deferred credit		
	£		£		£
Cost	100,000	Cost	100,000	Capital grants reserve	(20,000)
Grant (20%)	20,000				
	80,000				
Revaluation	150,000	Revaluation	150,000		
Surplus to		Surplus to			
capital reserve (1)	70,000	capital reserve (2)	50,000		(20,000)

(1) Automatically, in error, £20,000 grant has been transferred to revaluation reserve inside the shareholders' funds part of the balance sheet.

(2) The correct transfer of surplus to the revaluation reserve, i.e. the difference between the gross cost and the revalued figure.

Solution 2 – SSAP 4

Mr A P Grant
Managing Director
Small Company Ltd

Trump and Ace
Chartered Accountants
Dunstore

Date

Dear Mr Grant

Accounting treatment of government grants

With reference to the points raised in your letter of 12 October 2001 I am now in a position to reply.

(1) SSAP 4 is suitable for large companies only

The accounting treatment of SSAP 4 is applicable to all companies regardless of size. SSAP 4 requires the grant to be matched to revenue over the life of the asset. The grant is an aid to finance the purchase of the asset and a small company is just as likely as a large company to be able to finance its own expansion. It is wrong to treat the grant as a bonus and therefore it cannot be credited directly to profit and loss account in the period in which it is received.

(2) Grants are absolutely essential for survival

The purpose of capital grants is to provide finance to aid capital expenditure, not to provide working capital or cash to carry on business. It would be wrong to suggest that grants are absolutely essential for survival. They should be regarded as an aid to expansion. Any working capital or long-term finance should be provided by long-term loans or shareholders' equity.

(3) Grants should be recognised in the profit and loss account when received and not treated as a deferred credit

The key accounting concept in SSAP 4 is that of accruals. In essence this requires the matching of the grant and the useful life of the asset by spreading the grant over that useful life. For limited companies this must now only be achieved by the revised version of SSAP 4, i.e. by crediting a deferred credit reserve which can be released to profit and loss over the same period as depreciation. The net cost method (i.e. to credit the grant immediately against cost) is no longer available to companies. The ASC has taken Counsel's opinion that this would result in a netting off of assets against liabilities which is not permitted under company legislation.

(4) The cost of the asset should be apportioned but not the grant

The value of a grant is to provide an immediate cash flow benefit to the grantee in order to aid expansion and financing of capital expenditure. However, the benefit of the use of the capital asset will be felt over a number of years and under the matching concept the benefit of the grant should be set aside against those years. This is the accruals concept as opposed to adopting a cash basis of accounting. The concept has now been adopted in nearly all extant SSAPs as one of the fundamental accounting concepts.

(5) Two statements should be prepared, one for large companies and one for small companies

The accounting principles outlined in SSAP 4 are applicable to all companies regardless of size. The principles are similar in other SSAPs, FRSs and FREDs. However, over the last two years of its life the ASC attempted to make exemptions for small companies from certain disclosures. No exemptions have so far been made for the measurement of assets and liabilities or of profits/losses in the financial statements. It could also be argued that the fundamental concept of consistency would not permit different standards for different companies. The FRSSE (November 1997) now insists that SSAP 4 should be applied in full to smaller companies.

I hope that the above information will be of some benefit to you but please do not hesitate to contact me for any additional information.

Yours sincerely

T F Trump

Solution 3 – Non-depreciation

Internal memorandum

To: Managing director
From: Chief accountant   Date

Accounting treatment of investment properties

Standard accounting practice (FRS 15) requires us to depreciate all our fixed assets, with the exception of land, systematically over their finite useful life. This would normally entail a split of the cost of land and buildings into their two component parts with only the buildings proportion being depreciated. A failure to depreciate will mean that no charge for the use of the building is matched against the revenue it is helping to create.

Some companies have avoided this requirement on the grounds that their properties do not depreciate or if they do such depreciation charge would be immaterial. This is because of considerable monies being expended on repairs and maintenance. Credence has been given to this viewpoint by the decision of the Financial Reporting Review Panel (February 1992) to permit Forte plc to continue a policy of non-depreciation. However, this would seem to relate mainly to hotel properties and retail stores. FRS 15 retains the option but requires a compulsory annual impairment review, under FRS 11, to ensure that the property has not been impaired.

I believe that our company should instead look to SSAP 19 which permits investment properties to avoid depreciation under certain defined circumstances.

An investment property is defined as an interest in land or buildings which is:

(1)   complete so far as construction is concerned; and

(2)   held purely for its investment potential with any rental charges being negotiated at an arm's-length price;

(3)   not used by the company for its own purposes or let out to a fellow subsidiary or parent company.

The accounting treatment for investment properties is set out in SSAP 19. Investment properties are not depreciated except in the last twenty years of the leasehold life. Instead they are shown at their open market value in the balance sheet. Any change in that value is not recorded within the profit and loss account but instead is taken directly to an investment property revaluation reserve. However, if a fall in value were to exceed the balance in that reserve account then any excess must be charged to the profit and loss account. In addition, details of the movement in the reserve account should be disclosed in the notes to the accounts as well as details of the valuers and the basis of their valuation.

Solution 4 – Jupiter Ltd

(a)   *Notes to the accounts*

Tangible fixed assets

	Freehold land and buildings £'000	Plant and machinery £'000	Fixtures and fittings £'000	Motor vehicles £'000	Total £'000
Cost/valuation					
Balance 1.11.99	390	770	100	50	1,310
Additions	–	108	–	28	136
Disposals	–	–	–	(6)	(6)
Revaluations	400	–	–	–	400
Balance 31.10.00	790	878	100	72	1,840
Depreciation					
Balance 1.11.99	60	450	40	35	585
Charge for year (W1)	10	127.25	20	15.25	172.5
Disposals (W2)	–	–	–	(5.75)	(5.75)
Revaluations	(60)	–	–	–	(60)
	10	577.25	60	44.5	691.75
Net book value at 31.10.00	780	300.75	40	27.5	1148.25
Net book value at 31.10.99	330	320	60	15	725

Freehold land and buildings were revalued during the year by C Starr, chartered surveyor, at an open market valuation on an existing use basis.

(b)   *Revalued tangible fixed assets*

There is considerable inconsistency in the treatment of revaluations of fixed assets in annual company reports. Revaluations are permitted under the Companies Act 1985 and, until the advent of FRS 15, they were actively encouraged by the ASC/ASB. At present, revaluation is purely optional and tends to be adopted almost exclusively for land and buildings.

The main reason for revaluing land and buildings is that these assets are held for a long period, have long estimated useful lives and are usually appreciating in value. Also, the original cost is completely out of touch with the true value of the asset. This results in net assets being understated and possibly makes the company more susceptible to an unwanted takeover bid.

Revaluation under FRS 15 will result in an increased depreciation charge as it is important to match the charge to profit and loss with the related value in the balance sheet. The charge to profit and loss should be based on the carrying value of the asset (either cost or revaluation). Thus as asset values rise, so will depreciation charges. This provision was adopted to prevent the so-called 'Woolworth split depreciation policy'. Here all the revaluation surplus went to the balance sheet, with only historical cost depreciation being charged against profits, any excess being debited direct to the revaluation reserve. Another advantage of regular revaluations would be to make the directors more aware of the value of the assets being used by the company. If the value is less than open market value, it may be sensible to dispose of the asset.

The arguments against revaluation are put forward in FRS 15. Revaluations are not transaction based and therefore any value placed on the assets is subjective and should not be included under historical cost accounting.

Another argument against revaluation is its inconsistency in application. It appears that only assets which are appreciating are revalued and those depreciating are quietly ignored. FRS 15 now insists that, while not overly in favour of revaluation, if revaluation is to continue then directors must decide which classes of assets are to be revalued. They must then revalue all the assets within that class at least once every five years, albeit possibly on a rolling basis.

Even with this possible amendment there will still be a loss in comparability between companies. This must detract from the usefulness of the accounts for decision-making. FRS 3 has introduced a specific note to the accounts, a 'note of historical cost profits and losses', to ensure comparability between revaluing companies and historical cost based companies.

One of the major problems in adopting revaluation is how to account for the sale of revalued assets. FRS 15 has taken the view that if a company revalues an asset then that figure becomes its book value for all subsequent events, i.e. profit/loss on disposal will be calculated as the difference between the proceeds of sale and the revalued net book figure. Any balance remaining on revaluation reserve relating to that asset is now realised and must be transferred to the profit and loss account via an intra-reserve transfer.

The ASB in Chapter 6 of the Statement of Principles has opted for a long-term 'current value' revaluation policy for assets. In the interim the discussion paper *The Role of Valuation in Financial Reporting* (March 1993) proposed compulsory valuation for properties, quoted investments and commodities. However, FRS 15 *Tangible Fixed Assets* permits revaluation of certain classes of fixed asset, as long as these are updated at least once every five years.

Workings
W1 Calculation of depreciation charge for the year

	£000
Factory	
£240,000 ÷ 40 years (asset $^{30}/_{150}$ or 20% expired to 1.11.99)	6
Salesroom	
£150,000 ÷ 37.5 years (asset $^{30}/_{180}$ or 1/6 expired to 1.11.99)	4
	10

Depreciation amortised evenly over the asset's remaining useful life.

Plant and machinery
Balance 1.11.99
£475,000 ÷ 10 years   47.5
Additions (assume mid-year)
£100,000 ÷ 10 years × ½   5.0
                                                                                        52.5

Computer equipment   *£000*
Balance 1.11.99
£295,000 ÷ 4 years   73.75
Additions (assume mid-year)
£8,000 ÷ 4 years × ½   1
                                                                                       74.75

Furniture and fittings
Balance 1.11.99
£100,000 ÷ 5 years   20

Motor vehicles
Balance 1.11.99 less disposal
£44,000 ÷ 4 years   11
Disposal (mid-year)
£6,000 ÷ 4 years × ½   0.75
Additions (mid-year)
£28,000 ÷ 4 years × ½   3.5
                                                                                       15.25

W2 Calculation of accumulated depreciation on motor vehicle sold
                                                                                       £000
Balance 1.11.99   5
Charge to the date of disposal (W1)   0.75
                                                                                       5.75

Solution 5 – Assessment of depreciation

(a) The assessment of depreciation and its allocation to accounting periods requires consideration of the following three factors:

- The cost or valuation of the asset;
- The estimated useful life of the asset;
- The estimated residual value of the asset at the end of its useful life.

Legally, consideration must be given to Schedule 4, Companies Act 1985 as follows:

- The initial recording of the fixed asset must be at purchase price or production cost;
- A company may adopt alternative current cost or market value rules;
- If alternative rules are adopted, the comparable historical cost must be disclosed.

(b) Under FRS 15 (previously SSAP 12) if a company adopts historical cost accounting, depreciation should be based on this cost figure. Any attempt to provide for replacement should be appropriated from profits and transferred to a plant replacement reserve.

If a company revalues a fixed asset, then depreciation should be based on the revalued figure. This was adopted in SSAP 12 (revised) to stop what became commonly known as the

'Woolworth split depreciation policy'. With this policy companies would revalue their assets but charge only the historical depreciation to profit and loss, any excess being written off against the revaluation reserve. This was felt to be inconsistent because the charge to profit and loss did not match the newly revalued figure for fixed assets in the balance sheet. At the same time the excess depreciation, in an additional journal entry, could be transferred from revaluation reserve to realised revenue reserves. This is a process which is required even under FRS 15.

The problem is making a decision as to the exact purpose of depreciation. Is it a financing, valuation or accruals technique?

(1) If it is a financing technique, then it is important to retain profits in order to replace the asset at the end of its useful life.

(2) If depreciation is a valuation device, then it should represent the loss in market value.

(3) If it is an accruals technique, then its purpose is to match cost against revenue generated.

It could be argued that the use of market values meets all three purposes and should be encouraged. However, FRS 15 has now come to the conclusion that the use of market values is not transactions based and should not necessarily find a permanent place in traditional historical cost accounting.

(c) *To:* Managing director   Date

The selection of an appropriate method of depreciation

With reference to your memo of 12 November, the following is a summary of my views as to the most appropriate method for calculating depreciation.

The purpose of depreciation is not to provide for replacement of a fixed asset but to ensure that the cost or value of the asset is charged fairly to the profit and loss account. The aim is to allocate the cost or value as fairly as possible over the useful life of the asset and therefore match the depreciation charges against the revenues the asset is helping to generate. The decision to replace an asset is a separate issue and should not cloud the allocation procedure.

FRS 15 requires that the depreciation methods chosen are those which are the most appropriate to the types of assets used in the business.

The straight-line method is the most popular but not always the most appropriate. If you wish to change the method, not only must it give a truer and fairer view of the business, it must also apply the accruals or matching principle, i.e. the cost of using up the asset must be matched with the revenue it is expected to generate.

There is a wide variety of methods available and in order to choose the most appropriate, a number of factors should be considered.

(1) If the fixed asset is depreciating as production varies then a depletion unit method might best match costs against revenues.

(2) If the life of the fixed asset is determinate, e.g. leasehold building, then a straight-line method might be appropriate.

(3) The value of the fixed asset may be depleting in the early years more than later, caused by obsolescence and wear and tear, but not necessarily due to the volume of production. This is usually indicated by higher maintenance costs in the latter years. A reduced balance approach might be the most appropriate in this case. This balances low maintenance costs and high depreciation in the early years with high maintenance costs and low depreciation in later years. The sum of the digits approach adopts the same logic.

(4) If the fixed asset is likely to become technically obsolete fairly quickly, e.g. computer

equipment, then a more prudent view should be taken. Depreciation should be geared to high charges in the early years, adopting a reduced balance or sum of the digits approach.

(5) The charge for depreciation may not be material. A number of companies, especially in the retail sector and the hotel industry, are now no longer depreciating some of their freehold properties. They argue that depreciation is either insignificant or that maintenance has replaced depreciation, thus rendering the charge to be immaterial so that it is not necessary to make a charge to profit and loss.

Solution 6 – Arlington Ltd

(a) *Capitalisation of interest*

Under the Companies Act 1985, Sch. 4, it is permitted to include as part of the production cost of an asset:

(1) a reasonable proportion of the costs incurred by the company which are only indirectly attributable to the production of that asset; and
(2) interest on capital borrowed to finance the production of that asset, to the extent that it accrues in respect of the period of production.

The main arguments advanced in support of this capitalisation are as follows:

(1) Interest incurred as a consequence of a decision to acquire an asset is not intrinsically different from other costs that are commonly capitalised. If an asset requires a period of time to bring it to the condition and location necessary for its intended use, any interest incurred during that period as a result of expenditure on the asset is part of the cost of acquisition (IAS 23).
(2) A better matching of income and expenditure is achieved, in that interest incurred with a view to future benefits is carried forward to be expensed in the periods expected to benefit. A failure to capitalise would reduce current earnings artificially and not give a representative view of the benefits of the acquisition.
(3) It results in greater comparability between companies constructing assets and those buying similar completed assets. Any purchase price would normally include interest as the vendor would wish to recover all costs, including interest, on pricing the asset.

The main arguments advanced against capitalisation are as follows:

(1) Interest is incurred in support of the whole of the activities of the company. Any attempt to associate borrowing costs with a particular asset would be arbitrary.
(2) Capitalisation results in the same type of asset having a different carrying value, depending on the particular method of financing adopted by the enterprise.
(3) Treating interest as an expense leads to comparable information from period to period and provides a better indication of the future cash flows of an enterprise. Interest fluctuates with the amount of capital borrowed and with interest rates, not with asset acquisition.

In Arlington's specific circumstances, examination of FRS 15 reveals a number of specific conditions which should be applied:

(1) Where an entity's accounting policy is to capitalise borrowing costs, only those which are directly atttributable to the construction of a tangible fixed asset should be capitalised.
(2) The amount capitalised should not exceed the amount of borrowing costs incurred during the period.
(3) Capitalisation should commence only when:
   • borrowing costs are being incurred;
   • expenditure on the asset is being incurred; and
   • activity is in progress in getting the asset ready for use.
(4) Capitalisation should be suspended during extended periods in which activity is not taking place.

(5) Capitalisation should cease when all activities are complete. If the asset is built in parts, then capitalisation should cease on completion of each part.

(6) A weighted average of borrowing costs may be adopted, but no notional borrowing costs are to be included.

It is certainly fair to capitalise interest as the store is being built because this will bring the asset to its intended location and condition and thus ensure comparability between self-built and acquired stores. This has been adopted by most retail stores and hotel groups in the UK and Ireland, e.g. Marks and Spencer, Sainsbury, Jurys Hotel Group.

An additional problem is whether or not interest can be imputed to the balance sheet value for stock as the cost of financing those stocks once the store opens. This policy is common for stocks which mature over a long period of time (e.g. whisky), or for long-term work in progress when financing costs are a material element of total cost. However, the costs must be concerned with improving the condition of that stock. In Arlington's case this seems unlikely as the stocks would not change in condition once they have arrived in the store, while stock turnover should be fast enough to make any interest cost immaterial.

(b) Accounting treatment of Wilmette Ltd

Arlington's plan is to set up a credit card operation for its customers in line with other major department stores. A new company, Wilmette Ltd, will be set up with a share capital of £100. Arlington Ltd will hold 50 per cent of the share capital but will bear 100 per cent of the bad debt risk. The other 50 per cent will be financed by Winnetka Bank Ltd.

This could be argued to be an off balance sheet finance arrangement since it is proposed that Wilmette Ltd should be accounted for on an equity basis. Before the Companies Act 1989, FRS 2 and the ASB's Interim Statement on consolidation, this would have been defined as a 'controlled non-subsidiary'. This is a company which, although not fulfilling the Companies Act definition of a subsidiary, is directly or indirectly controlled by and is a source of benefits or risks for the reporting enterprise and its subsidiaries that are in substance no different from those that would arise if the vehicle was a subsidiary.

Under the new legislation, if it could be argued that Arlington Ltd held 'dominant influence' over the affairs of Wilmette Ltd, or had exercised significant influence so that both businesses were being operated on a 'unified basis', then legally Wilmette Ltd would be a subsidiary. As such, Wilmette Ltd would be a legal subsidiary of Arlington and should be consolidated in full. This would ensure that the commercial substance of the transaction was being recorded and not its legal form. Undoubtedly companies which previously have excluded their finance subsidiaries are now bringing them back into the fold for consolidation. There would also be no excuse for exclusion on the grounds of dissimilar activities, since the legislation and FRS 2 no longer permit exclusion unless it would destroy the true and fair view of the financial statements.

In addition, FRS 5 *Reporting the Substance of Transactions* requires that any special-purpose vehicle that is under the control of another party, even if not a legal subsidiary, be consolidated as a quasi-subsidiary.

Solution 7 – Toumey Enterprises plc

(a) SSAP 19 defines an investment property as an interest in land and/or buildings:

(1) in respect of which construction work and development has been completed; and

(2) which is held for its investment potential, with any rental income being negotiated at arm's length.

However, excluded from the definition are:

(1) properties owned and occupied by a company for its own purposes and not for investment purposes;

(2) properties let to and occupied by another member of the group.

These criteria can be applied to the individual properties of Toumey Enterprises plc.

(1) North is used as the head office of the group, therefore under exclusion (1) it would not be an investment property and would be accounted for under the rules of FRS 15.

(2) South is let to and occupied by a subsidiary, therefore under exclusion (2) it would not be an investment property.

(3) East is let to an associated company, but not part of the group. The property would appear to meet the definition of an investment property. Additional information required would include details of market rent to ensure that the asset is held for its investment potential.

(4) West is let to an outside company at an arm's-length rental over a period of fifteen years, being the unexpired period of the lease. This would appear to be an investment property.

(b) FRS 15 requires that all fixed assets, including buildings but not land, should be depreciated over their estimated useful economic life. This is regardless of the market value of those assets which may well be increasing.

SSAP 19, however, emphasises the concept of current values in determining the balance sheet valuation of investment properties. Paragraph 13 emphasises that changes in the value of investment properties should not go through the profit and loss account but should be disclosed as a movement in an investment revaluation reserve. FRS 15 is not applicable and SSAP 19 states that investment properties should not be subject to periodic depreciation charges. The only exception to this rule are those leasehold properties whose unexpired terms are twenty years or less.

The application of these principles would have the following effect:

(1) North and South are not investment properties, therefore they should both be depreciated as per FRS 15. The value of land and buildings should be separated because no depreciation is charged on land. The cost or revalued amounts for buildings should be depreciated over their estimated useful lives.

(2) East is an investment property, therefore no depreciation should be charged. The asset should be shown at open market value in the balance sheet.

(3) West is an investment property but the lease has less than twenty years to run. Therefore its revalued amount should be depreciated in accordance with FRS 15 over the remaining fifteen years of life of the lease.

Solution 8 – XY Group

(a) *What is meant by impairment?*

Tangible fixed assets are normally shown on balance sheet at historic cost or at valuation less any cumulative depreciation to date in order to arrive at net book value.

FRS 11 requires reporting entities to write down those tangible assets as well as goodwill and intangibles that have been impaired and have suddenly fallen in value. An impairment represents the decrease in the value of a fixed asset below its carrying value. This may be caused by sudden obsolescence, fire damage, current operating losses or even a rise in interest rates, which makes the future cash flows receipts much less valuable, when discounted to present value.

Under FRS 11, impairment is said to have taken place if an asset's recoverable value has fallen below its carrying value. The recoverable amount of an asset is taken as the higher of its net realisable value (NRV) and its value in use (NPV). NRV is defined as an asset's disposal proceeds less any disposal costs and NPV as the present value of cash flows expected to be generated from the asset's continuing use. Normally assets which are in normal use should have an NPV higher than an asset's NRV.

For example, if an asset's NBV is £100, its NRV £80 and NPV £90, then the impairment is the difference between NBV £100 less the higher of NRV and NPV, i.e. £90. The impairment of £10 is then written off as an operating loss unless it represents a revaluation downwards caused by external market forces.

Often it is not possible to identify an impairment on an individual basis as groups of assets tend to work together and if one asset is impaired then a whole group are impaired. In such circumstances, groups of assets known as income generating units (IGUs) should form the basis of assessment for an impairment review. The IGUs are identified subjectively by dividing the income streams of a group into units which have income streams that can be independently separated. FRS 11 provides guidance on this and takes an example of a transport company where the income streams can be specifically identified with trunk routes but not supporting routes. The latter are not regarded as independent IGUs since their income depends on the survival of the trunk routes.

In the IGU scenario the NPV requires reporting entities not only to identify the NBV of direct assets but it should also include its share of common assets and this total should be compared with the NPV of both direct cash flows and share of common asset cash flows. Like must be compared with like. The cash flow should normally be based on budgets and forecasts for the next five years but it can go beyond five years in exceptional circumstances, although the cash flows should be based on a growth rate that does not exceed the UK national growth rate. The discount rate normally chosen is the reporting entities weighted average cost of capital (WACC) as adjusted for the specific risks attached to the unit.

In the case of an IGU an impairment will have to be written off to either operating costs or to reserves using the same rules as for individual assets, i.e. internal to operating and external to reserves. The credit entry is more difficult as there are a number of assets involved. The FRS identifies a specific priority to write off the assets as follows:

(i)   Goodwill;
(ii) Intangible assets (but not recorded below their NRV);
(iii) Tangible assets (on a *pro rata* basis but again they should not be recorded below their NRV).

(b) Calculation of the impairment review loss of MH Ltd

On 31 December 1998

Fair value of purchase consideration		£2.0m
Fair value of net assets acquired		1.8m
Goodwill on acquisition		0.2m

On 31 December 1999

Net book value	(£1.75m + £0.19 goodwill)	£1.94m
Net present value	(given)	1.50m
Impairment		0.44m

(c) Allocation of impairment review loss

	Net book value	Impairment loss	Net present value
Goodwill	£0.19m	£(0.19)m	Nil
Capitalised development expenditure	0.20m	(0.20)m	Nil
Tangible fixed assets	1.30m	(0.05)m	£1.25m
Net current assets	0.25m		0.25m
	£1.94m	£(0.44)m	£1.50m

The journal entry should be as follows:

			£	£
Dr		Profit and loss account	0.44m	
	Cr	Goodwill		£0.19m
		Development expenditure		0.20m
		Tangible fixed assets		0.05m

The charge is to profit and loss account as it is due to operating problems and not to external factors.

Solution 9 – Redbingo Ltd

(i) Explanation of why impairment is caused and how it should be measured

Impairment is created because an event occurs which suddenly causes a drop in the value of the fixed assets over and above the normal depreciation rate. FRS 11 provides a number of examples of possible indications of impairment including sign of operating losses, significant drop in market values of fixed assets, physical damage, obsolescence and increase in interest rates, etc.

Impairment must be measured by comparing the net book value of an asset with its recoverable amount. Recoverable amount is defined as the higher of the net realisable value (NRV) of an asset and its future use value (NPV). The latter represents the present value of the future cash flows obtainable from the asset's continued use including the cash flow from its ultimate sale.

FRS 11 would prefer the impairment to be measured on an individual asset basis but it recognises that, in most circumstances, it will have to be measured using income generating units (IGUs), i.e. units which create income that can be independently measured of other IGUs. Any loss will have to be allocated in the strict order – goodwill first, intangible assets second and finally tangible assets on a *pro rata* basis. However, the latter group of assets should not be recorded below their NRV.

The loss should be charged to profit and loss if caused by internal factors or to reserves if caused by external market forces and there is a previous reserve to offset it against.

(ii) Red Ltd – Income generating unit

	£m	£m
Net book value		330
Net realisable value	240	
Value in use	230	
Higher of NRV and NPV		240
Impairment loss		(90)

Allocation of loss

	Total	Goodwill	Intangible assets	Tangible assets
	£m	£m	£m	£m
Net book value	330	80	70	180
Recoverable amount	240			
Impairment	(90)	(80)	(10)	Nil

The balance sheet will now be restated showing intangible assets valued at £60m and tangible assets at £180m, i.e. a total of £240m.

(iii)	*Bingo Ltd*	£m	£m
	Net book value (NBV)		5.9
	Net realisable value		
	Saleable value	2.5	
	Associated selling costs	(0.1)	
		2.4	
	Net present value		
	Present value of future cash flows		
	(£1.6m x 4 years = £6.4m x 0.8468)	5.42	
	Higher of NRV and NPV		5.42
	Impairment loss		(0.48)

Because the impairment is caused by operating problems the full loss must be charged to profit and loss and the net assets reduced by £0.48m.

Dr	Profit and loss	£0.48m	
	Cr	Fixed assets	£0.48m

The impairment should be included within the accumulated depreciation part of the fixed assets' schedule as a separate depreciation charge. Thus the cost will remain at £8.7m and the accumulated depreciation increased from £2.8m to £3.28m, leaving the book value at £5.42m. If the asset had been revalued then the movement would have been recorded at the top of the fixed assets schedule as part of the cost/revalued movement.

3

Asset Valuation:
Accounting for Intangible Assets

Solution 1 – SSAP 13 Accounting for Research and Development

(a) Definitions

Applied research

This is original or initial investigation undertaken in order to gain new scientific or technical knowledge and directed towards a specific practical aim or objective.

Development

The use of scientific or technical knowledge in order to produce new or substantially improved materials, devices, products or services, to install new processes or systems prior to the commencement of commercial production or commercial applications, or to improve substantially those already produced or installed.

(b) The distinction between applied research and development expenditure

Applied research is necessary to ensure that a company maintains its competitive position, but in general it is a part of ongoing activities and no single accounting period benefits. The research has not reached the stage at which commercial production could commence on any project. In contrast, development is normally undertaken in the expectation of specific commercial and technical success which will lead to a stream of future benefits. The distinction means that prudence would dictate an immediate write-off of research expenditure since any matching would be tenuous. On the other hand development expenditure would require a matching of costs with fairly certain future revenues. Development expenditure may therefore be deferred initially to be subsequently amortised to the profit and loss account over the life cycle of the commercially developed product.

(c) Specific accounting treatment

(i) Market research

SSAP 13 (revised) specifically excludes this item from the definition of research and development expenditure. It must therefore be written off immediately to the profit and loss account. It relates to the sale of products, not to their production.

(ii) Testing of pre-production prototypes

This is specifically mentioned as part of research and development expenditure. Such expenditure ensures that products are ready for commercial exploitation and it is therefore an essential part of the development process.

(iii) Operational research

Provided it is not tied to a specific research and development activity, this is argued to be operational expenditure and thus it is outside SSAP 13's definition of research and development expenditure.

(iv) Testing in search of process alternatives

This is clearly defined in SSAP 13 as part of research and development expenditure, since it is directly concerned with the enhancement of a company's existing production process.

Solution 2 – MWT plc

(a) *Project Alpha*

This is an item of applied research as the project is directed towards a specific outcome but that outcome has not reached the stage of producing a viable product. Under SSAP 13, therefore, the cost of £175,000 should be written off to profit and loss account and the amount disclosed in the notes to the financial statements along with other research and development immediately written off.

Project Beta

This is a long-term contract on which a profit of £14m is expected on completion. A formula based on cost to date over expected cost would suggest ($^{21}/_{61}$ or a third complete) so £25m could be taken as turnover at this stage,. The progress payment is deducted from turnover leaving a net debtor of £1m. Sales of £25m and matching cost of sales of £21m are included within normal sales and cost of sales for the period. (See appendix.)

Project Gamma

This is a long-term contract on which a profit of £2m (£7m – £5m) is expected on completion. A formula based on the cost to date over expected cost would suggest ($^{1.4}/_5 \times$ £2m) that £560,000 of the final profit can be taken to date. Sales of £1.96m and cost of sales of £1.4 will be recorded. Accordingly these amounts will be transferred from the contract account to the final profit and loss account and the balance of £440,000 will be carried forward as a creditor.

Project Delta

This a long-term contract with an expected loss of £6m on completion. This loss must be provided for immediately under the prudence convention. The loss on the contract will be debited to the profit and loss account via turnover of £20m and cost of sales £24m – £4m is recorded in the ledgers, so a provision for future losses of £2m should now be made to increase the cost of sales to £26m. Debtors of £1m would also appear in the balance sheet because the client has not yet paid all the invoices raised on this project.

Project Epsilon

This contract is at an early stage and it is too soon to take profit on the grounds of prudence, and of not being able to ascertain an eventual profit at this stage. The cost to date (£1m) is work-in-progress, but set off against the £3m invoiced to the client gives a net creditor for payments on account, and the £0.4m unpaid as a debtor.

Under SSAP 9, profits taken before completion of these long-term contracts must be based on prudent estimates of the profitable completion of the work, with reference to the rate of profitability for various parts of the contract.

(b) MWT plc – profit and loss account for year ended 31 March 2002

	£m
Turnover (25 + 1.96 + 20)	46.96
Costs (21 + 1.4 + 24)	46.40
	0.56
Provision for foreseeable losses	(2.00)
Loss on contracts	(1.44)
Research costs written off	(0.175)
Operating loss	(1.615)

Appendix

Workings

Project Beta	£m	£m
Total price		75
Costs to date	21	
Costs to complete	40	
		61
Estimated total profit		14

WIP

	£m			£m
Total cost	21	Cost of sales		21

Profit and loss

	£m			£m
Cost of sales	21	Sales		25

Debtors

	£m			£m
Sales	25	Bank		24
		Balance c/d		1
	25			25
Balance b/d	1			

Profit to record

	£m
1/3 costs completed ∴ 1/3 turnover	25
Less costs of sales	21
Profit to date	4

Balance sheet

Sales: £25m – £24m on account = £1m debtor

Project Gamma

	£m
Total price	7
Total cost	5
Estimated total profit	2

WIP

	£m		£m
Total cost	1.4	Cost of sales	1.4

Contract profit and loss

	£m		£m
Cost of sales	1.4	Sales (1.4/5.0 x 7m)	1.96

Debtors

	£m		£m
Sales	1.96	Bank	2.40
Balance c/d	0.44		
	2.40		2.40

Project Delta

	£m	£m
Total price		30
Costs to date	24	
Costs to complete	12	
		36
Estimated total loss		(6)

WIP

	£m		£m
Total cost	24	Cost	24

Contract profit and loss

	£m		£m
Cost	24	Sales	20
Provision for foreseeable losses	2		

Debtors

	£m		£m
Sales	20	Bank	19
		Balance c/d	1
	20		20
Balance b/d	1		

Project Epsilon

WIP

	£m		£m
Total cost	1	Balance c/d	1
Balance b/d	1		

Contract profit and loss

	£m		£m
Cost	–	Sales	–

Debtors

	£m		£m
Balance	2.6	Bank	2.6

MWT plc – balance sheet at 31 March 2002

The provision for profit in suspense will appear on the balance sheet under 'provisions and liabilities' – a deduction from assets which is not part of shareholders' funds.
Provision for future losses of £2m.
Creditors for progress payments on account = £0.44m + 2.6m = £3.04m
Stocks and work in progress £1m
Debtors (1 + 1) = £2m

Solution 3 – Newprods plc

(a) Accounting policy note

Research and development

Expenditure on pure and applied research is charged against profits in the year in which it is incurred.

Development expenditure incurred on specific projects is carried forward, when its recoverability can be foreseen with reasonable assurance, and amortised in relation to the sales from such projects. Such expenditure is treated as a deferred asset and included in fixed assets. All other development expenditure is written off in the year of expenditure.

Fixed assets acquired for use within research and development are capitalised and depreciated in the normal fashion. If part of the fixed asset expenditure relates to qualifying development expenditure, it may be carried forward to be amortised in the future.

The accounting treatment of items (1) to (5)

(1) New gas ionising plant, £750,000

This is a fixed asset which should be capitalised and subsequently depreciated over its estimated useful life. However, if the asset is used specifically for development, then the depreciation charge may form part of overall development costs. No information is available concerning its use during 2001; thus it can be assumed it is not used on qualifying development projects and depreciation should be written off to the profit and loss account. With a life of ten years and a charge for one month, depreciation should be £6,250 (£750,000 × 1/10 × 1/12) and the net book value is £743,750.

(2) Development of kiss-proof lipstick

Although this is research expenditure, it is a contract with a third party to provide a service to that party, albeit on a contract exceeding one year. It thus falls under SSAP 9's definition of a long-term contract. As such it is not part of development expenditure under SSAP 13. Turnover should be recorded on the basis of work carried out to date and cost of sales should be matched to the same period of time. As this is a straightforward cost plus 25 per cent contract, then cost of sales would be fairly charged at £90,000 and turnover at £90,000 × 125% = £112,500. As payments on account amount to £25,000 to date, then debtors would be recorded at £87,500 (£112,500 – £25,000). No amount would be recorded as work in progress. However, if a more conservative view is taken of the profit to date, the turnover and related cost of sales can be reduced, thus creating a balance of costs not transferred to cost of sales, i.e. work in progress.

(3) Employment of Dr Zod, £25,000

Dr Zod is a nuclear physicist and is probably an expert in the field of sub-atomic wave motions. However, the annual salary must be regarded as an expense unless it can be matched to a specific successful development project. If such a project cannot be identified then the cost of £25,000 should be written off straight to the profit and loss account.

(4)   New audio product, £250,000

This product would appear to meet the five qualifying conditions to enable development expenditure to be capitalised under SSAP 13. However, only 40 per cent (£100,000) is in respect of development and £150,000 will need to be written off immediately to the profit and loss account. The £100,000 may be carried forward in the balance sheet as an intangible asset, as well as the expected £400,000 when it is spent in future years. Assuming that £500,000 is eventually capitalised, this should be amortised to accounting periods on a systematic basis by reference to the periods over which it is expected that the new audio product will be sold. This could be on the basis of either time or units sold.

(5)   Wallop advertising (£20,000) and development costs (£300,000)

Development costs of £300,000 have already been capitalised in prior years. Amortisation should commence on 1 February 2001, the date of commencement of commercial production. With an expected market life of four years, annual amortisation will be £75,000 per annum assuming a straight-line allocation. For 2001, six months should be charged, i.e. £37,500. Development costs would be stated at £262,500 under intangible assets in the balance sheet. In addition, the movement for the year should be disclosed in the notes to the accounts. The advertising expenditure of £20,000 could be carried forward as an asset, provided that it meets the requirements of FRS 5, i.e. it is probable that future revenues will result from the expenditure and the asset has a cost or value which can be sufficiently reliably measured (general recognition tests). It would then be subsequently amortised to the profit and loss account over the period from which future benefits will derive. However, prudence would probably dictate an immediate write-off. For plcs and public interest bodies, this expenditure fits under the heading of *investment for the future* and should be disclosed in the *Operating and Financial Review*.

(b)   Critical evaluation of the accounting treatment and disclosure required by SSAP 13

SSAP 13 balances the accruals concept against the prudence concept. In allowing development to be carried forward as an asset, accruals have been given precedence over prudence in contravention of SSAP 2. However, under FRS 18 and the Statement of Principles, it is unlikely that this policy will continue.

However, this approach echoes similar stances in SSAP 9 and the former SSAP 24, in which the importance of matching costs with related revenues is considered crucial in stating the profit and loss account fairly. The alternative liability or balance sheet approach is now becoming more important. However, prudence is not totally ignored since development must be expensed unless it is reasonably certain that the expenditure will be recovered. There are obvious difficulties in determining what is technically or commercially viable, and whether or not sufficient resources are available, but these difficulties cannot be avoided.

Disclosure requirements include the following:

(1)   An accounting policy note must be provided.

(2)   Movements on the deferred development expenditure account for the year must be shown.

(3)   The profit and loss account charge must be analysed between direct write-off of expenditure and amortisation of previously capitalised development expenditure. Small companies are exempt provided they are less than ten times the size of a medium company for filing purposes.

(4)   The unexpired development expenditure must be shown under intangible fixed assets on the balance sheet.

Solution 4 – Flow Ltd

(a) Explanation of the terms finance lease/operating lease and how operating leases should be accounted.

SSAP 21 *Accounting for Leases and Hire Purchase Contracts* classifies all lease agreements into two distinct types – i.e. finance leases and operating leases. SSAP 21 was published in 1994 to ensure that reporting entities report the substance of their transactions in leasing contracts. In particular it was designed to ensure that where lessees retain control over an asset over substantially all of that asset's life, even though they never acquire legal title to that asset, it should be recorded as a fixed asset in the financial statements of the lessee. It is argued that the lessee bears most of the risks of ownership as well as the possibility of receiving most of the rewards of the asset.

A finance lease is a lease agreement which transfers substantially all the risks and rewards of ownership from the lessor to the lessee. On the other hand, an operating lease is any lease that is not a finance lease where, substantially, all the risks and rewards of ownership still remain with the lessor. The standard concentrates on trying to outline the boundaries of finance leases. Unfortunately the leasing companies have tried to set up agreements which fall outside the definition – by giving the impression that the risks still rest with the lessor.

The rationale behind the standard was to ensure that the substance of transactions was reported and not necessarily their legal form. The commercial reality of all transactions must be reported. In the case of a finance lease the asset is controlled by the lessee and should be reported as an asset on the lessee's balance sheet, not the lessors. In addition, the corresponding capital payments due should be recorded as a liability.

An important presumption is made in SSAP 21 that if the present value of the minimum lease payments amounts to substantially all (i.e. 90 per cent or more) of the fair value of the asset at the inception of the lease then the lease is regarded as a finance lease rather than operating. This is used by finance companies in drawing up contracts that 'deliberately' fail the 90 per cent test and therefore undermine financial reporting.

Operating leases are accounted for as if the assets are under the control of the lessor and thus lessees need only charge their rentals paid to the profit and loss account. These are essentially short-term agreements and the assumption is that there will be several users of the asset during its lifetime.

SSAP 21 requires the lessee to disclose the full leasing commitments on finance leases in the notes to the financial statements and these should be split between those due within one year, between two and five years, and those payable in over five years. SSAP 21 requires the lessee to disclose the annual operating lease commitments that are due to expire within one year, between one and two years, and in over five years.

(b) Journal entries to record the sale of property to River plc and the payment of the first rental

Date

			£	£
1 April 1998	Dr	Bank account	850,000	
	Cr	Loan account		300,000
		Disposal of property account		550,000

being the sale of property at market value

			£	£
	Dr	Disposal of property account	500,000	
	Cr	Property		500,000

being the cost of property sold transferred to disposal of property account

			£	£
	Dr	Accumulated depreciation – property	60,000	
	Cr	Disposal of property account		60,000

being accumulated depreciation on property sold

			£	£
	Dr	Disposal of property account	110,000	
	Cr	Profit and loss account		110,000

being profit on disposal of property

These journal entries record the sale and disposal of property to/from River plc in accordance with the requirements of FRS 5. The profit on sale is the difference between the fair value of the property and its carrying value at the date of sale.

				£	£
31 March 1999	Dr	Profit and loss account (leasing charges)		50,000	
		(interest 10.56% x £300,000)		31,680	
		Loan account			
		(Capital repaid £50,000 – £31,680)		18,320	
	Cr	Bank account			100,000

being the first rental payment to River plc, which is a combination of an operating lease and a repayment of interest and capital on the loan.

The rental repayment reveals the recording of the substance of the sale and leaseback transaction undertaken by River plc, which is a combination of an operating lease rental (for the continued use of the property) and the repayment of interest and capital on the loan.

Solution 5 – Lees Ltd

(a) Effect of the lease on projected profits

The decision must be taken as to whether the lease is of an operating or finance nature. Under SSAP 21 a finance lease is created if it transfers all the risks and rewards of ownership of an asset to the lessee. This would normally occur if at the inception of the lease the present value of the minimum lease payments would cover 90 per cent or more of the fair value of the leased asset. In this particular case four years' annual payments of £45,690 each discounted at the implicit rate of interest of 15 per cent would give a present value of £45,690 × 2.283 = £104,310 + £45,690 paid in advance = £150,000 which is exactly equal to fair value. This appears to be a finance lease.

In practical terms a finance lease would generally be indicated by the following circumstances:

(1) There is a primary period in which the lessor is repaid both the principal and the interest.
(2) There is a peppercorn or nominal rental in the secondary period.
(3) The lease cannot be cancelled at either party's option during the primary period.
(4) The legal title remains with the lessor.
(5) Maintenance and other risks are covered by the lessee.

Finance charge

	£
Total rental payments:	
4 × 45,690	182,760
Fair value of plant	150,000
Finance charge	32,760

This must be spread over three years because the first payment represents a repayment of capital since it has been paid in advance.

	Cost	Payment	Liability	15%	Liability
	£	£	£	£	£
30.11.99 to 29.11.00	150,000	45,690	104,310	7,823	112,133
	112,133			7,823	119,956
30.11.00 to 29.11.01	119,956	45,690	74,266	5,570	79,836
	79,836			5,570	85,406
30.11.01 to 29.11.02	85,406	45,690	39,716	2,979	42,695
	42,695			2,979	45,674
30.11.02	45,674	45,690		16	
				32,760	

Depreciation

Depreciation should be spread over the lower of the useful life of six years and the total lease term of four years plus secondary period. Assuming the secondary period is more than two years, then six years should represent the write-off period, i.e. £150,000 ÷ 6 = £25,000 per annum.

The effect of the finance lease on projected profits

Years ending 31 May	2000 (1/2 yr)	2001	2002
	£	£	£
Depreciation charge	12,500	25,000	25,000
Finance charge	7,823	(7,823 + 5,570 =) 13,393	(5,570 + 2,979 =) 8,549
	20,323	38,393	33,549

(b) Balance sheet extracts

	At 31.5.00	At 31.5.01	At 31.5.02
	£	£	£
Fixed assets			
Fixed assets under finance lease	150,000	150,000	150,000
Accumulated depreciation	(12,500)	(37,500)	(62,500)
Net book value	137,500	112,500	87,500

Liabilities

Amounts falling due within one year

Obligations under finance lease	30,044	34,550	39,716
Accruals and deferred income	7,823	5,570	2,979
Amounts falling due after one year	74,266	39,716	

Notes to the accounts

The future minimum payments to which the company was committed as at 31.5.XX was as follows:

	30.11.99	31.5.00	31.5.01	31.5.02
	£	£	£	£
Rentals due within 1 year	45,690	45,690	45,690	–
Rentals due between 2 and 5 years	91,380	45,690	–	–
Rentals due after 5 years	–	–	–	–
	137,070	91,380	45,690	–
Less finance charges in suspense	32,760	17,114	5,974	–
	104,310	74,266	39,716	–

Solution 6 – Queen Ltd

(a) A financial statement of Queen Ltd (see working at end of this solution)

(1) Profit on ordinary activities before taxation

Profit on ordinary activities before taxation is after charging the following:

	£
Depreciation (£4,000 + £2,500)	6,500
Hire of plant and machinery	18,000
Finance charges	1,625

(2) Tangible fixed assets

	Plant and machinery
	£
Cost	
Balance at 1.12.01	xxx
Additions	160,000
Disposals	(xxx)
Balance at 30.11.02	xxx
Accumulated depreciation	
Balance at 1.12.01	xxx
Charge for the year	6,500
Disposals	(xxx)
Balance at 30.11.02	xxx
Net book value at 30.11.02	xxx

Included within plant and machinery are assets held under finance leases £36,000.

(3)   Creditors: amounts falling due within one year

	£
Obligations under finance lease	13,669
Other loans	48,000

(4)   Creditors: amounts falling due after one year

	£
Obligations under finance lease	20,456
Other loans	60,000

(5)   Obligations under finance leases

	£
Amounts falling due:	
within one year (2 × £7,500)	15,000
between two and five years (3 × £7,500)	22,500
	37,500
Finance charges in suspense	
(5,000 – 1,625)	3,375
	34,125

(6)   Commitments under operating leases

Annual commitments under operating leases	
terminable at three months' notice	£18,000

(b)   The rationale for the accounting treatment in SSAP 21

SSAP 21 *Accounting for Leases and Hire Purchase Contracts* introduces the concept that economic substance should take precedence over the legal form of a transaction.

In the past leased assets were always held in the books of the lessor either as a fixed asset or as a debtor in the case of finance leases. However, the conditions of the contract in a finance lease would suggest that economically all the risks and rewards of ownership have passed to the lessee. The lessee is really 'purchasing' the asset using an alternative financing instrument, therefore it should be capitalised in the lessee's balance sheet.

SSAP 21 is geared to finance leases, in an attempt to stop what was a first attempt at off balance sheet financing, i.e. an asset and a liability left off the balance sheet. The consequence of this increasingly popular form of finance was an artificial reduction in gearing ratios and corresponding increases in ROCEs, which led to a possible lack of comparability with companies which purchased their assets outright.

The key to the standard is the definition of a finance lease, which is defined as a lease 'that transfers substantially all the risks and rewards of ownership of an asset to a lessee. It should be presumed that such a transfer occurs if at the inception of the lease the present value of the minimum lease payments amounts to substantially all of the fair value of the leased asset'.

These finance leases must be capitalised in the books of the lessee as from July 1987. As a result an additional depreciation charge will be required relating to the new fixed assets in the balance sheet. Also the interest element or finance charge, representing the difference between the rentals paid during the period of the contract and the fair value of the asset, should be charged through the profit and loss account so as to produce a constant periodic rate of charge. This entails the use of either the sum of the digits or actuarial methods to allocate interest costs over the financing period of the lease.

Identical accounting is required for hire purchase contracts, with the exception that with these contracts the legal title does pass hands.

Since the lessor has passed on the risks and rewards of ownership to the lessee then the asset is effectively sold and should be recorded as a debtor and not as a fixed asset in the lessor's books, i.e. the right to receive future lease rentals. Obviously the debtor should exceed the value of the asset sold, the excess representing the finance income on the contract. This income should be recognised in the profit and loss account over the period of the lease.

This is complicated by the ability of the lessor to attract capital allowances and capital grants which can accelerate the cash inflow from the contract. SSAP 21 suggests that although the interest should be spread (to mirror the lessee's accounting treatment), it should be spread having regard to the company's net cash investment in the lease so as to ensure a constant periodic rate of return on the lessor's net cash investment.

An operating lease is defined in SSAP 21 simply as 'a lease other than a finance lease'. By their nature, operating leases are short term with a number of lessees during the useful life of the asset. Therefore the rental payments are really expenses and should be charged by lessees directly to the profit and loss account, subject to the accruals concept. On the other hand the lessor should regard this as a fixed asset to be accounted for in the normal manner under FRS 15.

In summary, the accounting treatment in SSAP 21 was the first attempt by the ASC to address the problem of off balance sheet financing by reflecting the economic substance of transactions rather than their strict legal form. This means that comparisons between companies should not be affected by whether they have leased fixed assets or purchased them outright.

Workings

(1) Imperial Wizard

The agreement is terminable at three months' notice by either party and would therefore probably constitute an operating lease since the risks and rewards of ownership still rest with the lessor. The payments during the year (12 × £1,500 = £18,000) should be written off through the profit and loss account.

(2) Gandalf

This could constitute a finance lease as it would appear that the present value of the minimum lease payments of £45,000 would at least cover the fair value of the machine costing £40,000.

In addition the contract is non-cancellable and the lessee has responsibility for maintenance, indicating that the risks have passed to the lessee.

	£
Finance lease rentals 6 × £7,500	45,000
Cash price 1.6.01	40,000
Finance charge	5,000

	Opening balance £	Paid £	Liability £	Finance charge (5%) £	Closing balance £
30.11.01	40,000	7,500	32,500	1,625	34,125
31.05.02	34,125	7,500	26,625	1,331	27,956
30.11.02	27,956	7,500	20,456	1,023	21,479
31.05.03	21,479	7,500	13,979	698	14,677
30.11.03	14,677	7,500	7,177	323	7,500
1.12.04	7,500	7,500			

At 30.11.01 the balance sheet liability will be:

	£
Current: £7,500 × 2 = £15,000 − £1,331 =	13,669
Long-term: £7,500 × 3 = £22,500 − £2,044 =	20,456

The profit and loss account charges will be:

	£
Finance charge	1,625
Depreciation (£40,000 ÷ 5 yrs × $\frac{1}{2}$ yr)	4,000

Note: We must assume that the secondary period for the lease exceeds two years and therefore the useful life is less than the lease term for the Gandalf. The residual value of £5,000 has been ignored in calculating the depreciation charge.

(3) Merlin

This asset was purchased on 1 September 2001 and the quarterly instalments merely indicate a hire purchase agreement. The asset must be capitalised at £120,000 and the liability recorded at the same price, assuming that the loan is interest free.

The liability will be reduced by the instalments paid over the ten quarters.

	£
Total payments due	120,000
Paid 1.9.01	12,000
Due at 30.11.01	108,000

Split between current liabilities (4 × £12,000 = £48,000) and long-term liabilities (£60,000). Depreciation £120,000 ÷ 12 years × 1/4 year = £2,500.

Solution 7 – Lessor plc

(a) Principles of SSAP 21

SSAP 21 identifies separate accounting treatment for finance leases and operating leases. For a lessor, the treatment mirrors that for lessees, i.e. finance leases are capitalised in a lessee's records but recorded as a debtor in a lessor's books, and operating leases are recorded as expenses in a lessee's books but as a fixed asset in a lessor's records. This should lead to more consistency in the accounting treatment of leases.

For a lessor, the following are the detailed rules for recording annual post-tax income.

Finance lease

SSAP 21 requires gross earnings to be allocated to accounting periods so as to achieve a constant periodic rate of return on the lessor's net cash investment in the lease in each period. The debtor is recorded at the total of the minimum lease payments plus any unguaranteed residual value due to the lessor. The methods permitted to carry out the allocation are the 'post-tax actuarial method' and the 'investment period method'. The former takes cash flows into account, i.e. tax, grants, etc. Generally because of accelerated capital allowances and grants the lessor's net cash investment will fall in time and thus higher income will be recorded in the early years of the lease.

Operating lease

SSAP 21 requires the lessor to capitalise the assets and to charge depreciation in the normal manner. This should normally be on a straight-line basis unless another systematic or rational basis is regarded to be more representative. In addition, all rental income should be recognised immediately in the profit and loss account.

Hire purchase contracts

The accounting treatment is identical to that of a finance lease except that the legal title does pass to the hire purchasee.

(b) Financial statements

Profit and loss account (extracts) for years ended 31 December

	2000	2001	2002
	£	£	£
Rental income	16,000	16,000	16,000
Capital repaid (bal. figure)	9,498	11,508	13,529
Profit before tax (W2)	6,502	4,492	2,471
Taxation (bal. figure)	2,276	1,572	865
Net profit (W1 & 2)	4,226	2,920	1,606

Balance sheet (extracts) as at 31 December

	2000	2001	2002
Assets	£	£	£
Net investment in finance lease	40,502	28,994	15,465
Deferred taxation (W3)	–	–	1,970

Note:
    £50,000 – £9,498 = £40,502 – £11,508 = £28,994
    £28,994 – £13,529 = £15,465

Liabilities	2000	2001	2002
	£	£	£
Current tax (W1)	1,225	2,319	3,139
Deferred tax (W3)	1,051	304	–

Periodic rate of return on average net investment

	2000	2001	2002
	£	£	£
Profits before taxation	6,502	4,492	2,471
Average net cash investment			
2000 (42,000 + 36,268 ÷ 2)	39,134		
2001 (30,226 + 23,858 ÷ 2)		27,042	
2002 (18,371 + 11,363 ÷ 2)			14,867
Percentage return	16.6%	16.6%	16.6%

Workings

(1) Calculation of rate of return

Period	Net cash investment	Rental received	Tax effect	Average net cash inv.	Rate of return (5.4%)	Closing balance
	£	£	£	£	£	£
1	50,000	(8,000)		42,000	2,268	44,268
2	44,268	(8,000)		36,268	1,958	38,226
3	38,226	(8,000)		30,226	1,632	31,858
4	31,858	(8,000)		23,858	1,288	25,146
5	25,146	(8,000)	1,225	18,371	992	19,363
6	19,363	(8,000)		11,363	614	11,977
7	11,977	(8,000)	2,319	6,296	340	6,636
8	6,636	(8,000)				

Tax	Rentals	Capital allowances (25%)	Taxable profits	Corp'n tax (35%)
	£	£	£	£
2000	16,000	12,500	3,500	1,225
2001	16,000	9,375	6,625	2,319
2002	16,000	7,031	8,969	3,139
2003	16,000	5,273	10,727	3,754

(2) Calculation of annual profit

		Net		Gross
2000	£2,268 + £1,958 =	£4,226	$\times \frac{100}{65} =$	£6,502
2001	£1,632 + £1,288 =	£2,920	$\times \frac{100}{65} =$	£4,492
2002	£992 + £614 =	£1,606	$\times \frac{100}{65} =$	£2,471

(3) Calculation of deferred taxation

	2000	2001	2002
	£	£	£
Tax charge per profit and loss	2,276	1,572	865
Corporation tax	1,225	2,319	3,139
Transfer to/(from) deferred tax	1,051	(747)	(2,274)

Solution 8 – Trendy Clothes plc

(a) *Sporty Shirts plc*

(i)   *Entries in the profit and loss account of Trendy Clothes plc*

Profit and loss account for the year ended 31 December 2001

	£
Sales	160,748
Less cost of sales	126,000
Gross profit	34,748
Interest receivable under finance lease	18,855
Lease expenses ($\frac{1}{3} \times$ £8,400)	2,800

(ii) *Entries in the balance sheet of Trendy Clothes plc*

Balance sheet as at 31 December	*2002*	*2001*
	£	£
Current assets		
Amount receivable under finance lease	51,772	43,831
Prepayments	2,800	5,600
Non-current assets		
Amount receivable under finance lease	28,000	79,772

Workings

	£	£
Gross investment in lease		
Rentals 3 years @ £56,000 pa	168,000	
Guaranteed residual value	28,000	
		196,000
Net investment in lease		
Minimum lease payments (present value)		
£56,000 × (1.00 + 0.848 + 0.718)	143,696	
£28,000 × 0.609	17,052	
		160,748
Total finance income		35,252

Allocation of total finance income

Year	Opening net investment	Lease payments	Net investment outstanding	Interest income 18%	Reduction in net investment	Closing net investment
	£	£	£	£	£	£
2001	160,748	56,000	104,748	18,855	37,145	123,603
2002	123,603	56,000	67,603	12,169	43,831	79,772
2003	79,772	56,000	23,772	4,228	51,772	28,000

(b) Optimistic Sales Ltd

				£	£
(1)	Dr	Bank		124,575	
	Cr	Plant and machinery			75,000
		Deferred income			49,575

Being sale of machine back to leasing company at a price of £124,575.

			£	£
(2)	Dr	Paid under finance lease	124,575	
	Cr	Finance lease obligation		124,575

Being recording of loan received from the leasing company on leaseback of machine.

			£	£
(3)	Dr	Finance lease obligation	37,500	
	Cr	Bank		37,500

Being annual rental of £37,500 payable annually in advance.

			£	£
(4)	Dr	Finance lease interest	12,191	
	Cr	Finance lease obligation		12,191

Being the annual interest on the capital amount outstanding of (£124,575 − £37,500) × 14%.

			£	£
(5)	Dr	Depreciation – profit and loss	31,144	
	Cr	Accumulated depreciation		31,144

Being the annual depreciation charge £124,575 ÷ 4 years on a straight-line basis.

			£	£
(6)	Dr	Deferred income	12,394	
	Cr	Profit on sale and leaseback		12,394

Being overall profit on sale and leaseback of machine spread evenly over the leaseback period of four years.

Workings

	£
Sales price to Optimistic Sales Ltd	124,575
Net book value at date of sale	75,000
Capital gain	49,575

The lease entered into with Trendy Clothes plc is a finance lease. Therefore, in accordance with SSAP 21, para. 49, the profit on sale should be recorded and spread over the shorter of the life of the asset or the lease term, to provide an annual gain of £12,394. Depreciation is based on the same scenario and is also spread over four years in this case.

Solution 9 – FRS 10 *Goodwill and Intangible Assets*

(a) Prohibition of write-off of goodwill to reserves

There has always been deep controversy over the accounting treatment of goodwill. Some commentators have regarded goodwill as a once-off cost of acquisition which should always be written off to reserves whereas an equal number, on the other hand, believe that goodwill is an asset that should be capitalised on the balance sheet. Even within the latter camp there are differences of opinion as to whether that asset should be amortised or simply left alone as a permanent asset on the balance sheet.

The ASB itself was totally divided on the issue. After releasing a discussion paper which offered discussants a number of options, it was still unclear from the constituents in the profession which was the favoured method. It has been the only topic to date that the ASB has felt necessary to hold a three-day public hearing. Even then, after listening to over thirty submissions, the ASB realised that there would never be consensus in UK/Ireland as to the most appropriate accounting treatment.

The major problem with goodwill is that it is not an asset in the normal sense. It is intangible in nature, it is fugitive in that its value fluctuates on a daily basis and it is also very subjective. Certainly one can argue that it gives rise to future benefits but only if used in conjunction with other assets in the business. On the other hand it is not an immediate loss in value on acquisition but it will be replaced by the new inherent goodwill built up by the new owners of the business.

SSAP 22 *Accounting for Goodwill* was really a compromise standard. It permitted both options. In practice over 90 per cent of UK and Irish companies adopted the immediate write-off to reserves approach. This was simply adopted to avoid a substantial charge having to go through the profit and loss account each year for the amortisation of goodwill. As we move away from the manufacturing age to the information age it is clear that goodwill will form an even greater proportion of the purchase consideration than in the past. On average, surveys have shown that over 60 per cent of the purchase consideration is goodwill.

The real key issue behind the revision of SSAP 22, however, has been the need to enhance harmonisation of accounting standards throughout the world. Most countries have adopted the asset and subsequent amortisation approach and so the ASB has been under pressure to ensure that its standard falls into line. In particular, the IASC/IASB has banned the alternative immediate write-off solution.

FRS 10 has therefore taken the view that goodwill is an asset (albeit part of a larger asset, i.e. the investment in the subsidiary acquired) for which the management team must be made accountable. This accountability cannot be achieved if goodwill is written off immediately to reserves.

The new treatment for purchased goodwill required by FRS 10 is to capitalise it as an intangible fixed asset. This should then subsequently be amortised against post-acquisition profits over the assets' useful economic lives but those lives should not normally exceed twenty years. Goodwill will have to be reviewed for subsequent impairment, under FRS 11, in the first post-acquisition year and also thereafter if there is evidence that the asset has become impaired.

(b) *Charge for amortisation of goodwill for the year ended 30 April 1999*

Calculation of the goodwill acquired on the acquisition of Target Ltd at 1 May 1998

	£'000	£'000
Fair value of the purchase consideration		31,000
Fair value of the net assets acquired		
Net assets included at balance sheet at fair value	30,000	
Brand name acquired not included in net assets	3,000	
	33,000	
Group share (80%)		26,400
Purchased goodwill		4,600

Calculation of annual amortisation charge for goodwill on the acquisition of Target Ltd

Useful economic life of goodwill	40 years
Amortisation (straight-line approach)	£4.6m ÷ 40 years = £115,000 per annum

However, as the life exceeds the normal maximum life of 20 years permitted by FRS 10 the company must undergo an annual impairment review to ensure that the asset has not been impaired. This will be calculated in accordance with the rules in FRS 11 *Impairment of Fixed Assets and Goodwill*.

In addition the purchased brand name of £3m will also have to be amortised over its economic useful life. This should also not normally exceed 20 years. If the life does exceed 20 years then the annual impairment review process must take place, under FRS 11.

(c) Action for future years

FRS 10 demands an automatic impairment review in the period of acquisition. However, the review should be applied separately to the brand name.

As noted, because the useful life of the goodwill is over twenty years, a rigorous impairment review of goodwill must be undertaken. Similarly, because the directors believe that the brand name has an infinite life, that fact should be proved by undertaking a separate test each year on the value of the brand to ensure that it has not deteriorated.

Under FRS 11 all impairment reviews should test whether or not the carrying value of the asset should be written down to the asset's recoverable value. This amount is defined as the higher of its future use value (NPV) and its current selling value (NRV). The former will obviously require the need to forecast future cash flows and then discount them to their net present value. The impairment should be charged as a normal operating cost in the profit and loss account.

Solution 10 – Yukon plc

(a) Describe the requirements of FRS 10 regarding the initial recognition and measurement of goodwill and intangible assets

FRS 10 (formerly FRED 10) sets out the following recommendations for the initial recognition and measurement of goodwill and intangible assets:

(i)   Positive purchased goodwill should be capitalised as an asset on balance sheet. Negative purchased goodwill should be disclosed separately on the balance sheet, immediately below purchased goodwill.

(ii) Internally-generated goodwill should not be recognised.

(iii) Intangible assets, such as patents and brand names, should be capitalised at cost.

(iv) Acquired intangibles should be separated from goodwill where their value can be reliably measured. That value should be fair value.

(v)   If fair value cannot be measured reliably it should be subsumed under goodwill.

(vi) Internally-generated intangible assets may only be recorded if they have readily ascertainable market values. This effectively bans them from being recorded.

(b) Explain the approach in FRS 10 to amortise goodwill and intangible assets

FRS 10 seeks to amortise goodwill to profit and loss over the period of its estimated useful life. The useful economic life of purchased goodwill is the period over which the value of an acquired business is expected to exceed the values of its identifiable assets and liabilities. It is extremely subjective.

There is a rebuttable presumption in FRS 10 that the useful economic life of purchased goodwill and intangible assets are limited and do not exceed twenty years. If there are valid grounds for the life of the asset to exceed twenty years then a longer period may be adopted.

Where the useful life is believed to be twenty years or less the carrying value should be amortised, using the straight-line approach, over the asset's estimated useful life. If the useful life is believed to exceed twenty years but the value is insignificant and is not capable of future measurement, then a deemed economic life of twenty years should be adopted. If the economic life of goodwill or an intangible asset is believed to exceed twenty years and the value is significant and expected to be capable of future continued measurement, then:

(i)   if the useful economic life can be estimated, then goodwill or intangible asset should be amortised in the profit and loss account over that life;

(ii) if the useful economic life is indefinite, goodwill or intangible asset should not be amortised. However, in that case the goodwill/intangible asset should be reviewed for impairment each period. This is a very expensive and complex process, under FRS 11. Some companies that initially adopted this policy have now reverted to a life of less than twenty years. Under UITF 27 that change is regarded as a change in accounting estimate, and not a change in accounting policy.

The useful lives should be reviewed regularly and revised, if necessary.

(c) *Calculation of amortisation of goodwill on the acquisition of Yukon plc by Territory plc for the years ended 31 May 20X6 and 20X7*

Fair values of net assets acquired at 31 May 20X6 by Territory plc

	£'000	£'000
Fixed assets		
Intangible (no readily ascertainable market values – note i)		Nil
Tangible		
Land and buildings (note ii)		20,000
Other (note ii)		18,000
		38,000
Current assets		
Stocks (note iii)	20,000	
Debtors (note iii)	23,200	
Cash (face value)	8,800	
	52,000	
Creditors: amounts falling due within one year (note iii)	24,000	
Net current assets		28,000
		66,000
Creditors: amounts falling due after more than one year (note iv)		
(£11m + 1 year's interest £1.1 = £12.1m x 10% for 4 years		(13,147)
= £16,105,100 / 1.07³ = £13,146,559)		
Provisions for liabilities and charges (note v)		(886)
		51,967 x 80% 41,574
Purchase consideration		
Shares (note vi) 10m shares x 2.5/1 = 25m x £2.25 per share		56,250
Cash (note vi) 10m shares x £1 each		10,000
		66,250 x 80% 53,000
Goodwill		11,426

Amortisation year ended 31 May 20X6   11,426 ÷ 10 years = £1,143 per annum
Amortisation year ended 31 May 20X7

Net book value 20X6 (11,426 – 1,143)	10,283
Fair value adjustment (3,000 x 80% x 9 years/10 years)	(2,160)
Intangible assets, written off (7,000 x 80% x 9 years/10 years)	(5,040)
Revised goodwill	3,083
Amortisation (9 years)	343
Write-off of intangible assets	5,040
Total charge to profit and loss	5,383

FRS 7 *Fair Values in Acquisition Accounting* permits adjustments to fair values up to a full financial year following an acquisition. The valuation of land and buildings of £23m should be taken into account in the fair value exercise for 20X7, and not the original value of £20m.

Where an intangible asset cannot be measured reliably on acquisition, its value should be subsumed within purchased goodwill.

Stocks should be stated at current replacement cost but the fair value should not exceed the recoverable amount which is its net realisable value of £20m.

Provisions for future losses are expressly forbidden by FRS 7 but the reorganisation provision was set up prior to the acquisition so it can be included as part of the fair value exercise.

The deferred government grants should be ignored as the fair value of the assets to which they relate have already been included in the fair value exercise.

4

Asset Valuation: Accounting for Stocks and Work in Progress

Solution 1 – Beta Ltd

(a) Stock valuations

(i) Raw materials stocks

20,000 kg at £2 per kg   £40,000

Assume that this is lower than net realisable value (NRV). Even if NRV is lower, as long as the raw material can be incorporated into a finished product which will recover the £2 per kg, the cost is the correct value.

(ii) Work in progress stocks

	£
Material 8,000 kg × £2 per kg	16,000
Conversion costs 8,000 kg × ½	
= 4,000 kg × £1.21 per kg (W2)	4,840
	20,840

Assume that cost is lower than net realisable value.

(iii) Finished goods stocks

Total cost of production (W2)	£3.21 per kg
Net realisable value (W3)	£3.69 per kg

This stock must be valued at the lower of cost and net realisable value, i.e. 16,000 kg × £3.21 per kg = £51,360.

(b) Notes to the balance sheet

(1) Accounting policies (extract)

Stocks and work in progress
Stocks have been valued in accordance with standard accounting practice at the lower of cost and net realisable value. Costs include all those factory and other overheads required to bring the stocks to their present condition and location.

(2) Stocks
Stocks comprise the following:

	£'000
Raw materials and consumables	40
Work in progress	21
Finished goods	51
	112

(c) Trading and profit and loss account for the year ended 31 December 2001

	£'000	£'000	£'000
Sales			331
Cost of sales			
Material		160	
Labour (90 × 80%)		72	
Factory overhead (7.5 + 5.4 + 6 + 12) × 80%		24.7	
			256.7
Gross profit			74.3
Administration expenses			
Wages and salaries	48		
Rent and rates	2.5		
Heat and power	0.6		
Depreciation – office building & furniture	2		
Sundry overheads	4		
		57.1	
Selling expenses			
Wages and salaries	28		
Depreciation – salesmen's motor vehicles	2		
Sundry overheads	6		
		36	
			93.1
Net loss for the year			(18.8)

Workings

(1) Production

	kg
Sales	80,000
Closing stocks – finished goods	16,000
Closing stocks – work in progress	4,000
	100,000

(2) Factory cost of production

	£'000	£ per kg
Direct materials (£160,000 ÷ 80,000)		2.0
Wages and salaries – factory	90	
Rent and rates (75%)	7.5	
Heat and power (say 90%)	5.4	
Depreciation – factory	6	
Sundry overheads – factory	12	
	120.9	1.21
		3.21

(3) Determination of net realisable value

	£'000	£ per kg
Sales (80,000 kg)	331	4.14
Less selling expenses (80,000 kg)		
wages and salaries	28	(0.35)
depreciation – salesmen's motor vehicles	2	(0.03)
sundry overheads	6	(0.07)
	36	(0.45)
	295	3.69

The net realisable value of £3.69 per kg is greater than the cost of £3.21 per kg, therefore stocks of finished goods should be valued at the lower cost figure.

Solution 2 – Capsule Ltd

All limited companies are governed by the requirements of SSAP 9 when accounting for stocks and long-term work in progress. In SSAP 9 it is a requirement that all stocks must be valued at the lower of cost and net realisable value. Cost is further defined as that expenditure necessary to bring the asset to its present condition and location.

Often many of the problems surrounding stock valuation are concerned with which costs, especially overheads, can be included. Initially this will include all production costs and, in some instances, financing and administrative expenses but only to the extent that they relate specifically to the stock.

A major problem is also deciding how much overhead to absorb in stock valuation. SSAP 9 gives guidance on this and suggests that the absorption should be based on the normal level of activity of the business. What is considered normal is difficult to decide in practice but the decision should take account of past activity levels, budget activity levels and possibly also the maximum possible level of activity for the production machinery. The decision is obviously fairly subjective.

Material and labour costs can generally be more easily 'attached' to stocks, particularly if detailed wage analysis records are available.

Care is needed to ensure that all carriage inwards costs and non-recoverable customs duties are included in stock valuations but that trade discounts are excluded.

The definition of net realisable value (NRV) given in SSAP 9 is the actual or estimated selling price, net of trade but before cash discounts, less:

- all further costs to completion; *and*
- all costs incurred in marketing, selling and distribution.

The accounting treatment of each of the stocks is described below.

(1) Banoline stocks

In accordance with the definition of cost described above it would appear that the value of these stocks is overstated. It is incorrect to include a proportion of selling expenses as these have not been incurred in bringing the unsold stock to its present condition or location.

The inclusion of a proportion of factory overheads seems appropriate and therefore stocks would be valued fairly at £382,000.

Consideration of NRV is unlikely to change this value as the product is selling steadily and showing good profit margins.

The valuation of Banoline should be disclosed in the balance sheet under the heading of current assets. The accounting policy concerning the valuation of stocks should be included as part of the company's accounting policy section of the financial statements.

(2) Research costs – Calmdown

Although £348,000 has been spent on research into a new tranquilliser, it is to be reimbursed by a government agency. Therefore it should be accounted for as work in progress and not as research and development expenditure.

As the work is performed over the course of the contract then a proportion could be recorded as turnover representing cost plus 6 per cent, and the cost up to that stage could be written off to cost of sales.

However, if any of the debt is likely to become irrecoverable then provision should be made for the probable loss in accordance with SSAP 9's concept of foreseeable losses.

(3) Apentone stocks

As with the Banoline stocks, selling expenses should be excluded and thus the cost value of the stock is £706,000 – £59,000 = £647,000.

Under SSAP 9 it is a requirement to ensure that the NRV is not lower than cost. In the case of Apentone the NRV would be calculated as follows:

	£	£
Estimated sale proceeds		
(13,000 × 100 g packs at £35 each)		455,000
Less further packing costs	20,000	
additional advertising costs	30,000	
proportion of selling office expenses	59,000	
		109,000
Net realisable value		346,000

Since the NRV of £346,000 is lower than the cost of £647,000, stocks should be valued at that reduced amount. The stocks should be recorded under current assets in the balance sheet and the accounting policy must be disclosed in the financial statements.

(4) Laboratory costs

These are research costs which relate to the company's own products. As such they are not the subject matter of SSAP 9. This expenditure is governed by SSAP 13, and if the project is only in the embryo stages with no likelihood of future revenue then £265,000 should be written off immediately as an expense.

In addition any capital expenditure, albeit capitalised, should be depreciated and written off directly to the profit and loss account.

Under SSAP 13 research expenditure should be disclosed in the notes to the accounts unless the company comes under the small companies exemption from that standard. The net book value of the fixed assets should be included in the balance sheet under tangible fixed assets. The accounting policies for research expenditure should also be disclosed.

Solution 3 – Volt Ltd

Internal memorandum

To: Managing director
From: Financial controller   Date

The impact of stock valuation on reported profits to March 2002

I have included a draft manufacturing and trading account for the first three months of trading to 31 March 2002. This is shown in Appendix 1 together with stock valuations in Appendix 2. Under standard accounting practice we are required to include all costs that have been incurred in bringing the stocks to their present location and condition. However, any one-off or unusual items should be excluded. Appendix 1 shows that the effect of valuing stock at £116,000 has been to increase a £35,000 profit on PAR to £151,000. The main aspects of valuation are:

(1) The costs of raw materials consumed;
(2) Conversion costs, including direct labour and any manufacturing and other overheads necessary to bring the stock to its present location and condition.

The major problem has been to identify which overheads should be included in the stock valuation and how to calculate a fair absorption rate. In our own specific situation, the following costs should be included:

(1) Production overheads;
(2) Depreciation of equipment and factory buildings;
(3) Amortisation of development expenditure.

The absorption rate should be based on normal activity which is determined by reference to three factors: past experience, the current budget and productive capacity under normal working conditions. Since this is our first year, then only the last two can be considered. Our budget for 2002 is 100,000 units of PAR which also represents maximum normal working conditions. Therefore I have divided the £148,000 production overheads by a quarterly norm of 25,000 units to calculate a recovery rate of £5.92 per unit.

In addition to valuing stocks at cost, a further test must be carried out to ensure that the net realisable value (NRV) is not less than the cost figure. In the case of special order and raw material stocks, if the finished goods are obsolete then serious consideration may need to be given to this test. As regards normal PAR stocks, the likelihood is very small that the cost of £38.634 would be greater than NRV if the current selling price is £58.27.

Having weighed up all these points, I consider that the following accounting treatment is appropriate for our company:

(1) All labour and raw materials should be included in closing stock at their full cost. No start-up inefficiencies or wastage should be included in the value of closing stock and therefore there is no need for a write-off to profit and loss.
(2) For special stocks, a provision at the year end should be seriously considered to reduce stocks to NRV if it becomes obvious that the stocks are obsolete.
(3) The overheads in our PAR brand stocks should include the above items and should be absorbed based on our normal capacity of 100,000 units.

Appendix 1: The effect on reported profits of the valuation of stocks

	PAR		Other		Total	
	£'000	£'000	£'000	£'000	£'000	£'000
Sales (note 2)		641		109		750
Opening stocks:						
raw materials	Nil		Nil		Nil	
Purchases	333		107		440	
	333		107		440	
Less closing stocks:						
raw material (note 6)	49		5		54	
Cost of raw material						
consumed	284		102		386	
Direct labour costs	174		174		348	
Production overheads:						
Fixed	64		64		128	
Depreciation	51		51		102	
Amortisation of development	33		–		33	
Cost of manufacture	606		391		997	
Closing stock:						
finished goods	(116)		–		(116)	
Cost of sales		490		391		881
Net profit/(loss)		151		(282)		(131)

Appendix 2: Value of finished goods stock

At cost
3,000 units × £38.634 (working) = £115,902 (say £116,000)

Net realisable value
Average selling price of PAR = £641,000 ÷ 11,000 units sold = £58.27

Assuming that selling and distribution costs do not exceed £58.27 – £38.634 then production cost is lower than net realisable value.

Workings
Production costs relating to 14,000 units of PAR – 3 months ended 31 March 2002

	£'000	£'000	£'000
Wiring (purchases) (note 1)		92	
Less: special order transfer (note 3)	10		
closing stock (note 6)	7		
		17	
Cost of wiring consumed			75
Other raw material purchases (note 1)		348	
Less: special order transfer (note 3)	97		
closing stock (note 6)	42		
		139	
			209
Total raw materials consumed			284
Direct labour costs (£348,000 × 50%) (note 5)			174
			458

Production cost per unit of output £458,000 ÷ 14,000 = £32.714 per unit

Production overheads	*£'000*
Fixed production overheads £128,000 × 50% (note 5)	64
Depreciation of equipment and factory buildings	
£102,000 × 50% (note 5)	51
Amortisation of development expenditure	
£396,000 ÷ 3 years × ¼ year	33
	148

Overhead recovery rate £148,000 ÷ 25,000 units	
(normal capacity 100,000 units per annum – note 4) =	£5.92 per unit
Total cost of production for stock valuation	
£32.714 + £5.92 per unit =	£38.634 per unit

Solution 4 – Clam Ltd

(a) *Profit and loss account for the year ended 31 July 2001*

	£'000	£'000
Sales		2,480
Cost of sales (W1)		1,736
Gross profit		744
Less administration costs		110
Operating profit before taxation		634
Exceptional item: Redundancy and rationalisation (notes)		380
Operating profit before taxation		254
Taxation		127
Profits after taxation		127

Statement of movement in reserves

Opening balance as previously recorded	xxx	
Prior year adjustment (W5)	105	
Opening balance as restated		xxx
Retained profit for the year		127
Closing balance		xxx

Note to the profit and loss account

Note 1: Exceptional item £380,000.
In February 2001 the company closed its production facility in Bath and this has resulted in the laying off of 70 per cent of its workforce.

Note to the reader: Prior to 1993 this would have been treated as an extraordinary Item (net of tax).

(b) Report to the managing director

Mr T Swan	Todd, Makebelieve & Co.
Managing Director	Chartered Accountants
Clam Ltd	Main Street
Headfort Road	Limavady L7 4WX
Limavady L10 4JL4	Date

Financial statements for the year ended 31 July 2001

With reference to your letter of 19 August I am enclosing, as requested, a copy of your draft accounts for 2001. There are a number of matters that still need to be discussed:

(1) *Capitalisation of self-built specialised machinery*

Under FRS 15 it is permissible to identify all the costs required to bring self-built machinery to its present location and working condition and for its intended use. This will include materials and labour costs as well as any overheads, both manufacturing and others. As a result £138,642 of overheads has been capitalised.

The fact that the machinery would have cost £950,000 if purchased outside is not relevant. To take account of this saving would recognise profit on self-built work and would be in contravention of company legislation. However, in later years the machine may be revalued if the company adopts revaluation as a policy for plant and machinery. Any surplus would then be taken directly to a non-distributable revaluation reserve. However, the revaluation would have to take place every five years.

The machine should be depreciated over ten years, which is its estimated useful life. In accordance with normal policy, a full year's depreciation charge has been made in the year of acquisition/construction.

(2) *Valuation of closing stock*

In accordance with SSAP 9 all costs necessary to bring the stock to its present condition and location must be included in its valuation. This will include not only raw material and direct labour costs but also production overheads. In deciding the overhead absorption rate consideration must be given to the normal level of activity, which is the level of activity expected to be normally achieved based on past experience, budgets and production capacity.

Included in the overhead costs will be depreciation on the self-built specialised machinery described above. However, any one-off or non-recurring costs such as the rationalisation programme must be excluded.

I have therefore added £17,000 and £4,000 respectively to cover overheads and depreciation costs in stock, giving a total valuation of £73,000 for finished goods.

(3) *Exceptional/extraordinary items and prior-year adjustments*

In the 2000 accounts, a fundamental error was made in omitting stock valued at £210,000 from the closing stock valuation. This differs from the normal changes in estimates which occur when accruals and prepayments are different from actual payments and receipts.

Therefore this must be treated as a prior-year adjustment under FRS 3, i.e. the opening reserves and comparatives must be adjusted by an increase of £105,000 in reserves and opening stocks (£210,000 less tax charge 50 per cent).

I have adjusted the materials charged to plant from £190,000 to £140,000. Part of the stock value had been transferred at full cost of £106,000 but had been previously written down to its estimated realisable value of £56,000. Once written down it can never be restated back to cost, and thus the materials figures in fixed assets are overstated by £50,000.

The costs relating to the rationalisation and redundancy programmes are one-off items which will not recur and they are outside the ordinary activities of the business. Therefore these costs would have been treated as an extraordinary item under SSAP 6 and disclosed net of tax savings. SSAP 6 specified that the closure of a material segment of a business should be written off as an extraordinary item. However, under the new standard, FRS 3, it must be treated as an exceptional item and disclosed on the face of the profit and loss account, between operating profit and interest payable.

I hope that the above adjustments are acceptable to you and I would be grateful if you would confirm, at your convenience, that it is in order for the draft accounts to be finalised.

Yours sincerely

R W Todd

Note to the reader

Prior-year adjustments are, from June 1993, to be included within the primary statement of total recognised gains and losses under the terms of FRS 3.

Workings
(1) Calculation of cost of sales

	£'000	£'000	£'000
Opening stock 1.8.00		170	
Omission of stock 2000		210	
Purchases		820	
		1,200	
Less			
closing stock 31.7.01	307		
transferred to fixed assets			
(190,000 note 1 – 106,000			
note 2 + 56,000)	140		
		447	
Raw materials consumed			753
Direct labour			
(1,030,000 note 3 – 340,000			
transfer to fixed assets)			690
Production overheads (W2)			281
Depreciation (W3)			62
Costs of manufacture			1,786
Add opening stocks finished goods		23	
Less closing stocks finished goods (W4)		(73)	
			(50)
			1,736

(2) Calculation of production overheads

	Labour costs	Production overheads	Overhead recovery
	£1,030,000	£420,000	40.777%
Fixed assets:	£340,000 × 40.777% =	£138,642	
Production:	£690,000 × 40.777% =	£281,358	

(3) Own plant capitalised

	£
Materials (190,000 note 1 – 50,000 note 2)	140,000
Labour	340,000
Overheads (W2)	138,642
	618,642

Useful life of plant ten years. Assume a full year's depreciation of £61,864.

(4) Valuation of closing stocks – finished goods

	£'000
Material cost (note 4)	10
Direct labour cost (note 4)	42
Overheads 42 × 40.777% (W2)	17
Depreciation on own plant capitalised	
$42/690 \times £61,864$ (labour costs in stock as a percentage of total labour costs)	4
	73

(5) Prior-year adjustment

The omission of the parts stock of £210,000 at 31 July 2000 is so fundamental that if the company had been aware of its existence in July 2000 it would have adjusted the accounts. The truth and fairness of the accounts would have been destroyed. It is therefore a fundamental error under FRS 3 and requires a prior-year adjustment of £210,000 less 50 per cent tax effect.

Solution 5 – B & D Manufacturing Ltd

(a) *Closing stocks*

Finished goods	£
500 completed rugs at £37.50 per rug	18,750

Work in progress	Nil

Raw materials	
49,000 FF ÷ 7FF to £1	
(equivalent to 600 rugs – see W4)	7,000
	25,750

Note: Raw materials	
½ 300 rugs at full cost	3,500
½ 300 rugs at £11.67	3,500

In addition, a provision for the foreseeable loss on the latter equivalent 300 rugs should be provided of £7,749.

Workings

(1) Production units

Rugs sold	2,500
Closing stocks as at 31 March 2002	500
Production for the year	3,000

(2) Factory cost of production

	£	£ per unit
Raw materials 294,000FF ÷ 7FF/£1		
= £42,000 – £7,000 closing stock	35,000	11.67
Wages	25,000	8.33
Production overheads	52,500	17.50
	112,500	37.50

(3) Valuation at net realisable value (NRV)

	£ per unit
Selling price	55
Less selling and distribution expenses	Nil
NRV	55

All 500 units in closing stock will be disposed of and the NRV of £55 exceeds the cost of £37.50 per unit. Closing stock should therefore be valued at the lower cost figure, i.e. 500 units × £37.50 = £18,750.

(4) Raw material stocks

Materials utilised = 294,000 FF – 49,000 FF = 245,000 FF

Material in stock = 49,000 FF = 1/5 × 245,000 FF

Since 245,000 FF of stock produced 3,000 units, there is equivalent material in stock for 600 additional rugs of which there is a contract left to sell 300 (800 contracted – 500 rugs in closing stock).

The remaining raw material will be converted into 300 rugs which are expected to sell for £18 per unit. The raw material costs are £11.67 per unit which added to labour and overhead costs amount to £37.50. There is a case, therefore, for valuing material stocks at the lower of £18 and £11.67, i.e. £11.67. But should conversion costs of £25.83 × 300 be included as a projected loss and thus as negative stocks of £7,749? It is certainly foreseeable and should be provided, leaving raw material stocks at zero.

(5) Calculation of exchange gain/(loss) on translation

	£
Monthly liability at year end	
56,000FF ÷ 8FF closing rate	7,000
56,000FF ÷ 7FF average rate	8,000
Exchange gain (to profit and loss)	1,000

(b) Internal memorandum

From: Financial accountant
To: Financial director   Date

Stock valuation

With reference to your memorandum of 10 April, I detail below the procedures adopted by the company for the valuation of closing stocks.

(1) Total production was estimated at 3,000 rugs. This includes rugs sold as well as the closing stocks in our warehouse.

(2) Total factory costs of production were computed and the cost per unit was determined to be £37.50 per unit. Costs included not only materials and labour but also any factory overheads incurred in bringing the stocks to their present condition and location.

(3) The materials costs were calculated in accordance with standard accounting practice on foreign currency translation (SSAP 20) and the dual transaction approach was adopted, i.e. purchases were translated at the date of acquisition, not at the date of payment. Any movements in exchange rates between the date of purchase and the date of settlement have been written off to profit and loss account as exchange gains/(losses). In addition any monetary liability must be retranslated at the year end and this has led to a £1,000 exchange gain at 31 March 2002.

 A further £200 exchange gain will be recorded in the published accounts for next year when the cheque for £6,800 clears the outstanding creditor balance.

(4) Total cost per unit was then compared with net realisable value (NRV) and in accordance with SSAP 9, the lower figure has been extracted for the published accounts. Only 50 per cent of the raw material failed to reveal a higher cost valuation and this has been valued at the lower NRV of zero. In addition a provision has been made on that stock for future conversion costs.

Solution 6 – The definition of work in progress

(a) *The definition of a long-term contract*

SSAP 9 (para. 22) defines a long-term contract as one 'entered into for the design, manufacture or construction of a single substantial asset or the provision of a service where the time taken substantially to complete the contract is such that the contract activity falls into different accounting periods'. This would normally be a period exceeding one year but this is not an essential feature of the definition. A short-duration contract may be included as a long-term contract if it is sufficiently material to the activity of a period so that to omit the turnover and related cost of sales would cause a distortion of the period results and fail to give a true and fair view. However, this policy should be applied consistently from year to year within the entity.

(b) *Disclosure in the profit and loss account and balance sheet*

(1) *Profit and loss account*

 Under SSAP 9, para. 28, long-term work in progress should be assessed on a contract-by-contract basis and reflected in the profit and loss account by recording turnover and related costs as activity progresses. Turnover is ascertained in a manner appropriate to the stage of completion of the contract, the business and the industry in which it operates.

 If the contract can be reasonably assessed before its conclusion (para. 29) then a prudently calculated attributable profit should be recognised in the profit and loss account as turnover and related cost of sales.

(2) *Balance sheet*

 Work in progress (para. 30) should be disclosed as follows:

- If recorded turnover exceeds payments received on account — Separate the debtor as 'amounts recoverable on contract'.

- If excess payments are received in a contract then the balance is set off against long-term contract balances and if still greater — Separate the creditor as 'payments on account'.

- Long-term contract balances at cost less transferred to cost of sales, after foreseeable losses and excess payments not matched with turnover

  Separate the stocks as 'long-term contract balances'.

  Should be disclosed separately into
  (i) net cost less foreseeable losses
  (ii) applicable payments on account.

- If provision for foreseeable losses exceeds costs (after transfers to cost of sales)

  Include within 'provisions for foreseeable losses'.

(c) Specific disclosures

Trading account

	Contract X £'000	Contract Y £'000
Turnover	500	350
Cost of sales	450	400
Gross profit/(loss)	50	(50)
Provision for foreseeable losses		(60)

Balance sheet

	£'000
Recoverable on contracts (350 turnover – 200 payments)	150
Provision for foreseeable losses	60
Stocks: long-term work in progress (600 costs – 450 transfer to cost of sales – 25 excess payments)	125

Notes to balance sheet

Stocks are disclosed for Contract X at the net cost of £150,000 less applicable payments on account of £25,000.

Solution 7 – Druid Ltd

(a) Profit and loss account for the year ended 31 December 1999 and balance sheet as at that date

Profit and loss account for the year ended 31 December 1999 (extract)

	£'000
Turnover (£6,480 + £800 + £7,750)	15,030
Cost of sales (£5,290 + £800 + £7,750)	(13,840)
Provision for foreseeable loss	(1,324)
Gross loss	(134)

Balance sheet as at 31 December 1999

	£'000
Stocks and work in progress (£60 + £180 – £50 + £1,210 – £250)	1,150
Debtors – amounts recoverable on long-term contracts	650
Provisions for liabilities and charges – foreseeable losses	(1,324)
	476 Dr

Workings

Estimate of total profit/(loss) on contracts

	Contract 1	Contract 2	Contract 3
	£'000	£'000	£'000
Contract price	10,800	8,400	18,200
Costs to date	5,350	980	8,960
Estimated costs to complete contracts	3,250	5,900	10,200
Rectification work to complete (2% price)	216	168	364
Estimated total contract costs	8,816	7,048	19,524
Estimated total contract profit/(loss)	1,984	1,352	(1,324)
Stage of completion	12/20 months = 60%	2/14 months = 14%	–
Costs certified/estimated total costs	£5,290/8,816 = 60%	£800/7,048 = 11%	–
Attributable profit/(loss)	1,190	149	(1,324)

Turnover

	£'000	£'000	£'000	£'000
Costs certified to date	5,290	800	7,750	13,840
Attributable profit	1,190	–	–	1,190
	6,480	800	7,750	15,030

Stocks and work in progress

	£'000	£'000	£'000	£'000
Costs incurred to date	5,350	980	8,960	15,290
Cost of sales (certified to date)	5,290	800	7,750	13,840
	60	180	1,210	1,450
Deduct excess payments	–	(50)	(250)	(300)
	60	130	960	1,150

Debtors – amounts recoverable on contract

	£'000	£'000	£'000	£'000
Turnover	6,480	800	7,750	15,030
Payments on account	5,830	850	8,000	14,680
	650	(50)	(250)	350
Offset against work in progress	–	50	250	300
	650	Nil	Nil	650

(b) Application of fundamental accounting concepts in SSAP 9 Stocks and Work in Progress

Accruals

Key concept, as it attempts to match the costs incurred during the contract with the revenue earned on the contract to the same point in time as the contract progresses. Revenue is matched with the related costs to date.

Prudence

This is implemented in several ways in SSAP 9 as follows:

Contract 1   Profit only recognised in later stages;

Contract 2   No profit is incorporated within profits as the contract is only in its early stages;

Contract 3   Losses are recognised in full, immediately, to the end of the contract.

Consistency

The same accounting policies are adopted from year to year in the calculation of attributable profit and foreseeable losses and for all long-term contracts.

Going concern

This assumes that the company will be in operational existence for the foreseeable future and thus the assets are not computed on a break-up basis on any of the contracts.

Solution 8 – Athos Ltd

(a) SSAP 9 (original)

Balance sheet

	£'000
Current assets (see workings)	
Stocks – long-term work in progress	315
Trade debtors (progress payments unpaid)	50
Creditors – amounts falling due within one year	71

(b) SSAP 9 (revised)

Balance sheet

	£'000
Stocks – long-term contract work in progress at cost	Nil
Trade debtors (306 + 19)	325
Creditors – amounts falling due within one year (excess payments on account)	21
Provisions for liabilities and charges	
Provision for future losses on long-term contracts	10

Note:

Costs to date as a proportion of estimated total costs are charged to profit and loss and turnover is matched by crediting the same proportion of total turnover.

Profit and loss account

	£'000
Turnover (1,063 + 1,579 + 219)	2,861
Cost of sales (910 + 1,500 + 222)	2,632
Expenses	
Provision for future losses on contract	10

(c) *Advantages and disadvantages of SSAP 9 (revised)*

SSAP 9 (revised) was issued with the intention of removing the anomaly between the original SSAP and company legislation. The anomaly arose because an unrealised profit was included in the profit and loss account and a current asset (work in progress) was valued above cost, in direct contravention of Schedule 4 of the Companies Act 1985. The true and fair override had to be adopted for construction companies in order to comply with the original SSAP 9.

Other companies have taken the view that since payments on account must include a profit element they need only disclose the amount of profit included in the balance sheet, i.e. costs less payments on account. They argue that it is impossible to calculate how much profit is included in the balance sheet figure. They are therefore unable to quantify the effect of the departure from the statutory valuation.

The revised standard was also an attempt to integrate the profit and loss account and balance sheet more closely. SSAP 9 (revised) takes the approach that a long-term contract should be broken down into segments, each segment representing the work carried out to date during the accounting period. Any profit element will therefore normally be included in debtors and not work in progress, and this is acceptable under current company legislation.

ED 40 originally proposed that turnover and cost of sales should both represent work carried out to date. This meant that all attributable profit to date would be included in the profit and loss account. The Institute of Chartered Accountants of Scotland (ICAS) felt that this might be imprudent and that directors should be permitted to adopt a lower turnover figure if desired. SSAP 9 (revised) therefore allows directors to determine turnover as any figure up to the maximum of the value of work carried out to date. However, they must match costs transferred to cost of sales only up to the same period as turnover is recorded, i.e. the matching process is a priority.

This revised version can lead to a number of anomalous situations if a fairly conservative view is taken of turnover.

(1) If turnover exceeds payments received from the client to date, a debtor is created at the period end.

(2) If payments on account exceed turnover, then that excess must be set off against costs not yet transferred to cost of sales, the result being a reduction in work in progress.

(3) In extreme cases the set-off may be so high that it exceeds the balance of untransferred costs, the result being a creditor.

The new approach will certainly lead to full double-entry book-keeping and will link the two main financial statements closer together. In addition it will now comply with company legislation. The main practical advantage to users is likely to be a greater comparability between companies. However, as can be seen in (1) to (3) above, long-term contract information will be split into three parts of the balance sheet, i.e. debtors, work in progress and creditors. This could lead to confusion.

The increased flexibility given to the preparers of financial statements will probably result in manipulation of profit figures. This is because there is no guidance concerning the percentage of work done which is to be recorded as turnover.

Workings

Revised profit and loss account/balance sheet

(1) Calculation of overall profit/(loss)

		A		B		C
		£'000		£'000		£'000
Tender price		1,700		2,100		875
Cost to date	(62.5%) 910		(75%) 1,500		(25%) 222	
Future costs to complete	(37.5%) 545		(25%) 495		(75%) 666	
		1,455		1,995		888
Profit/(loss) on contract		245		105		(13)

(2) Original balance sheet

		A	B	C	Total
		£'000	£'000	£'000	£'000
Cost to date		910	1,500	222	
Attributable profit to date	(62.5%)	153	(75%) 79	–	
		1,063	1,579	222	
Foreseeable losses		–	–	(13)	
		1,063	1,579	209	
Progress payments received and receivable		757	1,650	200	
Long-term work in progress		306		9	315
Creditors			(71)		(71)

(3) Contract accounts

	A	B	C		A	B	C
	£'000	£'000	£'000		£'000	£'000	£'000
Cost to date	910	1,500	222	Cost of sales	910	1,500	222

(4) Contract profit and loss accounts

	A	B	C		A	B	C
	£'000	£'000	£'000		£'000	£'000	£'000
Cost of sales	910	1,500	222	Sales	1,063	1,579	*219
Provision for foreseeable losses			10				*25% × 875

(5) Contract debtor

	A	B	C		A	B	C
	£'000	£'000	£'000		£'000	£'000	£'000
Sales	1,063	1,579	219	Bank	757	1,600	200
Balance c/d		21		Balance c/d	306		19
	1,063	1,600	219		1,063	1,600	219
Balance b/d	306		19	Balance b/d		21	

Solution 9 – Wilkes Ltd

(a) Valuation of stocks and work in progress as at 31 July 2001

	£
Building material stocks	
Raw materials and consumables (W1)	116,435
Work in progress	
Long-term work in progress (W2)	106,750
Debtors (extract)	
Amounts due from long-term contracts	22,000

(b) Letter to Wilkes

Mr Wilkes
Managing Director
Wilkes Ltd
21 Headfort St
Wakingham

Tool and Fool
Chartered Accountants
121 Fetters Lane
London EC4

Date

Dear Sir

Valuation of stocks and work in progress in the annual published accounts for the year ended 31 July 2001

With reference to your letter of 9 October I have set out below the current procedure to value your stocks and work in progress for this year's accounts.

(1) Building materials stocks

These were originally valued at cost of £121,241 in the draft accounts. However, there are two adjustments which must be made in order to value the stock in accordance with SSAP 9:

(a) Type A blocks were incorrectly priced at £20 each instead of £20 per 100, therefore they have been overvalued in error by £2,970.

(b) Old-style windows are now obsolete and should be written off to zero value, unless there is any scrap value in which case they would be valued at that price less any disposal costs. It is a rule of SSAP 9 that stocks should be valued at the lower of cost and net realisable value. This will result in a reduction of £1,836 in the valuation of stocks.

The value of the interior doors which originally cost £20 each should not be adjusted as long as their recovery is assured in terms of sufficient revenues to completion. The current value of £18 is not relevant in this situation.

(2) Work in progress – Crooks Lane site

The potential revenue of £220,000 from the sale of the four houses on this site exceeds total cost by over £100,000 and the project is thus clearly profitable. However, the houses have still not been sold and it might be prudent not to take up any profit on this development until the sale is finally agreed. I have therefore valued the properties at their cost of £106,750 in the financial statements for this year.

(3) Work in progress – School site

This is more in the nature of a long-term contract with the Education Authority with the price fixed at £150,000. The contract is approximately one-third complete in terms of work certified, and profit should normally be taken up in this proportion. The contract will clearly be profitable but at present the cost of work certified exceeds its value. Therefore they are recorded as cost of sales and turnover respectively and a net loss of £27,510 is recorded in the accounts. No provision will be required for any further losses as the contract will ultimately be profitable. A debtor for £15,000 will be recorded as amounts due from the client but there will be a zero work in progress value.

(4) Work in progress – Smith Street site
This is similar to the school site contract and again the contract would appear to be ultimately profitable. It is only in its early stages and no profit should be taken up. However, costs of work completed to date exceed the value of work certified and a loss of £5,170 is recorded. Contract debtors are £7,000 and work in progress is zero.

(5) Summary
The following revised notes are required in your financial statements.

Note 14

Stocks	2001	2000
	£	£
Raw materials and consumables	116,435	xxx
Long-term work in progress	106,750	xxx
	223,185	xxx

Note 15

Debtors (extract)		
Trade debtors	22,000	xxx

I hope that these explanations will be sufficient for your needs but please do not hesitate to contact me if you have any additional queries.

Yours sincerely

Frank J Brano

Workings
(1) Building materials stock

	£
Raw materials (per draft accounts)	121,241
150 blocks (£20 per 100 = £30 priced at £3,000 in error)	(2,970)
102 old-style frames written off (obsolete) × £18	(1,836)
52 interior doors (no adjustment)	Nil
	116,435

(2) Work in progress

	Crooks Lane site (CL) £	School site (SS) £	Smith Street site (SmS) £
Land at cost	50,000	–	–
Materials used			
to 1 August	23,200	33,230	5,750
to 30 September	2,950	12,150	8,450
to completion	Nil	13,200	50,000
Plant, equipment, etc.	2,700	3,060	2,900
Labour and associated costs to date	31,150	43,260	6,420
to 30 September	6,560	10,300	5,230
to completion	Nil	12,400	70,000
	116,560	127,600	148,750
Contract price	220,000	150,000	200,000
Projected profit	103,440	22,400	51,250

All are ultimately profitable

	£
Valuation	
Crooks Lane site	106,750
School site	Nil
Smith Street site	Nil
	106,750

Contract accounts

	CL £	SS £	SmS £		CL £	SS £	SmS £
Land at cost	50,000	Nil	Nil	Cost of work	Nil	77,510	12,170
Materials used	23,200	33,230	5,750	Plant c/d	4,100	9,640	7,900
Plant at cost	6,500	10,660	7,900	Balance c/d	106,750	Nil	Nil
Labour & assoc. costs	31,150	43,260	6,420				
	110,850	87,150	20,070		110,850	87,150	20,070

Plant net book value

(Based on cost of work to date as a percentage of total expected costs.)

CL $\frac{£60,850}{£66,560}$ × £6,500 (cost) – £3,800 (RV) = c90%, therefore carry forward £4,100

SS NRV 14/11/01 £7,600
Cost £10,660
$\frac{1}{3}$ certified × £3,060 = £1,020, therefore carry forward £7,600 + £2,040 = £9,640.

SmS Carried down at net book value £7,900 because the value of the asset is increasing.

Contract profit and loss accounts

	CL £	SS £	SmS £		CL £	SS £	SmS £
Cost of sales	Nil	77,510	12,170	Turnover	Nil	50,000	7,000
				Profit and loss		27,510	5,170
	Nil	77,510	12,170		Nil	77,510	12,170

Contract debtor account

	CL	SS	SmS		CL	SS	SmS
	£	£	£		£	£	£
Turnover	Nil	50,000	7,000	Bank	Nil	35,000	Nil
				Balance c/d	Nil	15,000	7,000
	Nil	50,000	7,000		Nil	50,000	7,000

Solution 10 – Public holding company

Internal memorandum

To: Group chief accountant
From: Audit manager   Date

Valuation of subsidiary companies' stocks

(1) Introduction

It is imperative that the valuation of all stocks in the subsidiary companies complies with the requirements of SSAP 9 in order for the group's stocks to show a true and fair view and to ensure that they are consistently valued. SSAP 9 requires that stocks should be valued on the basis of the 'total of the lower of cost and net realisable value of the separate items of stock and work in progress or of groups of similar items'.

Each of the subsidiaries will be discussed in turn.

(2) Valuation of stocks in Screws Ltd

The adoption of a selling price less margin as the basis for stock valuation is not acceptable for a manufacturing company. SSAP 9, appendix 1, only permits this basis if it bears a 'reasonable approximation of actual cost'. It is traditionally used in the retail trade where the deduction of the mark-up will lead back to the actual purchase cost.

The company should adopt the principle of valuing stocks at the lower of cost and net realisable value. Cost should represent that expenditure which is needed in the normal course of business to bring the goods to their present location and condition. The costs should include, in addition to the costs of purchase, such costs of conversion as are necessary to achieve that purpose. Conversion costs should include all production overheads and labour costs which are specifically attributable and any other overheads which are incurred in bringing stocks to that location or condition.

It will be necessary to change the value of opening stocks and thus a prior-year adjustment (per FRS 3) will be necessary. In addition, under FRS 3 this must be recorded in the *statement of total recognised gains and losses.*

(3) Valuation of stocks in Brackets Ltd

Obviously the company is currently incurring losses and the question is posed: should this affect the valuation of the raw material? As long as the goods into which the materials are to be incorporated can still be sold at a profit then no reduction from cost is necessary.

Cost per tonne at 31 December

	£
Brass	500.00
Conversion costs (£120,000 ÷ 700)	171.43
	671.43

Net realisable value per tonne

	£
Market price	520.00
Less: selling costs (£30,000 ÷ 700)	42.86
	477.14

Stocks should therefore be valued at their net realisable value of £477.14 per tonne which is lower than actual cost. The total value is therefore 200 × £477.14 = £95,428.

(4) Valuation of stocks in Frames Ltd

Under SSAP 20, all foreign exchange transactions must be recorded at the exchange rate ruling at the time of the transaction, not at the date of payment. Therefore the purchases of windows would be recorded at £100,000 and if 95 per cent were still unsold then stocks would be valued at £95,000. The £20,000 movement in exchange between the transaction and payment dates would be treated as an exchange loss and written off to the profit and loss account. The proposed valuation of £114,000 would not be acceptable.

(5) Valuation of stocks in Concrete Blocks Ltd

SSAP 9 requires that all costs necessary to bring the stocks to their present condition and location should be included in the valuation, including all production overheads. Fixed overheads are just as necessary as variable costs in achieving this, therefore they should be incorporated within the valuation.

(6) Valuation of stocks in Providers Ltd

In this type of business, which carries a large range of merchantable goods, there is inevitably a strong likelihood of pilferage taking place. Despite your own computerised stock records revealing satisfactory percentages of gross profit, since there are rumours of substantial pilferage an investigation should take place. An independent stock count should be performed with particular emphasis on high-value stock items.

If you do not discover any major discrepancies, it would be reasonable to assume that there are no grounds for such rumours. The stock records can then be used as a basis for stock valuation in the financial accounts.

On the other hand, if substantial quantities of stock are found to be missing then it will be necessary to carry out a complete physical stocktake at the year end. The stock count would then be used as the basis for arriving at stock values in the financial accounts. In addition, a full investigation of the systems of internal control would be needed, plus an attempt to find out how the pilferage occurred and who is responsible.

5

Profit and Loss: Accounting for Taxation

Solution 1 – FRS 16 Current tax

(a) *Explanation for changes in the accounting standard for current tax*

FRS 16 was published in December 1999 to replace SSAP 8 *Accounting for the Imputation System of Taxation*. The main rationale for the changes was the decision, in April 1999, by the Chancellor of the Exchequer, to abolish advance corporation tax (ACT). ACT had complicated the corporate tax system in the UK by insisting companies paid over ACT fourteen days after the calendar year quarter in which a dividend was paid. Thus, for proposed dividends, it was reported as a current liability as it was paid within twelve months of the year end. However, it could only be recouped against mainstream corporation tax (MCT) of the accounting profits of the year in which it was paid, i.e. the following tax year. Thus it could be nearly two years before it could be recouped. Added to this problem was the restriction put on the amount that could be recouped against MCT.

As a result, many companies paying out large dividends could not see their ACT being recouped in the following year. SSAP 8 insisted that if the ACT could not be recovered either by going back six years or by going forwards one year then it should be written off to profit and loss as an additional tax charge, even though legally it could still be recouped eventually. This was an application of the prudence concept.

The accounting treatment under FRS 16 is much simpler because of the demise of ACT and its replacement by an instalment system of paying corporation tax. However, for those companies still with unrecovered ACT, there is a shadow system set up by government to allow those companies to recover ACT, but FRS 16 will only permit that recoupment as an asset on balance sheet if it is certain to be recouped in the following twelve months.

(b) *The main principles and disclosures contained in FRS 16*

There are basically five core principles enunciated in FRS 16, which companies should follow when computing their current corporation tax charges. These are:

1. Current tax should normally be recognised in the profit and loss unless the gain to which it relates has already been credited to reserves, in which case the tax must follow the gain also to reserves and to the STRGL.

2. Outgoing dividends paid and payable should be recorded without the inclusion of any tax credits as these are assumed to have already been taxed.

3. Dividends received and receivable should be recorded at the amount receivable or received without the inclusion of any tax credits, for the same reason.

4. If any income or expenses have been charged/credited with a lower than normal tax charge no adjustment should be made to those figures to pretend that they have actually suffered the normal rate of tax. No grossing up is permitted for tax.

5. The current tax charge should be measured at the amounts expected to be paid or recovered using the tax rates and laws that have been or are substantially enacted by Parliament, i.e. the Finance Bill must have passed the House of Commons stage.

Companies also have very little additional information to disclose under FRS 16. Essentially they are required to split their overall current tax charge between foreign and domestic tax but also to recognise the tax on the current year's profits as separate from any adjustments recognised in respect of prior periods. Domestic tax should be disclosed before and after any double tax relief.

An illustration of the required disclosure is provided below:

Illustration of profit and loss account disclosure

	£'000	£'000
UK corporation tax		
Current tax on income for the period	A	
Adjustments in respect of prior periods	B	
	C	
Double tax relief	(D)	
		E
Foreign tax		
Current tax on income for the period	F	
Adjustments in respect of prior periods	G	
		H
Tax on profit on ordinary activities		I

Solution 2 – FRS 19 Deferred tax

(a) Description of deferred tax

Deferred tax has been provided on the liability method. It arises mainly due to differences in the timing of the recognition of certain items (particularly depreciation) in the financial statements and by the Inland Revenue. The provision has been provided on all temporary timing differences with the exception of revaluation gains and unremitted earnings of subsidiaries at the current rate of tax. The balance of deferred tax has not been discounted as the time value of money is not considered to be material.

No provision has been made for tax due on chargeable gains arising from property disposals as any liability will be postponed by the application of rollover relief.

(b) Note to the balance sheet – provision for deferred tax

	Full provision £'000
Excess of capital allowances over depreciation	1,400
Other timing differences	120
Loss carried forward	(80)
ACT recoverable	(30)
	1,410

The movement on deferred taxation	£'000
Balance 1.1.X1	160
Profit and loss charge	1,040
	1,200
ACT	30
Balance 31.12.X1	1,170

Factors affecting tax charge for the period

The tax assessed for the period is lower than the standard rate of corporation tax in the UK (30%). The differences are explained below:

	£m
Profit on ordinary activities before tax	300
Profit on ordinary activities multiplied by standard rate of corporation tax in the UK (30%)	90
Effect of:	
Expenses not permitted by tax authorities	10
Excess capital allowances over depreciation	(30)
Utilisation of tax losses	(15)
Adjustments to previous periods	5
Current tax charge for period	60

(c) Liability method – balance sheet or profit and loss perspective

The liability method requires that deferred tax should be computed on the basis of the current rate of tax, and if tax rates change then an adjustment to the deferred tax account is required. Clearly the balance on the account is the best estimate of a future tax liability. It is a balance sheet perspective. If the full provision basis had been adopted then the liability method would result in a smoothing charge to profit and loss and the latter would be regarded as the key document. It was pressure from the CBI, among others, that forced the ASC to abandon their full provision basis. They considered that liabilities were being overstated and that this was adversely affecting gearing ratios. The 'partial provision' basis concentrated on ensuring that only the liability due to be paid in the foreseeable future was provided for.

The deferral method enables the tax charge to be based only on the current year's profits and the charge is unchanged until it reverses in future years. Profit and loss is therefore charged fairly but the balance sheet liability is unlikely to be correct if corporation tax rates change in the future. The deferral method is clearly taking a profit and loss and not a balance sheet perspective.

Solution 3 – Harmonise plc

(a)(i)(i) *Flow-through method*

	Profit before dep'n and tax	Capital allowances	Taxable profit	Corporation tax (33%)	Deferred	Total tax
	£	£	£	£	£	£
2000	1,250,000	400,000	850,000	280,500	Nil	280,500
						24.0%
2001	1,200,000	80,000	1,120,000	369,600	Nil	369,600
						35.5%
2002	1,100,000	80,000	1,020,000	336,600	Nil	336,600
						35.0%
2003	1,000,000	560,000	440,000	145,200	Nil	145,200
						17.2%

There will be no liability for deferred taxation on the balance sheet but the various corporation tax liabilities of £280,500, etc., will be classified as 'creditors: falling due within one year' as they will become payable within nine months of the year end.

(a)(i)(ii) *Full-provision method (FRS 19)*

	Taxable profit	Corporation tax (33%)	Deferred tax	Timing diffs. CA + dep'n	Total tax
2000	850,000	280,500	105,600	(400,000 – 80,000 × 33%)	386,100
					(33%)
2001	1,120,000	369,600	(26,400)	(80,000 – 160,000 × 33%)	343,200
					(33%)
2002	1,020,000	336,600	(52,800)	(80,000 – 240,000 × 33%)	283,800
					(33%)
2003	440,000	145,200	132,000	(560,000 – 160,000 × 33%)	277,200
					(33%)
			158,400		

The liability for deferred tax on the balance sheet will vary from £105,600 in 2000, to £79,200 in 2001, £26,400 in 2002 and ending up with £158,400 at the end of 2003. This represents the net timing differences of excess capital allowances of £480,000 × 33%.

(a)(i)(iii) *Partial-provision method (SSAP 15)*

Net reversals in the foreseeable future at the end of 2000 are £26,400 + £52,800 = £79,200 and only this figure should be accrued. In 2001 only £52,800 should be accrued and zero at the end of both 2002 and 2003.

There will therefore be a need to provide a note to the accounts detailing all the potential deferred tax still outstanding, i.e.

	Full potential – Provided	= Unprovided
2000	105,600 – 79,200	= 26,400
2001	79,200 – 52,800	= 26,400
2002	26,400 – zero	= 26,400
2003	158,400 – zero	= 158,400

(a)(ii) *Debentures*

	Profit and loss (accruals)		Paid	
2001	£1m × 10%	£100,000	100,000	(1/5/00, 1/11/00 = £1m × 10%)
2002	£1m × 10%	100,000	120,000	(1/5/01, 1/11/01 = £1m × 10% + £0.4 × 10% × 1/2, 30/4/02)
2003	£0.6m × 10%	60,000	70,000	(1/5/02, 1/11/02 £0.6m × 10% = £60,000 + £0.2 × 10% × 1/2, 30/4/02)
2004	£0.4m × 10%	40,000	40,000	(1/5/03, 30/11/03) £0.4m × 10%)
		300,000	330,000	

Deferred tax asset is £330,000 − £300,000 = £30,000 × 33% = £9,900. At 30 April 2000 the timing difference is £1m × 10% × 1/2 = £50,000 accrued of which only £30,000 × 33% is provided. £20,000 × 33% = £6,600 is therefore not incorporated on balance sheet. However, under FRS 19, that amount would need to be provided under the full-provision method.

(b) The following discussion considers the arguments for and against each of the methods:

The flow-through method

This method is based on the principle that only the corporation tax payable in respect of a period should be charged in the profit and loss account of that period. The effect on the balance sheet would be that it would only show the current liability relating to the tax payable.

On grounds of commercial reality, flow-through avoids the need to make assumptions about the future, which are uncertain as to outcome; on revenue grounds, recognising income tax when assessed is consistent with the government's policy of assessing tax for the time period in accordance with the fiscal policy of the time. On accounting principle grounds, the flow-through method complies with the matching principle whereby the amount charged in the profit and loss account is based on tax payable in relation to the taxable profit of the accounting period.

If the reporting entity is able to plan its tax affairs so as to substantially reduce its liability then that fact should be reported to shareholders, i.e. the accounts should 'tell it as it is'.

The arguments against the method are that the commercial reality is that tax has been deferred, i.e. a temporary cash flow benefit, and not eliminated and the uncertainties surrounding deferred tax provisioning are similar to many other areas where management exercise judgement. Eventually the tax will have to be paid and therefore this liability should be recorded on the balance sheet. On the question of accounting principle and the matching concept, it is argued that the tax should be matched against the operating results of the accounting period and not the taxable profit. A particular problem is that the EPS is affected by any deferred tax charge. EPS can therefore be distorted by fiscal policy rather than give a fair reflection of operating performance which it is supposed to measure.

Full-provision method

This method has strong support based on the accounting principles of matching and prudence. The tax charge is matched with the operating results and is prudent because the amount is the full potential tax liability based on the timing differences known at the date of the accounts.

The arguments against the method are largely based on commercial reality in that the result of full provisioning may be to accumulate provisions over time to the extent that they become a material item in the balance sheet without representing a genuine liability of the business. This occurs if the reporting entity has a policy of continual replacement and the originating timing differences always exceed any reversals thereby postponing the ultimate date of payment of tax almost indefinitely. There has been discussion about the advisability of discounting the provision, which would reduce its significance in the profit and loss account and balance sheet. However, it could be argued that discounting an accounting allocation is invalid and even if cash flows were identified they would be a subjective estimate of both the amounts and the years of reversals and a subjective choice of the most appropriate discount rate to use. However, this is the method that has been adopted by FRS 19 *Deferred Tax* and by the IASC, The provision may be discounted if the time value of money is material.

Partial-provision method

The approach (until January 2002) in the UK was to apply the partial-provision method calculating the charge using the liability method.

The arguments in favour of this method are largely based on realism. The tax charge reflects the amount of tax that will become payable based on current knowledge and intention; the provision in the balance sheet is a realistic estimate of the tax liability that will need to be discharged in the next three or four years.

The arguments against the method are mainly based on the need to consider the foreseeable future with a prediction of future events. This is subjective and can result in differing treatments of identical situations depending on the business's forecasts of future activity and profitability. It is too easy to manipulate and fails to comply with the definition of a liability under the Statement of Principles.

In conclusion, it is unclear whether a decision should be based on commercial reality or accounting principles. There is a conflict between the two, which SSAP 15 had attempted to resolve. Similar debates to that in the UK have occurred in other countries and within the IASC. The UK was out of step with international practice which overwhelmingly uses full provisioning and it is largely the reason why the ASB now require the implementation of the full-provision method.

(c) Assuming that all of the shares in Harmonise plc were acquired for cash by Grab plc on 1 May 1999, explain the factors that would be taken into account in determining the fair value of deferred tax as at the date of acquisition.

Determine on a group basis

Until the publication of FRS 19, FRS 7 provided that deferred tax assets and liabilities recognised in the fair value exercise be determined on a group basis by considering the enlarged group as a whole. At the end of the accounting period in which the acquisition occurred, the enlarged group's deferred tax provision was calculated as a single amount, on assumptions applicable to the group, and to determine the deferred tax of the acquired company as at the date of acquisition using different assumptions from those applying to the group as a whole would result in the post-acquisition profit and loss account reflecting the change from one set of assumptions to another, rather than any real change in the circumstances of the group. FRS 19 now insists that any fair value adjustments should not be recognised on non-monetary assets acquired at their fair value on acquisition.

Solution 4 – Clamp Ltd

(a) *Explanation as to accounting treatment of permanent differences*

There are two differences arising between profit as computed for accounting purposes and that for taxation purposes. These can be categorised into those which are defined as permanent and those which are attributed to timing differences. Permanent differences arise for two reasons:

(i) Certain income recognised in the accounts is not assessed for tax; and
(ii) Certain types of expenditure are not allowed for tax.

Permanent differences will always exist and therefore tax will have to be increased or saved immediately. No deferment of tax can take place.

On the other hand, timing differences arise because certain items are included in the financial accounts for a period which is different from that in which they are allowed/credited for tax purposes. There is no permanent reduction or increase in the amount of tax payable. In an effort to match the tax charge in the financial accounts with the taxable profit reported in the financial accounts, adjustments are made for such timing differences through a deferred taxation provision. No such matching is possible with permanent differences; therefore no account is taken of such differences in the calculation of the deferred taxation provision.

(b) Profit and loss account charge/credit for the year ended 31 December 1997

Profit and loss charge   £25,000 (W1)

This represents the increase in the deferred tax liability at the end of the year from the start of the year.

(c) Balance sheet as at 31 December 1997

Provisions for liabilities and charges
Deferred taxation   £60,000 (W1)

Under SSAP 15 this merely represents the tax due to be paid (i.e. reversed) in the foreseeable future (i.e. next three to four years). Under the proposed revision to deferred tax, FRS 19, the full provision of £66,000 would need to be provided. However, as it is not reversing in the next twelve months the balance needs to be discounted to present value using a government bond rate as the appropriate discount rate.

(d) Note to the financial statements

Apart from the amount provided, the company must disclose the full potential liability to tax. It must state that the amount of deferred tax not provided arising on accelerated capital allowances computed at 30 per cent was £6,000 (W2 less W1).

Land is shown in the accounts at a cost of £xx and has a market value of £xx, resulting in a gain of £330,000. If the land is sold, a tax liability of £99,000 would arise. No provision for deferred tax has been made as there is no intention to sell the land.

Workings
W1 Deferred tax account

Balance as at 1 January 1997	£35,000
Transfer from profit and loss account	25,000
Balance as at 31 December 1997	60,000

W2 Full provision for deferred taxation

Capital allowances	£520,000
Accumulated depreciation	(260,000)
Balancing charge	(40,000)
	220,000
Tax at 30%	66,000

W3 Calculation of maximum reversal of timing differences

Year	Depreciation	Capital allowances	Difference	Cumulative
	£'000	£'000	£'000	£'000
31.12.1998	360	400	(40)	(40)
31.12.1999	400	240	160	120
31.12.2000	450	330	120	240
31.12.2001	270	360	(90)	150
	1,480	1,330	150	

On a partial-provision basis the provision required is calculated by reference to the maximum reversal of £240,000 less the increase in the difference of £40,000 in 1998. Therefore the partial deferred tax balance would be £60,000 (i.e. £200,000 × 30%).

Solution 5 – Construct Ltd

(a) *(i)* *Partial-provision method*

Year ending 31/12	Capital allowances differences	Depreciation	Originating timing differences	Reversing timing differences	Cumulative future timing differences
	£'000	£'000	£'000	£'000	£'000
1998	600	700		(100)	N/A
1999	500	700		(200)	(200)
2000	450	720		(270)	(470)
2001	600	740		(140)	(610)
2002	800	780	20		(590)
2003	950	820	130		(460)

Under this approach only the amount which is likely to reverse in the foreseeable future, i.e. next three to four years, should be provided. Under SSAP 15 *Accounting for Deferred Taxation*, the maximum estimated future reversal of timing differences is £610,000 and thus only £610,000 × 31% should be provided.

Deferred tax account

	£'000		£'000
Balance at 31 December 1998 (bal. fig.)	35.9	Balance at 1 January 1998	225.0
Balance c/d (£610,000 × 31%)	189.1		
	225.0		225.0

The balance has fallen from £726,000 (i.e. £225,000/31%) to £610,000. The difference of £116,000 × 31% = £35,900 needs to be deducted from the deferred tax provision as well as a corresponding credit being made to the profit and loss account.

(a) *(ii)* *Full-provision method*

Deferred tax account

	£'000		£'000
Profit and loss account		Balance at 1 January 1998	
(£100,000 RTD × 31%)	31.0	(£1,400,000 given × 31%)	434.0
Balance c/d (£1,300,000 × 31%)	403.0		
	434.0		434.0

Under FRED 19 *Deferred Tax*, the full timing differences should be provided regardless of when they are likely to crystallise. At 1 January the total timing differences of £1.4m should be provided in full at 31 per cent. However these should then be reduced by the reversal during the year of £100,000 at 31 per cent. The tax provision therefore needs to be reduced by £100,000 x 31 per cent.

(b) Review of SSAP 15 and the likely switch to use of the full-provision approach

The main rationale for the switch from a partial- to a full-provision basis is the need for international harmonisation, particularly as global markets increase in importance. The EC is now totally committed to enforcing international standards and member states are expected to introduce IASs by the year 2005.

There are, however, other reasons for its adoption:

(i) Compliance with the ASB's new Statement of Principles (1999). Under this statement all assets and liabilities must be fully recorded on the balance sheet in order to properly reflect a true and fair view. The accruals concept is now relegated into a secondary role.

(ii) It is easier to apply in practice as it does not require any subjective judgments as to when timing differences are likely to reverse. The partial provision requires management to estimate future capital expenditure, depreciation and capital allowances.

(iii) It retains the matching principle. This should result in a smoother taxation charge as well as complying with the definition of a liability.

(iv) Every major standard-setter, particularly the IASC and the FASB in the United States, have adopted the full approach. The UK/Ireland only adopted the partial approach as an *ad hoc* solution to a particular problem of creating massive tax provisions which never seemed to be payable, as long as the company were to continue capital expenditure programmes.

The UK is proposing a slightly modified version of the full approach. No tax will need to be provided on revaluations nor on unremitted earnings of subsidiaries. This is proposed on the grounds that there is no legal obligation to pay any tax until the related property is sold and any gain not rolled over and unless dividends are actually received by the entity.

However, the most serious difference between UK and IASC/IASB standards is the issue of discounting. It is expressly forbidden under IASC standards but is now being recommended by the ASB. This has been proposed on the grounds that all long-term liabilities are permitted to be discounted and thus it should be extended to deferred taxation. The ASB hopes that this will reduce deferred tax to a more manageable total and therefore more acceptable to reporting entities. As the discounts start to unwind, they should be charged as part of finance costs and not treated as part of the tax charge. The discount rate should be based on a government bond rate.

In addition to the switch to full provision there is now a requirement to disclose the tax reconciliation statement. This statement works out the profits before tax and multiplies it by the tax rate giving rise to the likely taxation due. This will be reduced by excess capital allowances, tax losses, etc., and thus the actual tax charge will be reconciled accordingly.

Solution 6 – Partial plc

(a) (i) Permanent differences and timing differences

Deferred taxation arises in a company's accounts because the taxation authorities treat certain income and expenditure items differently from the accounting policies adopted by the company. For example, a company is not permitted to charge depreciation in calculating taxable profits, but instead capital allowances are awarded. These allowances are unlikely to be the same as the depreciation charge in the accounts, and thus a difference emerges.

These differences can be segregated into two distinct types:

(1) *Permanent differences*

These are differences which will not give rise to any additional tax charge or which will not be allowed as a deduction for tax purposes in a future accounting period. They are *permanent* differences between taxable profits and accounting profits. For example, certain expenses are never allowed for tax (entertainment, certain legal fees, etc.) and certain incomes are never taxed (government grants). As these will never reverse in the future, there is no need to make any adjustment to the tax charge provided in the profit and loss account for the period. The tax charge will therefore vary as a percentage of reported profit but this merely reflects the commercial reality.

(2) *Timing differences*

These are differences which will reverse in future accounting periods. A taxation charge should be provided to ensure a proper matching of the tax charge to the accounting profit earned. An example will help to clarify the importance of this concept.

Assume that a piece of machinery is purchased for £300 with a three-year life and no residual value. If the company adopts a straight-line depreciation policy, £100 will be charged in the profit and loss account each year for depreciation. The Inland Revenue will permit a 25 per cent writing-down allowance. The results are as follows:

Year	Depreciation	Capital allowance	Timing difference	Cumulative
	£	£	£	£
1	100	75 (£300 × 25%)	25	25
2	100	56 (£225 × 25%)	44	69
3	100	42 (£169 × 25%)	(69)	–
		127 (balancing allowance)		

Assuming an annual accounting profit of £500 and a tax rate of 50 per cent, tax will be provided as follows:

Year	Profit	Depreciation	Capital allowances	Taxable profit	Taxation Corp	Def	Total
	£	£	£	£	£	£	£
1	500	100	75	525	263	(13)	250
2	500	100	56	544	272	(22)	250
3	500	100	169	431	215	35	250

The deferred tax (credit)/charge enables the overall tax charge in the profit and loss account to reflect an even matching of accounting profit to the tax charge at 50 per cent. Without the deferred tax adjustment, the tax rate would vary from 54.8 per cent in year 2 to 42.5 per cent in year 3.

(a) (ii) *Disclosure of the deferred tax provision in the balance sheet*

FRS 19 (paras 61–65) requires the following to be disclosed in order to identify the asset or liability associated with deferred taxation provisions:

(1) The deferred tax balance (before discounting) and its major components – balance sheet or notes.
(2) Impact of discounting.
(3) Transfers to and from deferred tax – note.
(4) The amount of a deferred tax asset and the nature of evidence supporting its recognition.

(a) (iii) Calculating the deferred tax provision for inclusion in the balance sheet

Paragraphs 7–33 of FRS 19 explain how the deferred tax provision should be calculated for inclusion in the balance sheet:

(1)   The liability method should be adopted to compute the tax.

(2)   Provision for tax should be made in full for all timing differences with the exception of unremitted earnings of subsidiaries and revaluation surpluses and revalued assets which have been sold and the gain rolled over against a replacement asset.

(3)   The assumptions should take into account all relevant information available to the board of directors up to the date on which the financial statements are approved. In particular the tax rate should be based on tax rates that have passed the House of Commons bill stage.

(4)   A deferred tax asset should not be carried forward as an asset unless it is likely to be recovered.

(5)   The full provision may be discounted if the time value of money is material using a government bond rate with similar maturity dates to the deferred tax liability/asset.

(b) (i) Balance sheet extract as at 30 November 2000

Taxation, including deferred taxation (extract)   £43,750

Notes to the balance sheet

Note 18: Deferred taxation   *Total*
Excess capital allowances   £43,750

Workings

Year	Depreciation	Capital allowances	Timing differences	Cumulative	Partial provision (SSAP 15)
	£'000	£'000	£'000	£'000	£'000
2001	234	265	31	31	
2002	253	303	50	81	
2003	276	193	(83)	(2)	
2004	278	192	(86)	(88)	× 35% = 30.8
2005	248	262	14	(74)	

Full provision 2000	£525,000	C. Allowances		or	£475,000	WDV
(FRS 19)	£400,000	Depreciation			£600,000	NBV
	£125,000				£125,000	

× 35% = £43,750

(b) (ii) Profit and loss account and balance sheet extracts as at 30 November 2001

Profit and loss account (extract)

Taxation (extract for deferred tax only £57,400 – £43,750)   £13,650

Balance sheet (extract)

Taxation, including deferred taxation (extract)   £57,400

Notes to the balance sheet

Note 18: Deferred taxation   *Total*
                                                            £57,400

Workings

Year	Depreciation	Capital allowances	Timing differences	Cumulative	Partial provision (SSAP 15)
	£'000	£'000	£'000	£'000	£'000
2002	250	289	39	39	
2003	278	197	(81)	(42)	
2004	275	193	(82)	(124) × 35% = 43.4	
2005	253	265	12	(112)	
2006	254	278	24	(88)	

Full provision 2001   £289,000 Cap. allowances   or   WDV XX
(FRS 19)   £250,000 Depreciation   NBV XX
                             ─────────   ──────
                             £39,000   XX

+ £125,000 = £164,000
× 35% = £57,400

(c) The effect on the provision for deferred taxation of the revaluation of fixed assets on which capital allowances are received

There was no specific guidance in SSAP 15 on this point. In practice two separate accounting treatments have developed:

(1) *The revaluation is a permanent difference*
     The revaluation and its subsequent reversal via depreciation have no effect on tax and therefore should be ignored for deferred tax purposes.

(2) *The revaluation is a timing difference*
     The revaluation has been regarded as a restatement of depreciation, thereby effectively reversing that charge. Therefore, the revalued book figure should be compared to the written-down value when computing the deferred tax liability.

Under FRS 19 the first treatment will now become standard practice as no legal obligation is created until the asset is sold and tax crystallises.

Solution 7 – XL plc

(a) The main reasons for the criticism of SSAP 15 *Accounting for Deferred Taxation* are as follows:

(i) The recognition rule of SSAP 15 is different from that of other standards. Deferred tax assets and liabilities are recognised only when they will not be replaced by equivalent assets and liabilities. If this rule were applied to current assets such as stock or debtors then a significant part of such assets may not be recognised in the financial statements, because in many companies these values remain static with a hard core of the asset remaining. This problem led to the issue of an amendment to SSAP 15 in 1992 in respect of post-retirement benefits.

(ii) SSAP 15 is dependent on future events and the intentions of management. It is thought that this may be contrary to the Statement of Principles, which defines assets and liabilities in relation to past events and states that management's intentions alone do not give rise to assets and liabilities. There must be a legal or constructive obligation.

(iii) There have been variations in practice in the application of SSAP 15. There are variations in practice over fair-value adjustments made in acquisition accounting, as some companies provide for deferred tax on such adjustments and others do not. Similarly, there is no specific guidance in SSAP 15 as regards the effects of revaluation on the calculation of deferred tax relating to timing differences between the depreciation charged in the financial statements and the tax allowances.

(iv) The partial-provision method is not internationally acceptable. It is required in only a small number of countries and the global trend is towards full provision, particularly where there is a conceptual framework similar to the Statement of Principles. Only under the full-provision method can the liability be properly recorded. However, there may well be a case for discounting that liability to its present value.

(b)(i) *Fair-value adjustment*

The issue is whether fair-value adjustments in acquisition accounting give rise to deferred tax if the full-provision method is used. At present, fair-value adjustments are not timing differences in SSAP 15, but permanent differences. It is felt that deferred tax should not be provided on fair-value adjustments because these adjustments are made as a consolidation entry only. They are not taxable or tax-deductible and do not affect the overall tax burden of the company. An acquisition does not, by itself, increase the tax.

It is argued that providing for deferred tax on fair-value adjustments is not an allocation of an expense but a smoothing device. Finally, the difference between the carrying value of the net assets acquired and their fair value is goodwill, and therefore no deferred tax is required.

The arguments in favour of deferred tax are conceptual by nature. If the net assets of the acquired company are shown in the group accounts at fair value, then this will affect the post-acquisition earnings of the group. For example, an increase in the stock value by £10,000 will result in profit being reduced by £10,000 in the post-acquisition period. It seems consistent, therefore, to exclude the tax on these profits from the post-acquisition period also. That stock is inherently less valuable than similar purchased stock as the baseline for tax will be the original and not the revalued figures.

Additionally, since an acquisition gives rise to no tax effect, the effective tax rate in the profit and loss account should not be distorted as a result of the acquisition. Providing for deferred tax ensures that distortion does not occur.

Some commentators feel that deferred tax should be provided on assets purchased in an acquisition as a 'valuation' adjustment. If the asset had been purchased in an arm's-length transaction – for example, stocks – then this cost would have been totally tax-deductible. As this is not the case, the asset is worth less to the company because it is not tax-deductible. Therefore, deferred tax should be provided as an adjustment to reflect the reduction in the true value of the asset. FRS 19 has expressly come down on the side of not making provisions for deferred tax in these instances.

(b)(ii)   *Revaluations of fixed assets*

The revaluation of a fixed asset can be seen as creating a further timing difference because it reflects an adjustment of depreciation, which is itself a timing difference. An alternative view is that it is a permanent difference as it has no equivalent within the tax computation. The revaluation is not seen as a reversal of previous depreciation, simply that the remaining life of the asset will be measured at a different amount. The additional depreciation charge has no tax equivalent and it would be incorrect to make any tax adjustments in respect of this amount. If, however, the revaluation takes the asset value above its original cost, then a chargeable gain may arise and a provision for tax should be considered if disposal is likely.

As with fair-value adjustments, it can be argued that deferred tax is a valuation adjustment and, while a revaluation does not directly give rise to a tax liability, the tax status of the asset is inferior to an equivalent asset at historical cost; therefore, provision for deferred tax should be made in order to reflect the true after-tax cost of the asset. The revalued asset would not attract the same tax allowances as an asset purchased for the same amount and, therefore, if deferred tax was not provided it would distort the post-revaluation effective tax rate. (This would only be the case if the asset is the type which is deductible for tax purposes. Rollover relief postpones rather than extinguishes any tax liability and therefore should not affect the recognition of deferred tax.) FRS 19 again does not require provision for deferred tax on revaluations.

(c)(i)   *Full provision*

	NBV	Valuation	Tax value	FRS 19 Full difference (NBV)	SSAP 15 Temporary difference
XL plc		£'000	£'000	£'000	£'000
Buildings (revalued)	33,500	50,000	7,500	26,000	42,500
Plant and equipment (revalued)	52,000	60,000	13,000	39,000	47,000
Healthcare benefits	(300)	(300)	–	(300)	(300)
	85,200	109,700	20,500	64,700	89,200
BZ Ltd					
Buildings	300	500	100	200	400
Plant and equipment	30	40	15	15	25
Stock	114	124	114	–	10
Retirement benefit	(60)	(60)	–	(60)	(60)
	384	604	229	155	375
	85,584	110,304	20,729	64,855	89,575

	£'000	SSAP 15 £'000	FRS 19 £'000	
Deferred tax liability	89,935 @ 30%	26,980	19,565	65,215 × 30%
Deferred tax asset	(360) @ 30%	(108)	(108)	(360) × 30%
	89,575 @ 30%	26,872	19,457	64,855 × 30%
Less: opening deferred tax liability		(9,010)	(9,010)	
Adjustment due to change in tax rate:				
$9,010 \times {}^{100}\!/_{35} \times 5\%$		1,287	1,287	
Deferred tax expense for year		19,149	11,734	

The deferred tax expense relating to the revaluation of assets would not be shown in the group profit and loss account as it relates to items credited to equity.

(c)(ii) *Partial provision – only permitted by SSAP 15 not FRS 19*

Group position based on carrying values before any fair-value adjustment or revaluation

	£'000
Balance at 30.11.01	
Buildings	
XL plc	33,500
BZ Ltd	300
Plant and equipment	
XL plc	52,000
BZ Ltd	30
	85,830
Tax values at 30.11.01	
Building	
XL plc	7,500
BZ Ltd	100
Plant and equipment	
XL plc	13,000
BZ Ltd	15
	20,615
Timing differences	65,215

Timing differences	30.11.01	30.11.02	30.11.03	30.11.04
	£'000	£'000	£'000	£'000
Depreciation		(7,040)	(8,432)	(7,594)
Tax allowances		8,040	4,536	3,030
	65,215	1,000	(3,896)	(4,564)
Cumulative	65,215	66,215	62,319	57,755

Maximum reversal: 65,215,000 – 57,755,000 = £7,460,000
Provision required: £7,460,000 @ 30% = £2,238,000

Therefore there will be a release of the existing provision if deferred tax were calculated using the partial-provision method. However, because the land and buildings had originally cost £45m and the revaluation takes the value above this amount, an additional provision of (£50m – £45m × 30% =) £1.5m must be provided.

Thus, the deferred tax provision will be reduced to:

£'000	
2,238	timing differences
1,500	tax on revaluation – chargeable gain
3,738	

The deferred tax released to the profit and loss account will be (9,010,000 – 3,738,000) = £5,252,000.

There will be no deferred tax consequences of the retirement benefit liability or healthcare costs under the partial-provision method as it is anticipated that there will be no movement in the balance sheet amount.

Profit and Loss: Earnings per Share and Reporting Financial Performance

Solution 1 – Earnit plc

(a) Computation of basic earnings per share

Profits after taxation	£45m
Appropriations to non-equity shareholders	11m
Basic earnings	£34m

Share structure

1.4.1999 Equity shares	500m
1.10.1999 Exercise of share options 50m x ½	25m
Basic share structure	525m

Basic EPS

$$\frac{\text{Basic earnings}}{\text{Basic share structure}} = \frac{£34m}{525m} \times 100 = \quad 6.48p$$

Computation of diluted earnings per share

As per basic earnings			£34m
As per basic share structure		525m	
Options 100m x ½ year =	50m		
Options 120m x ½ year =	60m		
	110m x 50p/£2	27.5m	
		552.5m	

$$\frac{\text{Dilutive earnings}}{\text{Diluted share structure}} = \frac{£34m}{552.5m} \times 100 = \quad 6.15p$$

(b) Usefulness of basic and diluted earnings per share to an equity shareholder

(i)   EPS is widely used as an investment ratio, particularly as the base figure for the calculation of the P/E ratio.

(ii)   The dilutive EPS is used to give an indication to existing equity shareholders what impact the options have on their share of the earnings which will obviously be reduced on the exercise of the options at a discount of 25 per cent from market values.

(iii) It provides shareholders with a useful comparison of performance over time.

(iv)   The calculation of EPS is now standardised across the world and this enables multinational comparisons.

(v)   In this particular case the dilution is only 0.33p (c.5 per cent), which is not material and thus existing equity shareholders need not be over-concerned with the exercise of existing share options.

Solution 2 – Hogg plc

(a) (1)&(2) Basic earnings per share

	2002		2003	
	£	£	£	£
Earnings				
Profits after taxation		1,106,161		1,183,930
Less minority interest	4,800		(5,600)	
extraordinary items	(117,300)		44,500	
preference dividend	40,000		40,000	
		72,500		78,900
		1,178,661		1,105,030

	2002	2003
	No. of shares	No. of shares
Ordinary shares		
Balance at 1.4.01 and 1.4.02	4m	8.4m (4 + 2.8 + 1.6)
1.10.01 Issue at full market price		
$2m \times \frac{7}{5}$ bonus issue = 2.8m $\times \frac{1}{2}$ yr	1.4m	
1.1.02 Bonus issue $4m \times \frac{2}{5}$	1.6m	
	7.0m	

$$\frac{\text{Fair value of all outstanding shares} + \text{total amount received from the rights issue}}{\text{Number of shares outstanding} + \text{number of shares issued in exercise}}$$

$$= \frac{8.4m \times £1.33 + 840,000 \times £1}{8.4m + 840,000} = \frac{£12.012m}{9.24m} = £1.30$$

Computation of adjustment factor

$$\frac{\text{Fair value per share pre rights}}{\text{Theoretical ex rights value per share}} = \frac{£1.33}{£1.30} = 1.023$$

Computation of earnings per share

$$\frac{£1,105,030}{(8.4m \times 1.023 \times \frac{8}{12}) + (9.24m \times \frac{4}{12})} = \frac{£1,105,030}{8.8088m} = 12.54p$$

Earnings per share

2002: $\dfrac{£1,178,661}{7,000,000} \times 100 = 16.84p$

2003: $\dfrac{£1,105,030}{8,809,231} \times 100 = 12.54p$

(a) *(3) Diluted earnings per share*

Increase in earnings attributable to ordinary shareholders on conversion of potential ordinary shares (assume average fair value of one ordinary share during the year was £2)

	Increase in earnings	Increase in number of ordinary shares	Earnings per incremental share
Options			
Increase in earnings	Nil		
Incremental shares issued for no consideration: 500,000 × ((£2 − £1.50) ÷ £2)		125,000	Nil ①
15% convertible loan stock			
Increase in net profit: £1m × 0.15 × (1 − 0.4)	90,000		
Incremental shares: 1m × (£1 ÷ £1.50)		666,667	£0.135 ②

Computation of diluted earnings per share

	Net profit attributable £	Ordinary shares	Per share	
As reported	1,105,030	8,809,231	12.54p	
Options	–	125,000		
	1,105,030	8,934,231	12.37p	Dilutive
15% convertible bonds	90,000	666,667		
	1,195,030	9,600,898	12.45p	Anti-dilutive

The 15% convertible bonds are ignored as these are anti-dilutive. Therefore, diluted earnings per share is 12.37p and *must* be disclosed.

(a) *(4)&(5) Basic earnings per share for the corresponding previous period*

2002
Basic EPS for 2001 = 15.00p
Bonus issue 2:5 therefore corresponding previous period EPS for 2002 = 15.00p × 5/7 = 10.71p

2003
Basic EPS for 2002 = 16.84p
Rights issue therefore corresponding previous period EPS for 2003 = 16.84p × 1.30 cum/1.33 ex = 16.46p

(b) *The significance and usefulness of the EPS figures*

Private and confidential

Mr J A Hall
Managing director
Hogg plc
Fort Road, Dunstore

Trump and Ace
Chartered Accountants
River St
Portbray

Dear Mr Hall
Date

The significance and usefulness of earnings per share
With reference to your letter of 15 August I am writing to outline the significance and usefulness of the earnings per share (EPS) figure contained within your 2003 financial statements.

The EPS is calculated after deduction of minority interests and preference dividends and after taking into account extraordinary items. As a result both the £44,500 extraordinary loss and the £117,300 extraordinary gain are included and have materially affected the reported EPS.

Standard accounting practice (FRS 14) requires the disclosure of EPS because of its importance as part of the price/earnings ratio (P/E ratio). This is used by analysts as a major stock market indicator. Standardisation of earnings means that companies will calculate and disclose EPS on a basis which is comparable between companies and between one period and another.

The disclosure for 2003 reveals an EPS of 12.54p and a comparative of 16.46p (2002). The 2002 figure has been adjusted to take into account the bonus element in the rights issue. This reveals a decrease of almost 4p per share despite an increase of over £170,000 in profits after tax. This implies that the cash generated from the October 2001 full market issue and the December 2002 rights issue did not yield as high a return to the company as had been earned on the existing capital employed.

The fall in EPS, assuming a P/E ratio of 10, would result in a share price fall in theory from 164.6p to 125.4p. For this reason listed companies are permitted to incorporate a second, alternative version if it is felt that this would better illustrate the trend. The alternative may be that suggested by the Institute of Investment Management and Research (IIMR) in their Statement of Investment Practice No 1 *Headline Earnings*, which excludes capital items from the calculation. This has been accepted both by the *Financial Times* and the Stock Exchange as the base for the price/earnings ratio quoted daily. I would suggest that you seriously consider its incorporation in this year's accounts. Under FRS 3, this will require a reconciliation between the two published EPS figures.

The diluted EPS for 2003 is 12.54p. This indicates the extent to which the company is committed to obligations which could dilute the EPS in the future. Normally an assumption is made that the obligations will be fulfilled at the earliest possible date or at their greatest benefit. If these obligations proceed then there will also be savings in interest costs on the convertible loan stock. The difference in the two EPS values for 2003 is less than 5 per cent of the basic EPS; therefore under SSAP 3 the fully diluted EPS would not have to be disclosed. However, under FRS 14, in future the diluted earnings per share will have to be disclosed even if equal to basic EPS.

I hope that the above will be sufficient for your needs but please do not hesitate to contact me if you have any further queries.

Yours sincerely

A. F. Trump

Solution 3 – Dantes plc

(a) *Calculation of basic earnings per share*

2000	£'000	£'000
Earnings		
Profits after taxation		1,224
Less minority interests	87	
preference dividends	35	
		122
		1,102

FRS 14: computation of adjustment factor

$$\frac{(10m \times 84p) + (2.5m \times 60p)}{10m + 2.5m} = 79.2p$$

$$\frac{\text{Cum } 84.0p}{\text{Ex } 79.2p} = 1.06$$

$$\frac{£1{,}102{,}000}{(10m \times 1.06 \times {}^{3}\!/_{12}) + (12.5m \times {}^{9}\!/_{12})} = 9.2p$$

(b) Calculation of diluted earnings per share

	FRS 14
2000	*£'000*
Earnings	
Basic earnings (as above)	1,102
Add saving on preference dividend	35
	1,137

Number of shares

Basic number of shares	12,027
Add preference shares 1.7.00	
£2.4m ÷ £1.20 = 2,000,000 × 1.3 (highest conversion)	
= 2,600,000 × ¼ year issued	650
Warrants 2,000,000 (as above) × ¼ year × $\frac{26p}{84p}$ discount	
	142.847
	12,819.847

FRS 14: calculation of diluted earnings per share

Increase in earnings attributable to ordinary shareholders on conversion of potential ordinary shares

	Increase in earnings	Increase in number of ordinary shares	Earnings per incremental share
	£'000	*'000*	*£'000*
Warrants			
Increase in earnings	Nil		
Incremental shares issued for no consideration			
2,000,000 × ((84p – 60p) ÷ 84p) × ¼		142.847	Nil[1]
Preferences shares			
Increase in net profit	35		
Incremental shares		650 (¼ × 2,600)	5.38[2]

Computation of diluted earnings per share

	Net profit attributable £	Ordinary shares	Earnings per incremental share
As reported	1,102,000	12,027,000	9.2p
Warrants	–	142,857	
	1,102,000	12,169,857	9.06p
Convertible preference shares	35,000	650,000	
	1,137,000	12,819,857	8.87p

The diluted earnings per share is 8.87p and *must* be disclosed under FRS 14.

(c) *Published EPS figures*

Usefulness

The EPS figure represents the earnings that each share has generated during the year. Shareholders can therefore see both the dividend and the capital growth of their investment contained within this figure. In particular, it can be compared with previous years to gauge the trend over time.

EPS also forms the basis for the calculation of the price/earnings ratio (P/E ratio), a widely used investment indicator both for existing and prospective investors. It is published daily in the financial press. The P/E ratio can be compared with other companies within the industry to enable investors to assess whether or not their shares are performing as expected.

The diluted EPS is a useful warning indicator to existing shareholders of the potential impact on future earnings if existing warrants/options/conversion rights are exercised.

Limitations

One of the major limitations of EPS in the past was its linkage to SSAP 6. Its calculation involved the inclusion of exceptional items but the exclusion of extraordinary items.

In practice, there had been many attempts to encourage a rising trend in EPS by defining exceptional items very loosely. This enabled companies to include as many 'profits/gains' as possible within EPS and to exclude many 'losses' below the line so that they did not affect the EPS. This subjectivity attracted severe criticism and the ASB attempted to solve the problem in two ways:

(1) By reducing the number of items which can be classified as extraordinary (in effect this was a practical ban).

(2) By requiring EPS to be calculated after taking into account extraordinary items.

This has undoubtedly led to more distorted annual figures, but investors should be able to see the total impact of 'all' transactions for the period in question and make their own adjustments in arriving at trend information. This has been considerably undermined by the IIMR's decision to exclude capital items in its alternative *Headline Earnings* definition.

Another limitation is the denominator, which includes only ordinary shares. Reserves and retained earnings are excluded.

Changes in accounting policies can distort the EPS over time. Corrections should be made in the five-year historical summaries to ensure that all years are presented on the same basis.

Solution 4 – Amas plc

(a) *Earnings per share for 2001*

Earnings	£'000
Profits after tax	645
Less preference dividend	60
	585

FRS 14: computation of adjustment factor

$$\frac{(4m \times £1.05) + (1m \times £0.80)}{4m + 1m} = £1$$

$$\frac{\text{Cum } £1.05}{\text{Ex } £1} = 1.05$$

Earnings per share

$$\frac{£585,000}{(4m \times 1.05 \times {}^{4}/_{12}) + (5m \times {}^{2}/_{12}) + (5.36m \times {}^{6}/_{12}) \times {}^{3}/_{2} \text{ conversion} = 7,370,000} = 7.94p$$

(b) *Comparative earnings per share for 2000*

EPS per published accounts	16.5p
Adjust: for bonus element in rights issue	× 1.00/1.05
for bonus issue	× 2/3
Comparative EPS	10.47p

(c) *Diluted earnings per share for 2001*

Earnings	*£'000*
Basic earnings	585
Interest savings £1m × 10% × 50% net of tax	50
	635

Number of shares issued and ranking for dividend	*No. of shares*
Basic EPS ordinary shares	7,370,000
Conversion at maximum conversion	
1m × 250/100 × 3/2 bonus issue	3,750,000
	11,120,000

Diluted earnings per share

$$\frac{£635,000}{11,120,000} \times 100 = 5.71p$$

The disclosure of diluted earnings per share is required whether or not the dilution is material, i.e. more than 5 per cent different from the basic EPS. Under FRS 14, diluted earnings per share *must* be disclosed.

The FRS states that the following should be disclosed:

(1) Both basic and diluted EPS must be shown on the face of the profit and loss account, usually at its foot.

(2) Equal prominence should be given to both basic and diluted EPS.

(3) The basis of calculation of diluted EPS should be disclosed, usually in a note to the accounts.

(4) A comparative figure for diluted EPS for 2000 should be disclosed even if the assumptions upon which it is based are not the same as in 2001.

Solution 5 – Mayes plc

(a) (i) Rationale for changes from SSAP 3 to FRS 14

The ASB were forced to review SSAP 3 due to international developments. Both the IASC and the FASB united to produce a world standard on how to calculate EPS and both moved very closely to the ASB's version. In the interests of comparability the ASB decided to slightly alter SSAP 3 to bring it totally into line with the rest of the world. It was such a minor change that the standard was fully effective within three months.

The main changes brought in by FRS 14 were:

(1) The number of shares in the denominator was widened to include those ordinary shares which did not rank for dividend at present.

(2) Convertible debt would be brought into the denominator from the date when interest ceases to accrue.

(3) Bonus issues occurring post year end but before the publication of the accounts should be included in the calculation.

(4) More specific guidance was provided on how to calculate diluted EPS, particularly the sequence in which potential ordinary shares should be incorporated. In particular, the treasury stock method was included in FRS 14 for dealing with options and warrants.

(5) The 5 per cent exemption for publication of a diluted EPS was dropped as was the need to publish both a net and a nil basic EPS.

(a) (ii) Why there is a need to disclose diluted earnings per share

Basic EPS only takes account of those shares which are in issue and fails to take account of obligations that could dilute EPS in the future. However, the company could have also issued certain securities that, although currently not ordinary shares, have the ability of becoming ordinary shares. These include convertible loan stock, convertible preference shares and stock options. Investors are interested in examining the impact of their possible conversion into future shares and how current earnings would be reduced (diluted) by their conversion.

The disclosure should help users to assess the potential variability of future EPS and the associated risks attached. It is an indicator that current profitability may not be sustained. It is a useful warning device to equity shareholders that future earnings will be affected by diluting factors.

(b) Earnings per share – basic

		£'000
Profit attributable to members of parent company		12,860
Less: Preference dividend	(210)	
Other appropriations – non-equity shares	(80)	
		(290)
Basic earnings		12,570

Weighted average number of shares ('000)

	Shares	Weight	No.
1 June 1998	10,100	1.0	10,100
1 January 1999 (Note i – non-ranking)	3,600	5/12	1,500
1 March 1999	1,200	3/12	300
1 April 1999	(2,400)	2/12	(400)
	12,500		11,500
Bonus issue (post y/end but prior to issue) (1:5)			2,300
			13,800

$$\text{Basic earnings over Weighted average shares} = \frac{12,570}{13,800} \times 100 = 91.08\text{p}$$

Diluted earnings per share

	£'000
Basic earnings	12,570
Add: Interest saved on 6% convertible bonds	234
Non-equity costs on preference shares	290
	13,094
Number of shares	29,340

$$\text{Diluted earnings per share} \quad \frac{13,094}{29.340} \times 100 = \quad 44.6\text{p}$$

Ranking of dilutive securities

	£'000 Increase in earnings	'000 Increase in shares		£ Increase in earnings/share
Options	Nil	$1,200 \times \dfrac{5-2}{5} \times 9/12$	= 540	Nil
		$2,000 \times \dfrac{5-3}{5}$	= 800	
		$1,000 \times \dfrac{5-4}{5}$	= 200	
Convertible preference shares	290	$3,000 \times 2/3$	= 2,000	£0.145
Convertible bonds	234			
(6% x 6,000 x 65%)		$6,000 \times 2$	= 12,000	£0.0112
			15,540	
Basic shares			13,800	
			29,340	

Ranking – 1 options, 2 convertible bonds and 3 convertible preference shares

Computation of dilutive/anti-dilutive EPS

	£'000	Ordinary shares	Per share
Net profit from continuing operations	18,270	13,800	132p
Options	Nil	1,540	
	18,270	15,340	119p dilutive
6% bonds	234	12,000	
	18,504	27,340	67.7p dilutive
Convertible preference shares	290	2,000	
	18,794	29,340	64.1p dilutive

	£'000
Net profit from continuing operations	
Profit as per basic	12,860
Add discontinued loss (1,120 + 100)	1,220
Loss on sale of operations (5,080 – 600)	4,480
Non-equity shares appropriations	(290)
Net profit from continuing operations	18,270

Solution 6 – FRS 3

Until the advent of FRS 3 *Reporting Financial Performance*, users of financial statements relied heavily on what was termed the 'bottom line' for evaluating performance. This was particularly the case with the emphasis placed on the earnings per share (EPS) disclosed at the foot of the profit and loss account of quoted companies. Investment analysts used the EPS as a base for the price/earnings ratio, which is argued to be the 'key' performance indicator.

As a result management regarded the EPS as a 'god' which must be looked after at all costs and ensured to be seen on a rising trend. Creative accounting was thoroughly tested in this field of financial reporting, and particularly on the interpretation of extraordinary versus exceptional items. There was clear evidence of 'bad news' finding its way 'below the line' as extraordinary items and, vice versa, of 'good news' being included above the line as exceptional items.

FRS 3 has attempted to address this issue by shifting the focus away from the emphasis on one figure. It has achieved this by the following changes in the reporting environment.

(1) Extraordinary items

Extraordinary items are more or less banned under FRS 3. They should possess a high degree of abnormality and should be very rare in practice. Every unusual item is now treated as exceptional. As Sir David Tweedie (Chairman of the ASB) humorously puts it, nothing is extraordinary 'unless Martians were to land on earth.'

The flexibility provided under the old SSAP is therefore taken away from directors.

(2) Earnings per share

This will no longer be calculated before the inclusion of extraordinary items. FRS 14 *Earnings per Share* now insists that all extraordinary items should be included in the calculation of EPS. However, companies are still left free to include a second calculation of EPS based on their own definition, but the 'official version' must be given equal prominence and companies will have to provide a reconciliation between the two EPS figures.

Unfortunately, the Institute of Investment Management and Research (IIMR) has persuaded the *Financial Times* and the Stock Exchange to take on board their own *Headline Earnings* version (which excludes capital-based items), under the Statement of Investment Practice No 1. This has undermined the attempt of FRS 3 to move investors away from their fixation with EPS.

(3) Changes in the format of the profit and loss account

A layered format is to be adopted for the profit and loss account in order to highlight a number of important components of financial performance.

Total operations are to be analysed into three sections:

(a) Results of continuing operations;
(b) Results of acquisitions (as part of continuing);
(c) Results of discontinued operations.

Detailed notes on the breakdown of total turnover, cost of sales and profit before interest and tax are required, either on the face of the profit and loss account or in the notes to the accounts.

(4) Statement of total recognised gains and losses

A new primary statement has been introduced to ensure that all gains and losses are considered by the user. The statement incorporates realised profits/losses from the profit and loss account as well as unrealised gains/losses. This should enable the reader to obtain a good overall picture of company performance.

Together with any prior-year adjustments, this statement should ensure that the total wealth created by the company is incorporated within the financial statements.

Unfortunately, one of the main proposals in FRED 1, which was to require disclosure of 'revenue expenditure' on items such as training, maintenance, research and development and advertising, has been dropped. These items, although clearly of a revenue nature, do lead to profit enhancement in future years and disclosure would help the user to assess their likely future impact. However, disclosure is to be included in the voluntary *Operating and Financial Review* statement issued in July 1993 as a statement of best practice.

Hopefully, these measures will encourage users of accounts to switch their analysis away from excessive concentration on one key performance ratio and instead to view the company after assessing a variety of performance indicators. There is a danger, however, that the increased disclosures could lead to 'information overload', but this will only become obvious over a period of some years' usage of the new standard.

Solution 7 – RST plc

Internal memorandum

To: Managing director
From: Financial director   Date

Review of JKL's financial statements

With reference to your memorandum of 29 August 2001, I would like to respond to the specific issues raised as follows.

(a) JKL's financial statements

JKL has recently published their financial statements. These have been presented in accordance with the latest financial reporting standards (FRSs) and in particular FRS 3 *Reporting Financial Performance*. This FRS has resulted in considerable changes to the profit and loss account and has introduced a number of new financial statements.

The objective of FRS 3 was to try to move investors and analysts away from their fixation on earnings per share (EPS) towards a more comprehensive review of a range of important components of performance. This has been achieved by the following changes:

(1) The banning of extraordinary items for all practical purposes (although these are still listed under the Companies Act Schedules).

(2) A layered approach is taken to the profit and loss account and thus turnover and operating profits have been broken down into three sub-sections under the headings 'continuing operations', 'acquisitions', and 'discontinued operations'.

(3) A number of exceptional items must now be disclosed on the face of the profit and loss account to avoid a large number of items being included simply in the profit before tax note.

(4) Earnings per share should be calculated after all expenses/incomes, thus incorporating both exceptional and extraordinary items. This will result in a fairly volatile EPS but we are permitted to present an alternative version based on our own definition. However, the Institute of Investment Management and Research (IIMR) has recently introduced a version of EPS called *Headline Earnings* which has excluded all capital-based items from its definition. I believe that we should, as a minimum, prepare both the official and the headline figures, since the latter has now been accepted by the Stock Exchange and the *Financial Times* as the base for calculating price/earnings ratios.

(5) The requirement to publish three new statements:
   • the *statement of total recognised gains and losses*, disclosing the total wealth generated by the reporting entity during the period;
   • the *reconciliation of movements in shareholders' funds*, disclosing how shareholders' funds have changed during the course of the period; *and*
   • the *note of historical cost profits and losses*, which reconciles the difference between actual profit computed and the profit that would have been achieved if strict historical cost accounting had been retained.

(b) What constitutes discontinued operations?

Discontinued operations have been defined in FRS 3 as those operations which satisfy the following conditions.

(1) The sale/termination must be completed either in the financial year or before the financial statements are due to be signed on 28 February, i.e. 14 months. If the latter is postponed then we have a further month to 31 March to complete the sale/closure.

(2) If the operation is terminated, there must be a permanent cessation.

(3) The sale/termination must have a material effect on the nature and focus of our operations. This means a material reduction in our operating facilities by withdrawal from a particular market, or a material reduction in turnover within existing markets.

(4) The assets, liabilities, results of operations and activities must be clearly distinguishable physically, operationally and for financial reporting purposes.

These conditions mean that only very large closures/disposals can ever be classified as discontinued operations, and this will not necessarily occur on a regular basis.

(c) Why is a statement of total recognised gains and losses included?

This new primary statement has been incorporated into the financial statements to ensure that all gains and losses (whether realised or unrealised) are included within a performance document.

Prior to the advent of FRS 3, increases/decreases caused by the revaluation of fixed assets were taken to the revaluation reserve but this was recorded in the notes to the financial statements. Similarly, foreign exchange gains and losses on the translation of subsidiaries are taken direct to reserves under SSAP 20 *Foreign Currency Translation*, as they are not regarded as realised or earned.

Various scandals, such as Polly Peck, have made it necessary to inform readers that there are potential unrealised gains/losses that could result in actual profits/losses in the future.

Thus the new statement tries to gather all gains/losses, whether realised or not, into one statement. It consists of earned wealth (from the profit and loss account), and unearned wealth (from reserves) in the form of a memorandum. It does not include transfers between reserves or changes in reserves which do not result in an increase/decrease in wealth (e.g. goodwill formerly written off to reserves under SSAP 22).

Solution 8 – D plc

(a) The four components of financial performance as described in FRS 3 are as follows:

(i) *The results of continuing operations (including the results of acquisitions).* This component is required in order to allow the user to identify the results of those activities which are likely to continue in the future. By distinguishing continuing operations in this way, there is little danger of the user being misled by the inclusion of the results of discontinued operations.

(ii) *The results of discontinued operations.* This component shows the income and costs directly related to parts of the business which have been sold or terminated during the year. By definition, these will not recur in the future, but must be included to provide the overall view of the performance of the business in the current year, and in previous financial periods. This will enable more realistic conclusions to be drawn about future performance. The comparative figures will need to be restated to exclude discontinued operations of this year from last year's continuing operations.

(iii) *The profits or losses on the sale or termination of an operation, costs of a fundamental reorganisation or restructuring and profits or losses on the disposal of fixed assets.* If a business has closed down part of its operations, or carried out a major reorganisation or restructuring during the year, the associated costs may be significantly high. As they are not recurring items, these should also be stripped out and shown separately. The presence of such items in the profit and loss account will alert users to the fact that changes have been made within the business, which may affect future results and cash flows. These are now commonly referred to as 'super-exceptional' items.

(iv) *Extraordinary items.* These are material, abnormal items which fall outside the ordinary activities of the business. As these are not likely to recur, they should also be shown separately from the results of ordinary activities, in order not to cause distortions. An extraordinary item may, however, have implications for the future operations and cash flows of the business, and it is important for users to be made aware of them. In practice, the FRS has defined ordinary activities so widely that it is almost impossible to identify an extraordinary item.

(b) *D plc – profit and loss account for the year ended 31 December 2000*

	Continuing operations £'000	Discontinued operations £'000	Total £'000
Turnover	820	150	970
Operating expenses	(470)	(98)	(568)
Operating profit	350	52	402
Costs of closure and reorganisation	(42)	(127)	(169)
Loss on disposal of fixed assets	(19)	(78)	(97)
Profit on ordinary activities before interest	289	(153)	136
Interest payable			(37)
Profit on ordinary activities before taxation			99
Tax on profit on ordinary activities			(24)
Profit on ordinary activities after taxation			75
Dividends			(30)
Retained profit for the financial year			45

(c) *Reconciliation of movements in shareholders' funds*

	£'000
Profit for the financial year	75
Dividends	(30)
	45
New share capital subscribed	180
Reduction in revaluation reserve	(70)
Net addition to shareholders' funds	155
Opening shareholders' funds	1,230
Closing shareholders' funds	1,385

Solution 9 – NBS plc

To: Assistant Accountant
From: Management Accountant
Date:
Subject: Treatment of three transactions for year ended 31 October 2001

Transaction 1 – Disposal of business

Under FRS 3, this withdrawal from a particular market is a material discontinued operation, if the termination has ceased permanently, and it is clearly distinguishable. It must be disclosed in the profit and loss account in a separate column down to operating profit. The remaining group turnover, cost of sales and other operating expenses would appear in a column headed 'Continuing operations'. The disposal is intended to take place after the year end, but if it is completed before the earlier of three months after the year end or the date on which the accounts are approved, then it should be accounted for in 2001. A board decision is not enough to cause the company to account for the disposal in 2001, but an announcement or an offer from a buyer making it difficult for the company to change its policy will influence the decision as to the accounting treatment of the disposal. FRS 3 also requires that the loss on disposal of £50m should be provided for and shown on the face of the profit and loss account as an exceptional item, in the discontinued column. This treatment recognises the expected loss on disposal when the decision is made.

Transaction 2 – Fundamental restructuring

Fundamental restructuring is considered by FRS 3 to be part of continuing operations, but such an infrequent, but material cost should be dealt with as a 'super-exceptional' item, and should be disclosed on the face of the profit and loss account. The old sales ledger balances and obsolete stock are not part of the restructuring and should be adjusted to the cost of sales in the continuing operations column. These items are material, but ordinary exceptional items and should be disclosed by a note to the accounts. This note should also disclose the taxation effects of the exceptional items.

Transaction 3 – Disposal of properties

FRS 3 states that material profits and losses on disposal of fixed assets should be treated as 'super-exceptional' items and shown on the face of the profit and loss account. FRS 3 requires that the difference between the sales proceeds and the written-down value should be disclosed as profit in 2001, i.e. £40m.

However, the revaluation surpluses should be transferred from revaluation reserve to distributable reserves and will now be available for distribution as a dividend. But they should not be incorporated in the profit and loss account.

Signed: Management accountant

Solution 10 – Premier Ltd

Premier Ltd – profit and loss account for the year ended 31 December 2000

	2000 £m	2000 £m	1999 £m	1999 £m
Turnover				
Continuing (W1)	408		386	
Acquisitions	22		–	
	430		386	
Discontinued operations	70		98	
Total turnover		500		484
Cost of sales (W2)		(396)		(360)
Gross profit		104		124
Distribution costs	(28)		(20)	
Administration expenses	(50)		(42)	
		(78)		(62)
Operating profit				
Continuing (W3)	48		64	
Acquisitions (Note 1)	4		–	
	52		64	
Discontinued operations (Notes 2, 3)	(26)		(2)	
		26		62
Exceptional items				
Loss on sale of property in continuing operations (W4, Note 5)	(1)		–	
Profit on sale of operations (W5, Note 2)	14		–	
Costs of discontinuance (W6, Note 3)	(6)		–	
		7		–
		33		62
Interest payable		(12)		(8)
Profit on ordinary activities before taxation		21		54

Workings

(1)	2000 £m	1999 £m
Turnover	500	484
Acquisitions (Note 1)	(22)	–
Discontinued operations		
retail (Note 2)	(40)	(50)
manufacturing (Note 3)	(30)	(48)
Continuing operations	408	386

(2)	2000 £m
Original cost of sales	388
Error in credit to cost of sales on disposal of retail division (Note 2)	14
Error in debit to cost of sales of continuance (Note 3)	(6)
	396

(3)

	2000 £m	1999 £m
Operating profit	34	62
Exceptional items (excl. property sale)	(8)	–
Discontinued operations		
retail (Note 2)	10	(10)
manufacturing (Note 3)	16	12
Acquisitions (Note 1)	(4)	–
Continuing operations	48	64

(4)   Loss on disposal calculated in accordance with FRS 3:

	2000 £m
Net sale proceeds	12
Balance sheet carrying value	13
Loss on sale of fixed assets	(1)

(5)   The profit on sale of operations should always be shown on the face of the profit and loss account.

(6)   The exceptional item relating to the costs of discontinuance should be interpreted in two ways:

(i)   as one of three specific non-operating 'super-exceptional' items to be disclosed on the face of the profit and loss account (as per solution given);

(ii)   the loss on disposal of fixed assets could be included on the face of the profit and loss account and the other items relating to the discontinuance charged to cost of sales, etc., with relevant disclosure in the accounts.

(7)   The closure of the hire depot is not expected to lead to a material reduction in turnover in the continuing market and therefore does not meet the conditions in para. 4c of FRS 3. The operations of the closed depot are not therefore discontinued. If the costs are thought to be material they may have to be disclosed in the notes. They do not appear to fall into one of the categories listed in para. 20 of FRS 3, as there is no material effect on the nature and focus of operations. The costs are therefore charged in arriving at operating profit.

Solution 11 – Brachol plc

(a) (i) Movements on reserves

	P&L account £'000	Share prem. account £'000	Revaluation reserve £'000	Total £'000
At beginning of year	2,700	2,025	4,050	8,775
Prior-period adjustment	(1,350)			(1,350)
Premium on issue of share capital		2,755		2,755
Realisation of revaluation reserve on disposal of property	810		(810)	
Revaluation of fixed asset investment			(405)	(405)
Currency translation difference	(270)			(270)
Revaluation of property			540	540
Retained profit for the year	135			135
	2,025	4,780	3,375	10,180

(ii) Statement of total recognised gains and losses for the year ended 30 November 2001

	£'000
Profit for the financial year	810
Unrealised surplus on revaluation of property	540
Unrealised loss on fixed asset investments	(405)
	945
Currency translation differences on foreign currency net investments	(270)
Total recognised gains and losses relating to year	675
Prior-year adjustment	(1,350)
Total recognised gains and losses since last annual report	(675)

(b) (i) The purpose of the statement of total recognised gains and losses

This is a primary financial statement which is of equal standing to the profit and loss account, balance sheet and cash flow statement. It is designed to highlight to users all recognised gains and losses of a reporting entity for the year. It reveals whether or not the total wealth of the entity has increased over the year. As such it incorporates both realised and unrealised changes in wealth from the profit and loss account and from other reserves respectively. The latter will mainly involve the revaluation of fixed assets and foreign currency translation losses under the closing rate method of translation (per SSAP 20).

When assessing the financial performace of the entity it is important to investigate both the profit and loss account and the statement of total recognised gains and losses in order to gain an overall view of how the entity is progressing.

This additional statement will only affect those companies that have invested in branches/subsidiaries abroad, and/or those entities that have decided to adopt a modified form of historical cost accounting by incorporating revaluations of their fixed assets into their financial statements on a regular basis.

(ii) The extent to which users can make better decisions

One of the reasons for the introduction of the statement of total recognised gains and losses was the demise of companies such as Polly Peck plc, where substantial unrealised foreign currency losses were written off directly to reserves (under SSAP 20), but were not recorded within a primary statement. It was only when the group collapsed that these losses crystallised and the accounting profession was found to be lacking in terms of providing adequate relevant information on those investments.

The extent to which a user will be able to make decisions on the basis of information from the statement of total recognised gains and losses rather than from the movement in reserves can be gauged by investigating the statement for Brachol plc. It is clear that, although earned/realised wealth for the year was £810,000, this is converted into a decrease in overall wealth of £675,000, mainly due to a prior-period adjustment and to foreign exchange translation losses. Comparing this to the positive movement in reserves of £1,405,000 (£10,180,000 – £8,775,000) the only major differences are the share premium of £2,755,000 and the dividends of £675,000.

The information is therefore substantially the same but the difference is that it is combined in a single primary statement which is both standardised and brought to the front of the published financial statements. The presentation along these lines should lead to better decision making.

(c) *(i)* *The reconciliation of actual profit before tax to historical cost profit before tax*

The objective of the new statement introduced by FRS 3, 'Note of historical cost profits and losses', is to restate the actual profit published by those companies which adopt a modified form of historical cost accounting back to a profit/loss based on original cost.

The main differences arising from the modifications are as follows:

(1) There will be a higher depreciation charge based on the revalued carrying value of fixed assets.

(2) The realisation of revaluation gains previously recorded as gains in the statement of total recognised gains and losses, and therefore not permitted to be re-recorded as a gain in the current year's profit and loss account.

(ii) *The usefulness of the note of historical cost profits and losses*

The main use of this statement will be to aid inter-company comparisons, i.e. to ensure that those companies that have adopted revaluations are required to restate their financial results on the same basis as those which still adopt strict historical cost accounting.

This is important as there is no mandatory requirement to uniformly revalue assets and there has been a tendency also to restrict revaluation to periods involving rising prices. The latter practice therefore overstates asset values in times of rising prices.

The statement will eventually become obsolete when and if revaluation becomes compulsory for all reporting entities and thus all financial statements would be restated on the same basis. This has already occurred in NHS Trusts, whose accounts manual requires compulsory revaluation on an annual basis.

Those entities that have retained the existing historical cost system are not required to produce the statement.

Solution 12 – Fresno Group plc

(a) (i) *Statement of total recognised gains and losses*

	£m
Profit for the financial year	165
Other recognised gains and losses for the year	
Unrealised surpluses on revaluation of fixed assets	375
Total recognised gains and losses for the year	540

(ii) *Reconciliation of movements in shareholders' funds*

	£m
Profit for the financial year	165
Dividends	(15)
	150
Other recognised gains and losses for the year after dividends	375
New share capital issued	600
Goodwill written off on acquisitions	(250)
Net additions to shareholders' funds	875
Opening shareholders' funds	1,395
Closing shareholders' funds	2,270

(Note: no longer permitted by FRS 10) — beside "Goodwill written off on acquisitions"

(iii) *Analysis of movements on reserves*

	Merger reserve £m	Revaluation reserve £m	Profit and loss £m	Total £m
Opening balance	55	215	775	1,045
Profit for financial year			165	165
Property revaluation		375		375
Total recognised gains and losses for year	–	375	165	540
Transfer of previous revaluation reserve surplus realised in year		(54)	54	–
Depreciation on revalued assets less historical cost depreciation		(9)	9	–
Adjustments to reported profit to give profit on historical cost basis	–	(63)	63	–
Issue of shares	450			450
Goodwill written off	(250)			(250)
Dividend for year			(15)	(15)
Closing balance	255	527	988	1,770

(iv) *Note of historical cost profits and losses*

	£m
Reported profit on ordinary activities before taxation	255
Realisation of property revaluation gains of previous year	54
Difference between historical cost depreciation and depreciation calculated on revalued amount	9
Historical cost profit on ordinary activities before tax	318
Historical cost profit for the period retained after taxation, extraordinary items and dividends	213

Workings

Extract from profit and loss account – 31 January 2001

	£m
Profit on ordinary activities before taxation – continuing operations	300
Provision for loss on operations to be discontinued	(45)
Profit on ordinary activities before taxation	255
Taxation	(90)
Profit for the financial year	165
Dividends	(15)
	150

(b)(i)   As the decision to close the subsidiary was made before the year-end, but the closure will not occur until the following year, a provision for loss on operations to be discontinued would be required in the financial statements for the year ending 31 January 2001. The provision would comprise any direct costs of closure and any operating losses up to the date of closure. In this case the provision will contain the estimated operating loss from 1 February 2001 to 31 May 2001 of £30 million and the redundancy costs, stock and plant write-downs of £15 million: a total of £45 million.

As the closure does not qualify as a discontinued operation for the year ending 31 January 2001, the results of the subsidiary should be included in continuing operations, with the provision being shown as an exceptional item. In the notes to the financial statements it may be appropriate to disclose separately the results of operations which, although not discontinued, are in the process of being discontinued. Thus, the results of Reno plc for the year ending 31 January 2001 will be given and classified as 'discontinuing', not 'discontinued'. It should not be disclosed on the face of the profit and loss account as a 'super-exceptional' item.

(ii)   In the year to 31 January 2002, the closure of Reno plc will qualify as a discontinued operation. The following figures will appear in the financial statements of Fresno Group plc in respect of the subsidiary, Reno plc.

Reno plc – 31 January 2002

	£m	£m
Turnover – discontinued operations		175
Cost of sales		(195)
Gross loss		(20)
Administrative expenses	(15)	
Selling expenses	(30)	
Less provision released	30	
		(15)
Operating loss – discontinued operations		(35)
Loss on disposal of discontinued operations	(12)	
Less release of provision	15	
		3
Loss on ordinary activities before tax		(32)

The provision of £45 million was provided for in the 2001 financial statements and it has to be allocated between the operating loss and the loss on disposal. The actual loss in the period to 31 May 2001 was £65 million and the provision made against this in the previous period's financial statements of £30 million would be offset against this loss. The turnover and operating profit for the period to 31 May 2002 would be classified as discontinued in the financial statements to 31 January 2002.

In the financial statements to 31 January 2002, the provision of £15 million would be released against the loss on the disposal of discontinued operations.

Solution 13 – Greenhouse plc

(a) *Greenhouse plc – Consolidated profit and loss account for the year ended 31 August 2002*

	£'000	£'000
Turnover (W1)		
Continuing operations	25,365	
Discontinued operations	1,300	
		26,665
Cost of sales (W1)		(22,576)
Gross profit		4,089
Net operating expenses (W1)		(2,521)
Operating profit		1,568
Continuing operations (W1)	1,828	
Discontinued operations	(310)	
Less 2001 provision	50	
	1,568	
Loss on disposal of discontinued operations	(300)	
Less 2001 provision	70	
		(230)
Profit on ordinary activities before taxation		1,338
Tax on profit on ordinary activities (W3)		(364)
Profit on ordinary activities after taxation		974
Minority interests (W4)		(222)
Profit for financial year		752
Dividends (600,000 × 5p)		(30)
Retained profit for the financial year		722
Earnings per share (W5)		125.3p

All workings are rounded to nearest £'000.

Group structure

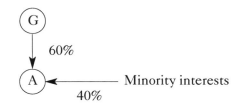

Workings

(W1) *Consolidated profit and loss schedule*

	Greenhouse	Airedale	Inter Co	Total	Discontinued	Continuing
	£'000	£'000	£'000	£'000	£'000	£'000
Sales	15,050	12,340	(725)	26,665	1,300	25,365
Cost of sales	12,679	10,622	(725)	22,576	1,225	21,351
Gross profit	2,371	1,718	–	4,089	75	4,014
Net operating expenses						
Distribution costs	1,042	824	–	1,866	100	1,766
Administrative expenses	730[1]	307	–	1,037	285	752
Other operating income						
Investment income (net)	(280)	(64)	(12)[2]	(332)		(332)
Net operating expenses	1,492	1,067	(12)	2,571	385	2,186
Net profit	879	651	(12)	1,518	(310)	1,828
Provision for discontinuance				50	50	
				1,568	260	1,828

Net operating expenses = 2,571 above – provision for discontinuance 50 = 2,521

1   Admin 766 – R&D 36 = 730
2   See working 2

(W2) *Inter-company dividend*
60% of 20 (200,000 × 10p) = 12 (net)

(W3) *Tax on profit on ordinary activities*

	£'000	
Greenhouse	268	
Airedale plc	96	
		364

(W4) *Minority interest*

	£'000
Airedale plc net profit after tax	555
Minority interest 40% thereof	222

(W5) *Earnings per share*

$$\frac{\text{Profits for financial year}}{\text{No. of ordinary shares}} = \frac{752}{600} = 125.3\text{p}$$

(b) *Group profit/loss account as at 31 August 2002*

	£'000	£'000
Greenhouse plc profit/loss account at 1.9.01		1,750
Airedale plc profit/loss account at 1.9.01	1,600	
Less profit/loss account at acquisition	(1,400)	
	200	
Group share thereof 60%		120
Profit and loss for year		722
Group resources at 31 August 2002		2,592

Solution 14 – Diva plc

Profit and loss account for the year ended 31 December 1996

		£m	£m
Turnover			
Continuing operations		225	
Acquisitions	(W6)	45	
		270	
Discontinued operations		30	300
Cost of sales	(W1)		(231)
Gross profit			69
Selling and distribution costs	(W1)		(12)
Administration expenses	(W1)		(9.5)
Operating profit			
Continuing operations		29.5	
Acquisitions		10	
		39.5	
Discontinued operations		8	47.5
Impairment of fixed assets	(W9)		(0.8)
Exceptional closure costs – plastic operations	(W8)		(15)
			31.7
Interest payable (1.2 + 0.5)			(1.7)
Profit on ordinary activities before taxation			30
Tax on ordinary activities			(10)
Profit on ordinary activities after taxation			20
Dividends proposed			(8)
Retained profits for the year			12
Retained profits brought forward at 1.1.1996			116.2
Retained profits carried forward at 31.12.1996			128.2

Balance sheet as at 31 December 1996

		£m	£m
Fixed assets			
Tangible assets	(W11)		177.7
Current assets			
Stocks	(30 – 1 (W3))	29	
Debtors		80	
Cash at bank		40	
		149	
Creditors: amounts falling due within one year (70 + 1 (W5) + 10)		81	
Net current assets			68
			245.7
Creditors: amounts falling due after more than one year			
12% debenture loans			(10)
			235.7
Provisions for liabilities and charges			
Deferred taxation			(5)
			230.7
Capital and reserves			
Called-up share capital			100
Investment property revaluation reserve	(W2)		2.5
Profit and loss account			128.2
			230.7

Statement of total recognised gains and losses

	£m
Profit for the financial year	20
Unrealised surplus on revaluation of investment properties	2.5
Total recognised gains and losses	22.5

Reconciliation of movements in shareholders' funds

	£m
Profit attributable to the members of Diva plc	20
Dividends proposed	(8)
	12
Other recognised gains and losses for the year	2.5
	14.5
Opening shareholders' funds	216.2
Closing shareholders' funds	230.7

Workings

W1 Allocation of costs

	Cost of sales	Distribution costs	Administrative expenses	
	£m	£m	£m	
Per the T/B	210	12	8.5	
Depreciation – buildings				
£100m / 50 years	2			Note 1
Depreciation – plant				
£120m / 10 years	12			
Depreciation – fixtures				
£30m / 5 years	6			
Stock obsolescence	1 (W3)			
Unfair dismissal claim			1	
	231	12	9.5	

W2 Investment property – SSAP 19

	£m		
Cost	5		
Surplus on revaluation	2.5	IP reserve	Note 2
Value on balance sheet	7.5		

W3 Stock valuation – SSAP 9

Headlights	NRV £2.2m – £0.2m selling costs = £2m		
	Cost	3m	Note 3
	Loss to profit and loss	(1m)	

W4 ACT

No longer required from April 1999   Note 4

W5 Unfair dismissal claim – FRS 12

This is an obligation – legal – and it is probable and can be reliably measured at £1m, therefore it should be provided under FRS 12.   Note 5

W6 Turnover and operating profits – acquisitions – FRS 3

Should disclose £45m as a separate sub-column for turnover and operating profit, as well as
£10m in operating profit   Note 6

W7 Cessation of manufacturing – FRS 3

Under FRS 3, the entity is in the process of discontinuing this activity but it is not actually
discontinued yet. It is also not really a change in the nature and focus of operations – it is still
subcontracting the operations. No adjustment should take place under FRS 3   Note 7

W8 Closure of manufacturing division – FRS 3

This is a major change in the nature and focus of operations; therefore under FRS 3, it should
be separately disclosed as a discontinued activity – turnover £30m, operating profit £8m   Note 8

W9 Provision for the closure of loss-making operation – FRS 12

The implementation of the closure decision has not yet commenced and no public announcement
has been made to that effect. It is not permitted to be provided in the financial statements,
under FRS 12   Note 9

W10 Capital commitments

Purely a legal disclosure in the notes to the accounts.

W11 Tangible fixed assets

	Land & buildings £m	Investment property £m	Plant & machinery £m	Fixtures & fittings £m	Total £m
Cost					
Balance at 1.1.1996					
and 31.12.1996	105	5	120	30	260
Surplus on revaluation	–	2.5	–	–	2.5
Balance at 31.12.1996	105	7.5	120	30	262.5
Accumulated depreciation					
Balance at 1.1.1996	16	–	36	12	64
Charge for the year	2	–	12	6	20
Impairment	0.8	–	–	–	0.8
Balance at 31.12.1996	18.8	–	48	18	84.8
Net book value 31.12.96	86.2	7.5	72	12	177.7

Solution 1 – Cash flow statements – FRS 1

To: Managing director
From: Chief accountant   Date

FRS 1 Cash Flow Statements

In response to your memo of 12 June with regard to the recent accounting standard on cash flow issued by the Accounting Standards Board (ASB), I have summarised some of the key issues as requested.

(a) Its stated objective

The objective of the new financial reporting standard (FRS 1) on cash flow statements is to require companies like ours to report their cash generation and absorption on a standardised basis. Companies must report their cash flows under nine headings:

- Operating activities
- Dividends received from associated companies
- Returns on investment and servicing of finance
- Taxation
- Capital expenditure and financial investment
- Acquisitions and disposals
- Equity dividends paid
- Management of liquid resources
- Financing

The nine headings must be disclosed in this sequence. The cash flow statement is intended to aid the reader's assessment of the liquidity, viability and financial adaptability of the enterprise. The standard headings should highlight the significant components of cash flow and will facilitate comparison with other companies.

(b) The required format

The cash flow statement must list the inflows and outflows of cash for the period under the nine headings in paragraph (a). A total should be produced for each heading as well as a separate total for the net cash inflows/outflows before financing. Examples of the formats are provided in the appendices to the standard and I have enclosed copies for your perusal.

In addition there are a number of back-up notes to the statement that must be produced. These include a reconciliation between operating profit and cash flow from operations, an analysis of the changes in net debt and details of any major non-cash transactions.

(c) The meaning of cash flow classifications

Operating activities

This represents cash flow from transactions arising from operating or trading activities. These are the net cash flows resulting from the operations shown in the profit and loss account in arriving at operating profit.

They may be reported using either the direct or the indirect method. The indirect method is compulsory and requires a back-up note to explain how operating profit is converted into cash flow from operating activity. The standard believes that the indirect method discloses the quality of profit generated in terms of cash generation. The reconciliation note must disclose any movements in stocks, creditors and debtors separately as well as any other differences between cash flow and profit. Since 1996 this note may be reported on the face of the cash flow statement as a prelude to the statement but not as part of it.

The direct method discloses the actual gross flows from trading activity, e.g. actual payments to suppliers and employees and actual receipts from customers, etc. It is purely a voluntary disclosure and to date very few companies have felt it necessary to disclose this second approach. Most accounting systems are geared towards accruals accounting and are not easily adaptable to the production of the direct information.

Investing activities
Under the original version of FRS 1 the cash inflows/outflows pertaining to investing activities consisted of:

(i)   receipts/payments on the sale/purchase of fixed assets; and
(ii) receipts/payments on the sale/purchase of subsidiaries/associates.

The revised version of FRS 1 now divides the category into three:

(i)   capital expenditure and financial investment – includes the cash flows in (i) above but also receipts/payments from the purchase and sale of investments not classified as a liquid resource or acquisition;
(ii) acquisitions and disposals – includes the cash flows only;
(iii) management of liquid resources – the cash flows relating to the purchase and sale of short-term investments sold in an active market.

Financing activities

These cash flows comprise receipts from and payments to external providers of finance in respect of principal amounts of finance. They include the following inflows/outflows:

• Receipts/repayments on the issue of shares
• Receipts/repayments on the issue of debentures/loans
• Capital element of finance lease payments
• Expenses/commission on the issue of shares/debentures, etc.

Cash flows from associated undertakings should be disclosed separately in between operating activities and returns on investment and servicing of finance.

Solution 2 – V Ltd

(a) *Cash flow statement*

V Ltd – Cash flow statement for the year ended 31 December 2000

	£'000	£'000
Net cash flow from operating activities (Note 1)		387
Returns on investment and servicing of finance		
Interest paid		(23)
Corporation tax paid (W2)		(76)
Capital expenditure		
Payments to acquire tangible fixed assets	(98)	
Proceeds on sale of tangible fixed assets (W3)	2	
		(96)
		192
Equity dividends paid (W1)		(46)
Net cash inflow before financing		146
Financing		
Repayment of loans	(250)	
Proceeds of share issue (30 + 61)	91	
Net cash outflow from financing		(159)
Decrease in cash		(13)

Reconciliation of net cash flow to movement in net debt

	£'000
Decrease in cash	(13)
Cash outflow from decrease in loans	(250)
Movement in net debt	(263)
Net debt at 1.1.00	301
Net debt at 31.12.00	38

Notes

(1) Reconciliation of operating profit to net cash flow from operating activities

	£'000
Operating profit	326
Depreciation	74
Loss on disposal	4
Increase in stock	(3)
Increase in debtors	(9)
Decrease in creditors	(5)
	387

(2) Analysis of changes in net debt

	At 1.1.00	Cash flows	At 31.12.00
	£'000	£'000	£'000
Bank	19	13	32
Long-term loans	(320)	250	(70)
	(301)	263	(38)

Workings

(1) Dividends

	£'000		£'000
Paid (balancing figure)	46	Balance 31.12.99	15
Balance 31.12.00	21	Profit and loss	52
	67		67

(2) Taxation

	£'000		£'000
Paid (balancing figure)	76	Balance 31.12.99	
Balance 31.12.00		(66 – 5 ACT)	61
(79 – 7 ACT)	72	Profit and loss	87
	148		148

(3) Disposal of machinery

	£'000		£'000
Fixed assets	18	Depreciation	12
		Loss on disposal	4
		Bank (balancing figures)	2
	18		18

(b) *Long-term profitability v short-term cash flow*

There is no single goal that managers should strive towards. Ultimately the long-term objective must be to maximise profits. However these profits are not likely to generate cash evenly throughout the life of the company. At times substantial negative cash flows will be created in periods of high investment, dividend payments, etc. Cash is therefore essential to meet these commitments, otherwise the business would cease to exist. It is important, therefore, to ensure that the short-term liquidity position is well controlled. The management of long-term profitability is extremely important but it is equally important to ensure that short-term liquidity is maintained.

Solution 3 – Blue Ting plc

(a) **Blue Ting plc – cash flow statement for year ended 31 May 2001**

	£m	£m
Net cash inflow from operating activities (note 1)		220
Returns on financing and servicing of finance		
Interest received	3	
Interest paid (7 – 3)	(4)	
Interest element of finance lease rental payment	(3)	
Net cash outflow from servicing of finance		(4)
Taxation		
Corporation tax paid (10 + 22 – 16)		(16)
Capital expenditure and financial investment		
Payments to acquire tangible fixed assets	(104)	
Receipts from sales of tangible fixed assets	21	
		(83)
		117
Equity dividends paid (12 + 8)		(20)
Net cash inflow before financing		97
Movement in net liquid resources		
Payments to acquire 8.5% Treasury Stock 2113	(60)	
Payments to acquire loan notes repayable on demand	(15)	
		(75)
Financing		
Issue of ordinary share capital	14	
Share issue costs	(1)	
Purchase of own shares	(12)	
Capital repayments under finance leases	(7)	
Net cash outflow from financing		(6)
Increase in cash		16

Reconciliation of movement in net cash flow to movement in net debt (Note 2)

	£m
Increase in cash for the period	16
Cash paid to increase liquid resources	75
Cash repaid on finance leases	7
	98
New finance leases	(28)
Conversion of 6% Debentures into shares	29
Movement in net debt in the period	99
Net debt at 1.6.00	(90)
Net funds at 30.5.01	9

Notes

(1) Reconciliation of operating profit to net cash inflow from operating activities

	£m
Operating profit	100
Depreciation	37
Amortisation of development expenditure	1
Profit on sales of fixed assets	(2)
Decrease in stocks	15
Increase in debtors	(20)
Increase in creditors	89
Net cash inflow from operating activities	220

(2) Analysis of changes in net debt

	1 June 2000 £m	Cash flow £m	Non-cash changes £m	Reclassification £m	31 May 2001 £m
Treasury Stock 8.5% 2113	–	60			60
Treasury Stock 12.75% 2001	20	–			20
Loan notes	–	15			15
		75			
Cash at bank	3	4			7
Bank overdraft	(20)	12			(8)
		16			
Obligations under finance lease (ST)	(3)	4		(6)	(5)
6% Debentures 2001–2007	(60)	–	29		(31)
Obligations under finance lease (LT)	(30)	3	(28)	6	(49)
		7			
	(90)	98	1	Nil	9

(b) The disclosure of forecast cash flow information would be advantageous to users of financial information for the following reasons:

(i) Disclosure of cash flow forecasts would provide users with the benefit of management's knowledge of the company's future cash flow and their views of the future outlook for cash flows. Further, it commits management to future planning and consideration of going concern issues.

(ii) Public disclosure of cash flow forecasts would reduce the benefits of insider dealing as relevant information would be made public.

(iii) Managerial performance could be evaluated by the disclosure of cash flow information.

(iv) Cash flow forecasts may help investors or creditors to assess the ability of the company to pay its way in the future.

The following disadvantages are also apparent if cash flow forecasts are published:

(i) Cash flow forecasts are subjective and uncertain. They will be based upon the opinions of the management of the company. However, users of financial information should be aware of the subjective basis for the forecasts and can take this into account when utilising them.

(ii) Forecast cash flow information can be manipulated by unscrupulous managers. However, if these forecasts are continually inaccurate then users will not use the information and no advantage will be gained by the managers.

(iii) The information will be difficult to audit because of its subjective nature. Auditors will only report upon the accounting principles used and the consistency of their application. The auditor will not report upon the 'truth and fairness' of the information.

(iv) Disclosure of information may be harmful to the interests of the company by giving information to their competitors. However, if all companies disclose forecast cash flow information, then it can be argued that little competitive advantage will be gained, although international competitors may gain advantage. Also it may be prejudicial in relation to disputed amounts.

Solution 4 – Carver plc

(a) **Consolidated cash flow statement for the year ended 30 September 2001**

	£'000	£'000
Net cash inflow from operating activities (note 1)		372
Dividend received from associates		
(1,000 + 495 – 145 tax – 1,100)		250
Returns on investments and servicing of finance		
Interest paid (150 + 30 – 40 – 40 discount)	(100)	
Dividend paid to minority interest		
(0 +100 P & L + 63 – 115)	(48)	
Dividend received from fixed asset		
investments (200 – 45)	155	
		7
Corporation tax paid (including ACT)		
(67 + 150 + 13 + 495 P & L – 87 – 375 – 30 + 17 Acq)		(250)
Capital expenditure and financial investment		
Payments to acquire tangible fixed assets		
(3,000 – 1,400 + 500 – 165 – 850)	(1,085)	
Proceeds on disposal of machine	500	
		(585)
		(206)
Acquisitions and disposals		
Cash consideration on purchase of Good Display Ltd	(14)	
Cash balances acquired on acquisition	112	
		98
Equity dividends paid (200 + 400 P&L – 300)		(300)
Net cash outflow before use of liquid resources		
and finance		(408)
Management of liquid resource		–
Financing		
Issue of shares (3,940 + 2,883 – 2,000 – 2,095 – 275 Acq)	2,453	
Issue of loan stock (1,460 – 500 – 40 Discount)	920	
Capital loan repayments (200 + 170 + 850 adds – 240 – 710)	(270)	
		3,103
Increase in cash		2,695

Reconciliation of net cash flow to movement in net debt

	£'000
Increase in cash	2,695
Cash Inflow from issue of loans	(920)
Cash outflow from lease repayments	270
	2,045
New finance leasing	(850)
Notional interest	(40)
	1,155
Net funds at 1.1.01	950
Net funds at 31.12.01	2,105

Notes

(1) Reconciliation of operating profit to net cash flow from operating activities

	£'000	
Operating profit	1,485	
Depreciation charges	325	W1
Profit on sale of machinery	(100)	
Increase in stocks	(943)	W2
Increase in trade debtors	(547)	W3
Increase in trade creditors	152	W4
Net cash inflow from operating activities	372	

(2) Analysis of changes in net funds

	At 1.1 2001	Cash flow	Acquisition (excl. cash & overdrafts)	Other non-cash changes	At 31.12 2001
	£'000	£'000	£'000	£'000	£'000
Cash	1,820	2,695			4,515
Obligations under finance lease	(370)	270		(850)	(950)
Loans	(500)	(920)		(40)	(1,460)
	950	2,045		(890)	2,105

Workings

(W1) Depreciation charges	£'000	£'000
Buildings		125
Machinery:		
Closing aggregate amount	1,200	
Less opening aggregate amount	(1,100)	
	100	
Add depreciation on disposal	100	
		200
		325

(W2) Stock	£'000	£'000
Closing balance		1,975
Less:		
Opening balance	1,000	
Arising from the acquisition	32	
		(1,032)
Cash outflow		943

(W3) Trade debtors	£'000	£'000
Closing balance		1,850
Less:		
Opening balance	1,275	
Arising from the acquisition	28	
		(1,303)
Cash outflow		547

(W4) Trade creditors	£'000	£'000
Closing balance		500
Less:		
Opening balance	280	
Arising from the acquisition	68	
		(348)
Cash inflow		152

(b)(i) *The treatment of capitalised interest and liquid resources.*

FRS 1 requires capitalised interest to be shown within the interest paid heading in the *Returns on investments and servicing of finance* section of the cash flow statement.

The effect of this will be to increase the interest paid from £100,000 to £105,000. The purchase of tangible fixed assets will be reduced by the same amount from £1,085,000 to £1,080,000.

(ii) *The treatment of cash and liquid resources*

We have noted that the cash figures comprised the following:

	1.10.00	30.9.01
	£'000	£'000
Cash in hand	10	15
Bank overdrafts	(770)	(65)
Bank	1,080	1,890
10% Treasury Stock 2000	1,500	–
Bank deposits	–	1,125
Gas 3% 1997–2002	–	1,550
	1,820	4,515

Applying the FRS 1 definition of liquid resources as current asset investments held as readily disposable stocks of value which are:

- The 10% Treasury Stock 2000 was acquired on 1 September 2000 and redeemed on 31 October 2000 and falls within the FRS definition of a liquid resource.
- The bank deposits were made on 1 January 2001 and the amount deposited will become available on 31 December 2001. However, they will not be treated as a liquid resource: they are cash.

- The Gas 3% was acquired on 1 June 2001 and matures on 30 September 2003. It should be recorded as a liquid resource.

The effect on the consolidated cash flow statement is:

- The management of liquid resources section will include the 10% Treasury Stock and Gas 3% as a purchase of liquid resources at a figure of £50,000.
- The revised cash flow statement totals will be:

	£'000
Operating activities	372
Dividends received from associates	250
Returns on investments	2
Taxation	(250)
Capital expenditure and financial investment	(580)
	(206)
Acquisition and disposals	98
Equity dividends	(300)
	(408)
Movement in liquid resources	(50)
Financing	3,103
Increase in cash	2,645

Solution 5 – Sweet plc

Consolidated cash flow statement for the year ended 31 December 1998

Reconciliation of operating profit to net cash flow from operating activities

	£m
Operating profit	1,050
Goodwill amortisation	16
Depreciation	750
Decrease in stocks (1,280 – (1,220 – 300 acq.))	360
Increase in debtors (1,440 – (1,740 – 240 acq.))	(60)
Increase in creditors (680 – (750 – 160 acq.))	(90)
	2,026

Cash flow statement

	Working	£m	£m
Net cash flow from operating activities			2,026
Returns on investments and servicing of finance			
Interest paid (40 + 10)		(50)	
Dividend paid to minority interests	3	(96)	
Interest element of lease rentals (given)		(150)	
			(296)
Taxation	4		(256)
Capital expenditure and financial investment			
Purchase of fixed assets	5	(161)	
Proceeds on disposal of plant and machinery		–	
			(161)
			1,313

	£m	£m
Acquisitions and disposals		
Cash element in acquisition of Gentle Ltd	(365)	
Net bank balances acquired on acquisition of Gentle Ltd	(256)	
		(621)
Equity dividends paid (OB 192 + 240 charge – 240 CB)		(192)
Cash flow before the use of liquid resources and financing		500
Management of liquid resources		-
Financing		
Capital element of finance lease rentals		
(OB 360 + 960 = 1,320 + 480 additions = 1,800 – CB (400 + 1,040))		(360)
Net cash inflow for the year		140

Reconciliation of movement in net cash inflow to the movement in net debt

Increase in net cash inflow for the year	140
Reduction in net debt – finance leases	360
	500
Finance lease acquired	(480)
Decrease in net debt	20
Net debt at 31.12.1997	(1,484)
Net debt at 31.12.1998	(1,464)

W1 Analysis of changes in net debt

	31.12.1997 £m	Cash flow £m	Non-cash £m	Acquisition £m	31.12.1998 £m
Bank overdraft	(164)	140			(24)
Obligations under finance lease	(360)				(400)
Obligations under finance lease	(960)	360	(480)		(1,040)
	(1,484)	500	(480)		(1,464)

W2 Calculation of goodwill on takeover of Gentle Ltd

Purchase consideration	(£365m cash + £50m shares at £1.50)	£440m
Net assets acquired	(75% x £480m)	360m
Goodwill		80m

Amortisation: £16m per annum over 5 years

W3 Minority interests

	£m
Balance at 31.12.1997	496
Acquisition of Gentle (25% x £480m)	120
Share of profits for the year	80
	696
Balance at 31.12.1998	600
Dividends paid to minority	96

W4 Taxation

	£m
Balance at 31.12.1997 (164 + 184)	348
Acquisition of Gentle tax	64
Profit and loss charge	290
	702
Balance at 31.12.1998 (190 + 256)	(446)
Taxation paid	256

W5 Tangible fixed assets

	£m	
Balance at 31.12.1997	2,960	
Acquisition of Gentle fixed assets	420	
Finance lease acquired	480	
Capitalisation of interest	10	(included in interest payments)
Revaluation surplus	25	
	3,895	
Depreciation charge for the year	(750)	
Loss on disposal of fixed assets	(26)	
	3,119	
Balance at 31.12.1998	3,280	
Purchase of fixed assets	161	

Solution 6 – Holmes plc

(a) *Cash flow statement for the year ended 30 September 1999*

Reconciliation of operating profit to net cash inflow from operating activities

	£m
Operating profit	150
Depreciation charges (note 4)	58
Amortisation of goodwill (W1)	10
Decrease in stocks (CB 105 – 30 acq. = 75 – 90 OB)	15
Decrease in debtors (CB 120 – 25 acq. = 95 – 100 OB)	5
Decrease in trade creditors (CB 40 – 15 acq. = 25 – 30 OB)	(5)
Investment income	(6)
Net cash inflow from operating activities	227

Cash flow statement

	£m	£m
Net cash inflow from operating activities		227
Dividends received from associates (W2)		7
Returns on investments and servicing of finance		
Investment income	6	
Interest paid (W3)	(50)	
Dividends paid to minority interest (W4)	(5)	
		(49)
Taxation		
UK corporation tax (W5)		(32)
Capital expenditure and financial investment		
Receipts from the sale of freehold property (W6)	100	
Payments to acquire tangible fixed assets (W6)	(8)	
		92
Free cash flow		245
Acquisitions and disposals		
Cash payments on acquisition of subsidiary (W7)	(100)	
Cash and bank balances acquired with the subsidiary (W7)	10	
		(90)
Equity dividends paid (W8)		(25)
Cash inflow before the use of liquid resources and financing		130

	£m	£m
Management of liquid resources		
Net proceeds on disposal of current asset investments		
(70 OB – 20 CB)		50
Financing		
Capital element of finance lease payments (W9)	(25)	
Repayment of loan stock (90 OB – nil CB)	(90)	
		(115)
Increase in cash for the period		
(OB 5 – (80) = (75) – CB 10 – (20) = (10))		65

Workings

(1)   Acquisition of Watson plc

	£m		£m
Fair value of purchase consideration	100	Goodwill b/f	19
Fair value of net assets acquired (80% x £105m)	84	Watson plc	16
Goodwill	16		35
		Goodwill c/f	25
		Amortised year	10

(2)   Investment in associates

	£m
Opening balance	70
Share of associates profit (40 – 15 interest – 8 tax)	17
	87
Closing balance	80
Dividends received	7

(3) Interest paid

	£m
Group only (no accruals)	50

(4)   Minority interests

	£m
Opening balance (40 + prop. dividend 5)	45
Profit and loss	10
	55
Acquisition of Watson plc (20% x £10.5m)	21
	76
Closing balance (65 + prop. dividend 6)	71
Dividends paid	5

(5) Taxation paid

	£m
Opening balance (8 + 24)	32
Profit and loss	35
Acqusition of Watson plc	5
	72
Closing balance (10 + 30)	40
Taxation paid	32

(6)   Tangible fixed assets

	£m		£m
Opening balance	280	Disposals at NBV	90
Acquisition of Watson plc	60	Exceptional gain	10
Finance lease (note 4)	40	Proceeds on disposal	100
	380		
Disposals at NBV	(90)		
	290		
Depreciation	(58)		
	232		
Closing balance	240		
Payments to acquire fixed assets	(8)		

(7)   Acquisitions and disposals

	£m
Cash consideration (given – note 3)	(100)
Cash balances acquired (given – note 3)	10

	£m			£m
(8) Equity dividends paid		*(9) Finance leases*		
Opening balance	25	Opening balance (20 + 70)	90	
Profit and loss	25	Additions (given – note 4)	40	
	50		130	
Closing balance	(25)	Closing balance (25 + 80)	105	
Paid	(25)	Capital repaid	25	

(b) Memorandum

To: Managing director
From: Management accountant
Date: 30 December 1999

RE: GROUP CASH FLOW STATEMENT – Rationale for notes to the statement

With reference to your memorandum of 16 December, the following are my comments on the rationale behind the supplementary notes to the cash flow statement:

(1)   Reconciliation of operating profit to operating cash flows

All published financial statements must adopt the 'indirect method' of accounting for operating cash flows, which last year generated a positive inflow of £227m. The cash flow statement is designed to link the three primary statements together – the profit and loss account, the cash flow statement and the balance sheet. The main rationale for this note is therefore to link the operating profit of £150m with the cash generated by those operations. There is a fundamental difference between profit and cash – the former adopting the accruals concept. The reconciliation therefore takes operating profit and adjusts for all non-cash expenses/income in the profit and loss and movements in net current assets so as to identify the underlying cash flow performance from operations.

The statement can be shown separately from the cash flow statement as a note to the financial statements or it can be disclosed as a preface on the same page of the statement, but not part of it. This is to ensure that no non-cash flow items are included in the statement. It must be pure cash. It should help investors interpret how good the company is in turning operating profits into positive cash flow.

(2)   Reconciliation of net cash flow to movement in net debt

The revised FRS 1 restricts the definition of 'cash' to real cash and bank balances. It is, however, out of line with international accounting standards and with the way that most large groups manage their treasury function. However, this particular reconciliation does link the movement in cash for the period with the movement in net borrowings for the period. It therefore provides a bridge between the balance sheets at the start and end of the period so that all three primary statements are 'speaking' to each other for the first time.

A cash flow statement should provide investors with information about liquidity and solvency. Net debt is a better indicator of liquidity than cash alone. The problem is that net debt is likely to be reported under several headings in the balance sheet. The rationale behind the note is to bring all the elements of net debt together in order to provide a broader picture of the management of liquidity and solvency.

(3)   *Summary of the effect of the acquisition of Watson plc*

The purpose behind this note is to provide investors with full details of the fair values of consideration paid to acquire other companies, the fair values of the net assets acquired and details of goodwill so created. In many cases the purchase consideration does not contain much cash and the cash flow statement should only include cash elements in the statement. The only cash that would appear in the statement would be the cash and bank balances taken over and any cash element in the purchase consideration. The note should provide users with a broad picture of how any acquisition has affected the liquidity and solvency of the company.

8

Accounting Disclosure Standards: Post Balance Sheet Events, Provisions and Contingencies, Pensions and Segmental Reporting

Solution 1 – Omega Ltd

Mr A. D. Shannon
Managing Director
Omega Ltd

Twig & Tree
Chartered Accountants
Main St, Belfast

Dear Mr Shannon,

Date

Standard accounting practice relating to post balance sheet events

With reference to your letter of 10 April 2002, I should like to explain what is meant by post balance sheet events. These are defined in SSAP 17 as those events which occur after the balance sheet date but before the date on which the financial statements are approved by the board of directors. They include both favourable and unfavourable events.

Post balance sheet events may be of an *adjusting* or *non-adjusting* nature. The main difference between the two is that the latter does not exist at the year end.

Adjusting events are those which provide additional evidence relating to conditions existing at the balance sheet date and which require the revision of previous estimates used in the preparation of the financial statements. Typical examples of such events include the liquidation of a debtor, obsolescence in stock leading to its value falling below cost, and perhaps the crystallisation of liabilities.

Non-adjusting events are those arising after the year end which do not affect the condition of the assets or liabilities at the balance sheet date but which are so material that their non-disclosure would give a misleading picture to users of the financial statements. They are disclosed in the notes and do not adjust the actual financial statements. Examples of such events include the nationalisation of a subsidiary, major acquisitions/disposals and substantial uninsured losses.

The main principle is that financial statements should be prepared on the basis of conditions existing at the year end.

A material post balance sheet event requires adjustments to be made in the financial statements where:

(1) It is an adjusting event (as above).

(2) The application of the going concern concept is in doubt. In this case the accounts should instead be prepared on a break-up basis.

(3) The event is such that prudence would require it to be included in the accounts.

As mentioned earlier, a material non-adjusting post balance sheet event should be disclosed if it is so material that its non-disclosure would affect the ability of users to reach a proper understanding of the financial position. It should also be disclosed if it happens to be the reversal or maturity after the year end of a transaction entered into prior to the year end, the substance of which was primarily to alter the appearance of the company's balance sheet, i.e. window dressing.

For each non-adjusting event requiring disclosure, the following must be disclosed in the notes to the financial statements:

(1)   The nature of the event.

(2)   An estimate of the financial effect or a statement to the effect that it is not practicable to make such an estimate.

The financial estimate should be calculated before taking taxation into account. Any tax implications should be noted separately if this is necessary for a proper understanding of the financial position.

Any events which occur after the date of approval of the financial statements by the directors are not within the ambit of SSAP 17. This date should be disclosed in the financial statements, usually at the foot of the balance sheet or as a separate note to the financial statements.

However, if the board of directors subsequently becomes aware of some material event it should consider publishing this information, perhaps in the chairman's report, so that users of the financial statements are not misled. Pro forma accounts are now a popular addition to the annual report so that the impact of non-adjusting events can be clearly identified.

After signing the audit report, the auditors might occasionally draw the board's attention to information which materially alters the view of users of the financial statements. In extreme circumstances, if the board refuses to act, the auditors are entitled under company legislation to make a statement about the event at the AGM.

I hope that the above adequately explains current accounting practice for post balance sheet events but please do not hesitate to contact me for any additional information.

Yours sincerely

A. P. Twig

Solution 2 – Cooper plc

(a)   *The need for an SSAP*

Under SSAP 17, events arising after the year end should be reflected in the financial statements if they provide evidence of conditions which existed at the year end and they materially affect the amounts to be included.

It is also a requirement that material non-adjusting events must be disclosed by way of notes, i.e. those events which do not affect conditions at the year end but which are so material that their non-disclosure would prevent a proper understanding of the financial statements.

Without the SSAP, it would not be possible to put an adequate valuation on accruals and prepayments and the financial statements would not show a true and fair view.

The following are the recommendations for the accounting treatment to be accorded in the accounts of Watt Ltd:

(1) Stock destroyed

The event (i.e. the flood) occurred after the year end and is therefore non-adjusting. The net loss after insurance is expected to be £100,000. This should be disclosed if its non-disclosure would affect the user's ability to reach a proper understanding of the financial statements. As this represents over 55 per cent of the profits before tax, it is certainly material and should be disclosed. In next year's accounts it should be written off as an exceptional item within the figure for profit before tax.

(2) Debtor in receivership

The event (i.e. the debtor of £34,000) existed at the year end and the subsequent evidence indicates that the debt may not be recovered due to the receivership of the company. The provision for bad debts should be based on the likely non-recovery at the time of the accounts being approved but prudence may dictate 100 per cent provision if no evidence exists at that time.

The additional sale of £40,000 occurred after the year end and should be matched against a bad debt provision in the next year. No provision should be made at this stage as the event did not exist at the year end. However, this represents over 20 per cent of profits and therefore could be considered to be sufficiently material to be disclosed as a non-adjusting event.

Note 19. Post balance sheet events

(1) Subsequent to the year end, a severe flood at our warehouse in Romcard destroyed stock to the value of £350,000. Insurance proceeds have recovered £250,000 of this loss but a net loss of £100,000 has been incurred.

(2) One of Watt's major customers, Brickbat Ltd, went into receivership after the year end. Full provision has been made in the accounts for amounts owing at the year end but £40,000 sales since then have not been provided as they relate to next year.

(b) Listed building

Under SSAP 19 *Accounting for Investment Properties*, if an asset is held by the group purely for investment potential with a rental income at arm's length, then it need not be depreciated. It should be recorded in the books at its open market value of £1m. This is an uplift of £150,000 from its original cost, which must be credited to a separate investment property revaluation reserve.

Stracey Ltd was set up this year to acquire the listed building and it is 100 per cent owned by the group. The company should be consolidated as it is no longer permissible, under the Companies Act 1989 and FRS 2 on subsidiary undertakings, to argue that Stracey's activities are so dissimilar that consolidation would be misleading. It is now necessary to prove that, if the subsidiary is included, the group accounts would no longer show a true and fair view. If that were the case, then the company would be equity accounted and neither the asset nor its related revaluation reserve would appear in the group accounts.

The proposal to move group head office would mean that the building no longer meets the criteria as an investment property because property let to another group company is specifically excluded. The building would then need to be depreciated unless maintenance expenditure renders the charge immaterial or residual values are considered to be as high as cost. The building need no longer be revalued, but if it is, then the revaluation should follow the rules set out in FRS 15 and revaluation should take place on a regular basis, i.e. once every five years.

(c) The impact of the proposed dividend policy

To: Managing director
From: Chief accountant   Date

The impact of the proposed dividend policy

A dividend of £550,000 used to result (prior to April 1999) in a payment of Advance Corporation Tax (ACT) of £183,333 (25/75 × £550,000), payable fourteen days after the end of the quarter in which the dividend was paid. This ACT could be set off ultimately against the mainstream corporation tax but only to the extent of 25 per cent of taxable profits.

Since the dividend was paid in 2001/02 then relief would only be available against 2002 profits and, to enable a full set-off, taxable profits would need to be £733,332 (£183,333 × 100/25). If profits are less, then any surplus ACT was carried back for up to six years, creating a repayment of corporation tax. However, the 25 per cent restriction must be maintained for those years. If carryback is not possible then it could be carried forward indefinitely. However, FRS 16 states that it is prudent to set up a debtor only for recovery in the next period. Any ACT left over should be treated as irrecoverable and therefore written off.

Any irrecoverable ACT was treated as an additional tax charge and as a result the earnings per share (EPS net basis) would fall. In order to show what EPS would have been if no dividend had been declared, a nil basis EPS was calculated. (FRS 14 has abandoned both the nil and net basis).

SSAP 3 required that the result of the nil basis of calculating EPS should be shown in addition to the result of the net basis. This was only necessary if there was a material difference between the two figures. Materiality was not defined but could be either 5 per cent or 10 per cent.

If irrecoverable ACT written off is in fact recovered in future years, then the effect will be a credit to the tax charge in the year of recovery. This would increase the EPS. Since 1999, an instalment system of corporation tax has been in place and ACT has been abolished. However, previously written off irrecoverable ACT may still be recovered, under transitional rules, as long as it can be recovered in the next accounting period.

Solution 3 – Trunfair Ltd

To: Directors, Trunfair Ltd   Date
From: J. Swale, Financial controller

Post balance sheet information – year end 31 July 2001

With reference to the finalisation of our annual accounts, the following material information has come to light and will require a revision of the accounts:

(1) Withdrawal of faulty design products

The major design fault was discovered on 1 September 2001, one month after the year end. Therefore, although the event did not exist at (i.e. was not discovered before) the year end, it could be argued that the stocks did exist in a faulty state at that time. It would therefore be treated as an adjusting post balance sheet event under SSAP 17.

The committed advertising expenditure of £300,000 should be written off and fully accrued by the year end as it is unlikely to be recovered. However, if the unspent £150,000 could be avoided or switched to other products then only the £150,000 expenditure incurred to date would need to be expensed. The write-off may be so material that it is abnormal in relation to usual expenditure and it should therefore be disclosed as an exceptional item in the annual accounts, as per FRS 3. However, under FRS 12 the committed but unspent expenditure of

£150,000 would be treated as a mere intention and not an obligation. Therefore it may not be provided as a liability in 2001.

The stocks returned will be refunded in full to the customer but hopefully this will be countered by a refund to Trunfair from its own suppliers. This is a counterclaim contingency. If it is probable that a refund will be received and thus no loss crystallises, then the financial statements should record the liability and separately a probable asset. If, however, it is only possible that a refund will be received, then the liability should be accrued and any possible gain ignored, following the prudence concept. These recommendations are in accordance with FRS 12 *Provisions, Contingent Liabilities and Contingent Assets*. Under FRS 12 a counterclaim should be treated completely separately from the accounting treatment for the claim, as it is argued to be illegally offsetting an asset against a liability.

It is important to understand that the likelihood of success and the probable amounts of the claim/counterclaim must be separately assessed and disclosed, if appropriate. Only if the possibility of the loss is remote should no disclosure be made. If a possible material contingency is disclosed, the following are required:

(a) The nature of the contingency.

(b) Any uncertainties expected to affect its ultimate outcome.

(c) A prudent estimate of its financial effect or a statement to the effect that it is not practicable to make such an estimate.

In addition, under the *Statement of Principles* and FRS 5 it is unlikely that the advertising expenditure would result in future economic benefits. Therefore it must not be capitalised and should be written off to the profit and loss account.

(2) Flood at warehouse destroying stock

The uninsured stock loss of £200,000 was caused by a torrential downpour of rain resulting in a flood at the company's new riverside warehouse. This event occurred after the year end, therefore the condition did not exist at the year end. The loss would be considered as non-adjusting under SSAP 17 unless it could affect the going concern of the business. If the latter were the case then the accounts would need to be prepared on a break-up basis.

However, assuming that the company is a going concern, the non-adjusting event would require the following disclosures if non-disclosure would affect the user's ability to reach a proper understanding of the financial statements:

(a) The nature of the event.

(b) An estimate of the financial effect before accounting for taxation, and any tax implications, to effect a proper understanding of the financial position.

(3) Bills dishonoured

The bills were discounted by the bank two weeks before the year end. They subsequently became dishonoured on maturity after the year end. This is a post balance sheet event and gives additional evidence of a condition existing at the year end. It should be treated as an adjusting event under SSAP 17 and the loss of £120,000 should be accrued in the financial statements.

The company would obviously take action to make a counterclaim. If success is probable then, under SSAP 18, the probable gain would have been offset against the liability to the bank. However, if success is no more than possible then, under the prudence concept, no disclosure can be made. FRS 12, however, has effectively banned the offsetting procedure and the claim liability must be kept separate from the probable counterclaim asset.

Solution 4 – Diverse plc

(a) Explanation of principles outlined in SSAP 24

The basic objective of SSAP 24 *Accounting for Pension Costs* is to ensure that the accruals concept is applied to accounting for pension costs in the profit and loss account and so ensure the matching of revenue with its related employee remuneration (inclusive of pension costs).

Defined contribution schemes

Sometimes known as 'money purchase' schemes, they represent schemes in which the benefits paid out are determined by the contributions made and the cost to the employer is known with certainty as it is simply the contributions due for the period. The ensuing risk therefore lies with the employee and not the employer. The accounting treatment for the employer, therefore, is fairly simple and employers only have to charge the contributions payable for each period to the profit and loss. There are no hidden assets or liabilities.

Employer/Employee ⟶ contributions ⟶ pension fund ⟶ pensioners

(Risk)

Defined benefit schemes

These are sometimes known as 'final salary' schemes. In these schemes the risk lies with the employer. The employer needs to ensure that funds in the scheme will be sufficient to meet the fund's requirements. Actuaries will determine, on a triennial basis, whether or not there are sufficient funds to pay for the long-term liability based on such assumptions as rate of increase in salaries, rate of return on investments, the rate of inflation, etc. Frequently the amounts of assets in the scheme are not sufficient or are in surplus, in which case the accounting treatment should be to spread the deficits/surpluses over the average remaining service lifetimes of the employees in the scheme. The funding treatment, on the other hand, would probably result in the company paying additional lump sums into the scheme or taking a contribution holiday. It will undoubtedly differ, however, from the accounting objective.

As the risk is borne by the employer, defined benefit schemes do give rise to considerable uncertainty in assessing the pension contributions due in accounting periods, particularly when deficits/surpluses are identified. This has resulted in many instances, in recent years, of companies deciding to switch all new employees to enter defined contribution schemes and closing down defined benefit schemes except for existing employees.

Employer/Employee ⟵ pension fund ⟵ pensioners

(Risk)

(b) Profit and loss charge for the year ended 31 December 1998

	£m
Normal contribution cost	5
Variations	
Deficiency 1994 (£6m) less surplus 1997 (£4m – £3m exceptional) = £5m / 20 years	0.25
Experience surplus 1997	(3.0)
Total pension cost	2.25

The deficit arising from the actuarial valuation at 31 December 1994 will continue to be recognised in the year ended 31 December 1998, having already been recognised for the three previous years.

The cumulative net deficit needs to be accounted from the year ended 31 December 1998.

The £3m surplus should be recognised immediately rather than be matched over the useful service life of the remaining employees in the scheme as this is a one-off reduction in the number of members in the scheme and this is one of the exceptions to the normal spreading rule.

(c) Pension cost asset/liability in the balance sheet as at 31 December 1998

| Year | Funding | Profit and loss account | | | | | Balance sheet |
| | | Exceptional charge | Normal | Deficit/surplus | Total | | prepayment |
	£m	£m	£m	£m	£m		£m
1994	5	–	5	–	5		Nil
1995	11	–	5	0.3	5.3		5.7
1996	5	–	5	0.3	5.3		5.4
1997	5	–	5	0.3	5.3		5.1
1998	5	(3)	5	0.25	2.25		7.85] S/t
1999	5	–	5	0.25	5.25		7.60 L/t asset]

Valuation

1994	£6m/20 years	=	£0.3m per annum
1997	£(6m – 1m)/20 years	=	£0.25m per annum

The closing balance will be disclosed under debtors within the current assets section of the balance sheet.

Under UITF Abstract 4, the amount of the prepayment due within one year (£7.85 – 7.60). i.e. £0.25m. should be disclosed separately from the £7.6m long-term asset. If it is so material in the context of the company's total net current asset position that it could mislead readers then it must be disclosed separately on the face of the balance sheet.

Solution 5 – Richlieu plc

(a) Profit and loss account, balance sheet and notes

Profit and loss account for the year ended 31 December 2001

| | SSAP 24 | FRS 17 |
	£	£
Regular pension cost (£800,000 + £750,000 – see workings)	1,550,000	1,550,000
Variations from regular cost (£500,000 – £200,000)	300,000	–
	1,850,000	1,550,000
Exceptional charge	2,000,000	2,000,000

Note: Under FRS 3 this would be separately noted as an exceptional item on the face of the profit and loss account, between operating profit and interest payable.

Balance sheet as at 31 December 2001

	£	£
Prepayment	1,700,000	1,450,000
Provisions for liabilities and charges	550,000	3,300,000

Notes to the accounts

The company operates two main pension schemes, works and staff, providing benefits based on final pay. The assets in both schemes are held separately from those of the company.

The company's accounting policy is to charge the cost of the pensions against profits on a systematic basis over the average expected service lives of the employees in the schemes.

The pension cost is assessed in accordance with the advice of professionally qualified actuaries, and in respect of the principal schemes the pension cost for the year ended 31 December 2001 was:

	£'000
Regular pension cost based on a constant percentage of earnings over the employees' service lives with the group	1,550
Variations from regular cost based on a constant percentage of current and estimated future earnings over the average remaining service lives of current employees	300
Net pension cost to operating profits	1,850

The closure of the Buckingham division entailed an immediate contribution of £2,000,000 to ensure that the assets of the works scheme were sufficient to cover the liabilities in respect of the accrued benefits of the former employees at that location. This has been treated as an exceptional item.

Details of the most recent valuation of the pension scheme:

Date of most recent valuation	1 January 2001
Methods used	Accrued benefits
	Prospective benefits
Main assumptions	
Rate of price inflation	X %
Real return on investments relative to price inflation	X %
Increase in earnings relative to price inflation	X %
Market value of investments at last valuation date	£X
Actuarial deficiency at last valuation date	£3.3m
Level of funding being the actuarial value of assets expressed as a percentage of the accrued service liabilities	X %

Workings

(1) Works scheme (excluding Buckingham division)

	Funding	Regular		Variation	Total	Balance sheet prepayment
	£'000	£'000		£'000	£'000	£'000
2001	3,000	800	+	500	1,300	1,700
2002	2,700	800	+	500	1,300	3,100
2003	1,000	800	+	500	1,300	2,800
2004	1,000	800	+	500	1,300	2,500
2005	1,000	800	+	500	1,300	2,200
2006	1,000	800	+	500	1,300	1,900
2007	1,000	800	+	500	1,300	1,600
2008	1,000	800	+	500	1,300	1,300
2009	1,000	800	+	500	1,300	1,000
2010	800	800	+	500	1,300	500
2011	800	800	+	500	1,300	Nil

Variation from regular cost £5,500,000 ÷ 11 years = £500,000 p.a.

Under FRS 17, the full deficit of £5.5m would be charged directly to reserves (and reported as a recognised loss in the statement of total recognised gains and losses). The profit and loss would still be charged with £800,000 as a normal service cost. The difference between the funding of £3m and charge of £6.3m, i.e. £3.3m, will be recorded as a provision on the balance sheet.

(2) Staff scheme

	Funding	Regular	Accounting charge Variation	Total	Balance sheet provision
	£'000	£'000	£'000	£'000	£'000
2001	–	750	–	200	550	550
2002	–	750	–	200	550	1,100
2003	400	750	–	200	550	1,250
2004	400	750	–	200	550	1,400
2005	750	750	–	200	550	1,200
2006	750	750	–	200	550	1,000
2007	750	750	–	200	550	800
2008	750	750	–	200	550	600
2009	750	750	–	200	550	400
2010	750	750	–	200	550	200
2011	750	750	–	200	550	Nil

Variation from regular cost £2,200,000 ÷ 11 years = £200,000 p.a.

Under FRS 17, the full surplus would be recorded as an asset (provided recovery probable). Thus, although the normal service cost of £750,000 would go to the profit and loss, an asset of £1.45m would be recorded and separately disclosed under current assets. That surplus would be a recognised gain in the statement of total recognised gains and losses.

(b) *The importance of the assumptions made in actuarial valuations*

Pension costs represent a substantial percentage of any company's total expenditure and can be significantly affected by the actuarial assumptions adopted. It is therefore essential that the assumptions are as accurate as possible so as to minimise the differences between actual events and those assumptions, otherwise very large surpluses/deficiencies will arise. Small changes in assumptions cause dramatic changes in the size of the surplus/deficit and could result in over-payments or over-refunds in specific instances.

Key assumptions include: rates of inflation, earnings increase, real return on investments, rates of labour turnover, life expectancy, etc.

(c) *The relative merits of the treatments of actuarial surpluses/deficits*

SSAP 24 normally requires actuarial surpluses/deficits to be spread over the average remaining service lives of the employees in the scheme. However, where there is a significant reduction in the number of employees any difference should be written off immediately, and if this is caused by unusual events it should be treated as an exceptional item under FRS 3.

Two other exceptions to the normal spreading rule can occur:

(1) When prudence dictates that a material deficit should be recognised over a shorter period because of a major event/transaction not previously allowed for in the actuarial assumptions.

(2) When a refund is received in accordance with the Finance Act 1986, then the refund should be credited to the profit and loss account in the period in which it occurs.

The principle behind the normal spreading rule is to ensure that the cost of pensions is charged against profits on a systematic basis over the employees' service lives in the scheme, thereby producing a charge which is not subject to wide fluctuations. It is a 'profit and loss or income' approach, i.e. the balance sheet entry represents residuals not yet charged to profit and loss.

An alternative 'balance sheet' approach has been adopted in the USA which ensures that the asset/liability is correctly valued at the start and end of each accounting period, any residual being written off to the profit and loss account. It is argued that this is the approach adopted in SSAP 15 on partial provision for deferred tax. However, this will lead to wide fluctuations in the annual charge. There is a new FRS on the subject which will move pension costing from the current 'profit and loss' approach closer to that above.

A third possibility for treating surpluses/deficiencies is to deal with any actuarial surplus/deficit as a prior-year adjustment and spread it retrospectively over the three years since the previous valuation. However, under FRS 3 this should only occur if there has been a fundamental error or a change in accounting policy. Since the differences are caused mainly by changes in estimates, FRS 3 would seem to preclude this proposal.

The approach adopted in SSAP 24 would seem to be the best solution since it concentrates on the matching principle, i.e. that all costs incurred, including pension costs, should be matched against the revenue which they are trying to create.

Solution 6 – Renmore Ltd

(a) (i) *Accounting and funding implications of a surplus – option 1*

Funding	Year 1	Refund £3m (£5m less tax charge of 40% = £2m)
		Normal contribution £1.2m
	Years 2-3	Payment £1.2m
Accounting		No spreading occurs when a refund is taken. The accounting treatment would be as per the contributions paid.
		FRS 17 results in the same accounting treatment as SSAP 24 as it insists that all surpluses/deficits must be recorded immediately.

(a) (ii) *Accounting and funding implications of a surplus – option 2*

Funding	Years 1 and 2 – no funding	
	Year 3 £825,000.	
Accounting	Under SSAP 24 the surplus of £5m should be spread evenly over the 12 remaining average years of service resulting in a reduction of £416,667 in the overall charge for each year.	

Funding	*Profit and loss*			*Balance sheet*
	Normal	*surplus*	*Total*	*provision*
–	£1.2m	(£0.4167m)	£0.7833m	£0.7833m
–	£1.2m	(£0.4167m)	£0.7833m	£1.5667m
£0.825m	£1.2m	(£0.4167m)	£0.7833m	£1.525m

Under FRS 17 the surplus would need to be created immediately as an asset on the balance sheet as follows:

Funding	*Profit and loss*			*Balance sheet*
	Normal	*surplus*	*Total*	*asset*
–	£1.2m	(£5m)	(£3.8m)	£3.8m
–	£1.2m	–	£1.2m	£2.6m
£0.825m	£1.2m	–	£1.2m	£2.225m
£0.825m	£1.2m	–	£1.2m	£1.850m
£0.825m	£1.2m	–	£1.2m	£1.475m
£0.825m	£1.2m	–	£1.2m	£1.100m
£0.825m	£1.2m	–	£1.2m	£0.725m
£0.825m	£1.2m	–	£1.2m	£0.35m

(a) (iii) Accounting and funding implications of a surplus – option 3

Funding Years 1–12 £650,000 contributions paid

Accounting Under SSAP 24 the surplus of £5m should be spread evenly over the remaining average years of service resulting in a reduction of £416,667 in the overall charge for the year.

Funding	Profit and loss			Balance sheet
	Normal	surplus	Total	asset
£0.65m	£1.2m	(£0.4167m)	£0.7833m	£0.1333m
£0.65m	£1.2m	(£0.4167m)	£0.7833m	£0.2667m
£0.65m	£1.2m	(£0.4167m)	£0.7833m	£0.4000m
£0.65m	£1.2m	(£0.4167m)	£0.7833m	£0.5323m
£0.65m	£1.2m	(£0.4167m)	£0.7833m	£0.6657m
£0.65m	£1.2m	(£0.4167m)	£0.7833m	£0.7989m

Under FRS 17 the profit and loss should be charged with the normal contribution of £1.2m per annum and the STRGL credited with £5m of a surplus. This would lead to an asset of £5m – £1.2m + £0.65 = £4.45m being created. Each year the asset will fall by £0.55m (difference between funding of £0.65m and £1.2m charge).

Option (1) results in a refund in year 1 but results in an additional tax liability of 40 per cent which would normally make this option unattractive. The charge for years 2–10 will be more expensive than options (2) and (3).

Option (3) is attractive as no pension contributions occur for two years but the charge in the subsequent ten years will not be as expensive as option (1). The third option results in the same charge as option (2) but results in each year having the same lower funding.

(b) Deferred tax implications

SSAP 24 is expressed mainly in terms of matching income and expenditure in the profit and loss account and the asset/liability in the balance sheet as a balancing figure. This is in direct contrast to FRS 17 which will reverse the procedure and instead concentrate on getting the assets and liabilities right before matching income and expenditure. SSAP 24 is the cumulative difference between the amount charged in the profit and loss and the amount that has been paid. It will result in the creation of an artificial asset or liability.

Since companies will generally continue to have contributions allowable for tax when paid, that figure will also represent the cumulative timing difference which has to be taken into account for deferred tax, i.e. the balance sheet figure represents the amount by which the recognition of pension costs in the profit and loss account has been cumulatively more or less than contributions paid to date.

Under FRS 19 *Deferred Tax* companies are required to provide deferred tax in full in relation to pension costs.

This recognises that the balance sheet has become the primary statement and therefore it is important that all assets and liabilities are properly determined on the balance sheet. FRS 19 extends the balance sheet argument to accounting for pension costs and insists that all surpluses/deficits be immediately recorded as assets/liabilities on the balance sheet and will therefore, in the future, not be spread forward over the employees' average remaining service lives.

If the profit and loss figure is greater than actual contributions, there is a need to make a deferred tax provision for this difference because it will reverse, unless continually replaced by new surpluses.

As the accrual is increased or decreased over the service lives during the time the payments differ from the charge to profit and loss, this will be reflected in the deferred tax account.

Under FRS 19 companies are permitted to discount their full provisions for deferred tax to present value although this is expressly forbidden in IAS 12 *Income Taxes*.

Solution 7 – SSAP 25 Segmental Reporting

(a) The purpose of segmental reporting

The purpose of segmental reporting (Paragraph 1, SSAP 25) is to provide information to assist users of financial statements:

(1) to appreciate more thoroughly the results and financial position of the entity by permitting a better understanding of the entity's past performance and thus enabling a better assessment of its future prospects; and

(2) to be aware of the impact that changes in significant components of a business may have on the business as a whole.

This is because many companies now operate in several geographical markets, carry on different classes of business and offer different growth opportunities and degrees of risk. The overall group results do not provide sufficient detailed information for a user to make an informed judgement about an entity's different activities.

(b) The criteria adopted to identify separate reportable segments

Segments must be classified under SSAP 25 (Paragraphs 7–10) in two ways:

- Class of business
- Geographical

In identifying separate reportable segments the directors should have regard to the overall purpose of presenting segment information (see (a) above) and the need for users to be informed about where an entity carries on business, in different activities or geographical areas.

In particular the following separate segments should be identified:

(1) Those that earn a return on investment out of line with the rest of the business.
(2) Those that are subject to different degrees of risk.
(3) Those that have experienced different rates of growth.
(4) Those that have different potentials for future development.

Each significant class of business or geographical segment should be identified. A normal cut-off would be if third-party turnover is 10 per cent or more of the total or if the segment's results are 10 per cent or more of all segments in profit or in loss or if its net assets are 10 per cent or more of the total net assets of the entity.

The directors should review the definitions annually and redefine them when appropriate.

(c) What information should be disclosed for each reported segment

The following must be disclosed for each reported segment:

(1) *General* (Paragraph 17)
The definition of each reported class of business and geographical segment.

(2) *Turnover* (Paragraphs 18, 34)
Distinguishing between external sales and inter-segment sales.

(3) *Result* (Paragraphs 21–22, 34)
Profit/(loss) before taxation, minority interests and extraordinary items.

(4) *Net assets* (Paragraphs 24–25, 34)

In addition, for geographical turnover only, segmentation by origin and destination is required unless there is no material difference between the two, in which case only the former is required.

Segment results are normally recorded before interest.

If group accounts are presented then segment information should be presented on the basis of those consolidated financial statements.

Associated undertakings' results should normally be incorporated if they account for at least 20 per cent of the entity's results or 20 per cent of the total net assets.

The total of the segment information should reconcile with the related total in the financial statements and comparatives should also be provided.

(d) The main difficulties with the disclosure of segment information and the arguments against its disclosure

Difficulties

(1) The precise definition of a reportable segment is extremely subjective. It can change over time and there is a need to redefine if appropriate.

(2) The treatment of common costs. Should they be arbitrarily apportioned to segments or netted against total segment net profits/(losses)?

(3) The identification of the occasions when it is better to classify interest as a segment expense rather than to net it off against total profits.

Arguments against disclosure

(1) Segmental reporting results in the disclosure of sensitive information to competitors, especially to overseas entities who do not have the same disclosure requirements.

Exemption is available for directors if they believe that disclosure would be seriously prejudicial to their interests.

(2) Individual investors do not invest in segments but in the business as a whole.

(3) The additional cost of providing the information may well exceed any benefits to be derived from its disclosure. Accordingly, entities below the criterion of ten times the size of a medium-sized company under S248 Companies Act 1985 are exempt.

Solution 8 – Innovations plc

(a) Segmental reporting

(i) The case for segmental reporting

(1) Shareholders are better able to assess earnings potential and risk and they can more accurately predict future earnings potential. Knowledge of the constituent parts is relevant in assessing total performance in terms of the quality of the earnings.

(2) Segmental reporting should improve capital market efficiency and help to eliminate one form of insider dealing.

(3) The consumer could benefit in terms of reduced prices because of the increased competition encouraged by the disclosure of competitive information.

(4) With better knowledge of their competitors, management could be stimulated to become more innovative and efficient.

(5) Government and the public in general may have a better explanation of the allocation of public investment funds.

(ii) The case against segmental reporting

(1) The costs of collecting the data, processing and auditing it could well exceed any tangible benefits to be derived from its disclosure.

(2) Investors can only participate in the company as a whole, not in its constituent parts. Management attention may be directed away from maximising wealth for the business as a whole to maximising the wealth of constituent parts with consequent sub-optimum results.

(3) The choice of definition of a segment is arbitrary and could lead to information of low reliability.

(4) If errors are disclosed then management may be reluctant in the future to experiment and innovate. Ultimately this will lead to poor performance and dissatisfaction with management.

(5) Government intervention could be encouraged by segmental disclosure if a large degree of concentration was revealed in certain industries.

(6) Competitors will assimilate segment information and profitable segments will be under pressure to perform.

(b) Published segment report for inclusion in the annual report

Classes of business

	Fruit		Canning		Bureau		Other		Group	
	2001	*2000*	*2001*	*2000*	*2001*	*2000*	*2001*	*2000*	*2001*	*2000*
	£'000	*£'000*	*£'000*	*£'000*	*£'000*	*£'000*	*£'000*	*£'000*	*£'000*	*£'000*
Turnover	13,635	15,188	20,520	16,200	5,400	4,050	2,700	1,350	42,255	36,788
Inter-segment	1,485	1,688	2,970	3,105	—	—	—	—	4,455	4,793
Third party	12,150	13,500	17,550	13,095	5,400	4,050	2,700	1,350	37,800	31,995
Profit before taxation	2,565	3,375	4,725	3,600	412	540	—	—	7,702	7,515
Inter-segment profits	—	—	—	—	—	—	—	—	(7)	(765)
	2,565	3,375	4,725	3,600	412	540	—	—	7,695	6,750
Common costs									5,130	4,104
Group profit before taxation									2,565	2,646
Net assets										
Segment net assets	33,750	32,400	40,500	33,750	18,765	17,563			93,015	83,713
Unallocated assets									13,500	11,003
									106,515	94,716

Geographical

	UK		USA		Other		Unallocated		Group	
	2001	*2000*	*2001*	*2000*	*2001*	*2000*	*2001*	*2000*	*2001*	*2000*
	£'000	*£'000*	*£'000*	*£'000*	*£'000*	*£'000*	*£'000*	*£'00*	*£'000*	*£'000*
Turnover by destination										
Sales to third parties	XX	XX	XX	XX	XX	XX	XX	XX	XX	XX
Turnover by origin										
Total sales	29,700	26,190	8,910	6,345	1,350	1,215	2,700	1,350	42,660	35,100
Inter-segment	2,700	1,890	2,160	1,215	—	—	—	—	4,860	3,105
Third party	27,000	24,300	6,750	5,130	1,350	1,215	2,700	1,350	37,800	31,995
Profit before taxation	5,130	4,590	2,430	1,890	270	405			7,830	6,885
Inter-segment profits									(675)	(405)
									7,155	6,480
Common costs									4,590	3,834
Group profit before taxation									2,565	2,646
Net assets										
Segment	43,200	40,500	32,400	24,300	18,360	19,683			93,960	84,483
Unallocated									12,555	10,233
Total net assets									106,515	94,716

(c) The identification of trends from segment reports

(1) The definition of a segment

The directors are responsible for defining both geographical segments and class of business segments. It would be useful to know whether there are more than just three main segments which might be material. For example, one segment, Canning, represents almost 50 per cent of total external sales. Could this not be broken down further?

(2) Associated undertakings

No mention is made of these investments in Innovations' report but users would be better informed if details of associated undertakings could be obtained within the segment report. Materiality is approximately 20 per cent of total external sales/results.

(3) Inter-segment sales

A substantial part of sales (in the USA approximately one-third) are internal. Therefore an analysis of sales by destination as well as by origin would be helpful and would also comply with SSAP 25.

(4) Interest and common costs

Both of these items could be said to be generally regarded as material but not specific to any one segment. However, there are situations where these costs should be identified to a particular segment as they are segment specific. To exclude them would reveal a misleading picture of the segment and its total results.

(5) A matrix form of presentation

The consultative paper originally subscribed to the view that the user might benefit from a matrix presentation which combines both geographical and class of business analyses. One form could have looked like this:

Turnover	UK	USA	Other	Total
Fruit growing	XX	XX	XX	XX
Canning	XX	XX	XX	XX
Bureau	XX	XX	XX	XX
Other	XX	XX	XX	XX
	XX	XX	XX	XX

This was not included in the final SSAP as it was felt that this form of presentation would be too complex for the general reader to understand and interpret.

Solution 9 – Mushroom plc

Issue 1 Impairment of power generation income stream – FRS 11

	Power generation unit
	£m
Direct net assets attributable to power generation	160
Share of head office net assets (£15m x 40% given)	6
Net book value (NBV)	166
Recoverable amount is the higher of NRV and NPV	
Net realisable value (NRV) (£110m – £10 selling costs)	100

Higher figure is £140.468m

Net present value (NPV)
  £20m per annum x 10 years x 7% WACC
  £20m x 7.0234   140.468
  (Cash flows relating to tax and financing should not be considered)

Under FRS 11 *Impairment of Fixed Assets and Goodwill*, the fixed assets should not be carried at more than their recoverable amount, which is the higher of NRV and NPV. The impairment at 31 December 1999 is £166m – £140.468 = £25.532m.

This write-down should be reflected within operating costs, and if material, it should be recorded as an exceptional item in the notes to the financial statements. The impairment should be recorded within cumulative depreciation since the fixed assets have been carried on an historic cost basis.

The company should disclose the discount rate adopted. Impairment losses recognised when FRS 11 was first implemented should be recorded as changes in accounting estimate and should not be treated as changes in accounting policy. The ASB believes that the FRS is simply codifying existing practice and thus any adjustments should be treated as adjustments to current estimated lives and therefore treated as additional depreciation.

Issue 2 Provision for reorganisation of nuclear waste plant – FRS 12

FRS 12 *Provisions, Contingent Liabilities and Contingent Assets* states that a provision should only be created when an entity has a present obligation (i.e. either legal or constructive) as a result of a past transaction or event. It should also be probable (i.e. more than 50 per cent chance of occurring) and be capable of being reliably measured.

In the case of a reorganisation, a provision should only be created if a constructive obligation exists. This is deemed to have arisen when an entity not only has a detailed formal plan but has actually started to implement the plan or at least has announced the main features of the plan to those people affected by the decision. It must raise a valid expectation in those affected that it will carry out the restructuring.

FRS 12 notes that, by actually starting to implement the plan, it makes those people affected realise that the plan will be carried out. Examples of such events that trigger constructive obligations include the decommissioning of plant, the selling off of assets or the making of a public announcement. The announcement, however, must be outlined in sufficient detail, setting out main features of the plan so that it gives rise to a valid expectation in other parties, e.g. customers, suppliers, employees, trade unions, etc., that the entity will actually carry out the restructuring.

It is not acceptable, post-implementation of FRS 12, simply to include the £15m provision because, at the year end, Mushroom plc has not started to implement the plan or announced its main features to those affected by it. The company, therefore, does not have a constructive obligation.

FRS 12 does not permit the inclusion of certain costs in restructuring provisions. These include retraining or relocation costs. These relate to the future operation of the business.

The standard expects that there will not be a long delay between creating the provision and commencing the reorganisation. If there were a significant delay, it is unlikely that the plan would raise an expectation on the part of others that the entity was committed to the restructuring. Under the disclosure requirements of FRS 12, reporting entities must now disclose when the provision is likely to crystallise.

Issue 3 Fitting of special filters – FRS 12

At 31 December 1999, there is no obligation for the costs of fitting the filters because no obligating event has occurred (i.e. the fitting of filters). However, the appendix to FRS 12 suggests that an obligation to pay fines does exist due to non-compliance with the regulations. The company should therefore provide for £1m in fines but should not provide for the additional £750,000 as there is not a present obligation at the balance sheet date.

However, an opposing opinion would suggest that the entity must ultimately comply with the new legislation and therefore £5m should be provided at once. This may be discounted to its present value if it is unlikely to be paid in the near future.

The disclosures required under FRS 12 include a brief description of the obligation, the expected timing of any resulting transfer of economic benefits and an indication of the uncertainties about the amount or timing of those transfers.

Details are also required of the carrying amount at the start and end of the accounting period, any additional provisions created or reversed in the period and the discount rate applied.

Issue 4 Provision for decommissioning costs – FRS 12

Under FRS 12, Mushroom plc has a legal obligation to restore the seabed at the end of the contract. This should be provided at once. However, it may be discounted to its present value. It could be argued that the correct double entry would be to create a fixed asset which is then depreciated over the period of the contract. It is regarded as a 'negative' residual value because when the entity enters the contract it has to put the seabed back to its original state and it is therefore part of the cost of purchasing the contract in the first place.

The measurement of the liability at present value means that interest has to be accounted for to unwind the discount. The finance cost is purely notional as no interest is paid. However, it must be regarded as part of interest payable and it should not be treated as an operating expense.

The details of the costs to be charged to profit and loss and the balance sheet assets and liabilities are computed as follows:

Year	Operating costs	Finance costs	Fixed assets (NBV)	Fixed assets (provision)
31.12.1999	£986,280	£197,256	£3,945,120	£5,128,656
31.12.2000	986,280	205,146	2,958,840	5,333,802
31.12.2001	986,280	213,352	1,972,560	5,547,154
31.12.2002	986,280	221,886	986,280	5,579,040
31.12.2003	986,280	230,960	Nil	6,000,000
	4,931,400	£1,068,600		

Depreciation   £6m x 0.8219 (annuity for 4 years at 4% risk-free rate) = £4,931,400/5 years = £986,280

Finance costs   £4,931,400 x 4% = £197,256 1999
                                5,128,656 x 4% = £205,146 2000
                                5,333,802 x 4% = £213,352 2001
                                5,547,154 x 4% = £221,886 2002
                                5,579,040 x 4% = £230,960 2003 (bal. fig.)

Solution 10 – World Wide Nuclear Fuels plc

(a) (i) *Why there was a need for more detailed guidance on provisions in the UK*

Until FRS 12 there were very few rules on how companies could account for provisions on their balance sheets, apart from the definition provided in the Companies Act as 'any amount retained as reasonably necessary for the purposes of providing for any liability or loss which is likely to be incurred, or certain to be incurred but uncertain as to the amount or as to the date on which it will arise'.

The main reasons for the publication of FRS 12 were broadly the following:

(i)   The deliberate creation of 'big bath' provisions to smooth earnings performance, many of which were totally spurious and would not actually occur. These would be reversed back to profit and loss in times of poor performance.

(ii)   The lack of narrative explanation of the reason why the provisions were created and when they were likely to be finally settled.

(iii) There was no accounting standard for that part of the balance sheet and thus it became a 'secret reserve' weapon for creative accountants.

There was a need to ensure that the accounting treatment for provisions followed the principles laid down in the Statement of Principles (December 1999) and in particular ensure that all provisions recorded on the balance sheet meet the definition of a liability.

(a) (ii) *Circumstances under which a provision may be recognised on balance sheet*

FRS 12 applies the Statement of Principles to accounting for provisions. It insists that, in order for provisions to be recognised on the balance sheet, they must pass the definition of a liability and also the recognition criteria in chapters set out in Chapters 4 and 5 of the Statement.

FRS 12 defines a provision as representing a liability of 'uncertain timing or amount'. Essentially it differs from normal liabilities as the latter tend to be fairly certain in terms of their amount, their timing and to whom they are paid.

A liability represents 'an obligation to transfer economic benefits as a result of a past transaction or event'. It must be more than a mere intention to pay. It must represent either a legal or constructive obligation, the latter of which has raised a valid expectation on behalf of those affected by the decision that it will actually take place.

The two recognition criteria are:

(i)   There must be sufficient evidence that a transfer of economic benefits will take place; and

(ii)   The liability must be reliably measured.

FRS 12 only makes reference to three specific provisions. In the case of foreseeable losses, these provisions are no longer acceptable as the company is under no legal or constructive obligation to pay off these losses. On the other hand, if the company is locked into an onerous contract from which they cannot legally withdraw, then any losses incurred right to the end of those contracts should be provided in full. The third example is a provision for restructuring. These are still permitted as long as the company is demonstrably committed to the reorganisation/reconstruction. This means that the reconstruction has already started to be implemented or employees informed. A board decision, by itself, is not sufficient for the provision to be created.

Any provision which meets the definition and recognition criteria of a liability must also be reliably measured. This should represent the entity's best estimate of the amount most likely to be paid to settle the provision and in those cases where there are a number of homogeneous items the expected value technique may be adopted. Objective evidence of future events may be taken into account and if the provision is not likely to be paid for a number of years then it should be discounted to reflect the time value of money.

(b) (i) *Provision for decommissioning costs*

FRS 12 *Provisions, Contingent Liabilities and Contingent Assets* has had a major impact on accounting for decommissioning costs. In the past most extractive/oil companies gradually built up a provision over the life of the associated mine/oilfield. The provision was often created on a unit of production basis so as to match the cost of decommissioning with the associated revenue being created from the sale of associated oil, etc. This was a profit and loss or accruals-based approach. This is the accounting treatment adopted by World Wide Nuclear Fuels plc.

Since the publication of FRS 12 these provisions must now comply with the balance sheet approach and it is argued that a nuclear energy company has an immediate obligation on the day that the damage occurs, i.e. on the opening up of the radioactive facilities, etc. A provision must be created in full immediately and, if not payable for several years, then it should be discounted to its present value. In the case of the group, the discount rate adopted is market rate. Under FRS 12 companies should adopt a real interest rate or future prices discounted by a nominal rate. A risk-free rate should be adopted where a prudent estimate of future cash flows already reflects risk (e.g. government bond rate).

The unwinding of the discount should be charged to profit and loss account, not as part of decommissioning costs, but as part of interest payable.

(b) (ii) *Provision for future operating losses*

Under FRS 12 no provision for future operating losses may be created. However, if the company has entered into an onerous contract then a provision should be created. An onerous contract is one in which the entity cannot avoid the excess costs over revenues of fulfilling a contract.

Clearly the company has entered such a contract and the provision of £135m should be set up for the uneconomic supply of oil.

FRS 12 does not spell out specifically any rules on environment liabilities. However, in the appendix, it is recommended that where legislation has been broken or if the entity has a dark green policy then provisions should be made for such costs on the grounds that they are clearly legal or constructive obligations. If the company has created a valid expectation that the environmental liabilities will be paid out then a provision should be set up. It will depend on the subjective judgment of both auditor and preparer.

The company only sets up a provision when a formal plan of action on the closure of an inactive site has been set up and when the expenditure on remedial work is probable and the cost can be measured with reasonable certainty. This would appear to be a satisfactory basis on which to set up a provision. The provision of £120m should therefore be permitted.

Solution 11 – Genpower plc

(a) (i) *Explain the need for an accounting standard for provisions*

Prior to FRS 12 *Provisions, Contingent Liabilities and Contingent Assets*, there were no rules on what could be incorporated within the section of the balance sheet entitled 'Provisions for liabilities and charges'. This enabled the 'creative accountant' to use provisions as a form of secret reserves which could be manipulated to smooth out profit performance. It became known as 'big bath accounting' and companies created spurious provisions for future losses, restructuring, maintenance, etc., in good years and then released them back to profit in bad years. It was designed to ensure a smooth EPS profile. These provisions were quite material and were also treated as exceptional items; thus readers would disregard them as non-recurring. These provisions were often based on management intentions rather than on a genuine legal or constructive obligation.

FRS 12 was instituted to put a stop to these practices but also to ensure that much more disclosure is provided in the financial statements about the provisions created – both in narrative and in numeric terms.

(a) (ii) *Principles of FRS 12*

FRS 12 effectively introduced the main principles contained in Chapters 4 and 5 of the Statement of Principles (SOP) to accounting for provisions. However, FRS 12 does not apply to reductions in asset values, e.g. bad debt and stock obsolescence provisions, nor to provisions which are governed by a more specific accounting standard, e.g. FRS 17 and 19.

A provision is defined as a liability of uncertain timing or amount. The word uncertainty distinguishes a provision from a normal liability which must be recorded within either short- or long-term creditors. It must also be distinguished from a contingent liability. The latter is basically a possible liability rather than a probable liability required by FRS 12 to be recorded as a provision.

Chapter 4 of the SOP defines liabilities as 'obligations to transfer economic benefits as a result of past transactions or events'. In order for a provision to exist, clearly a present obligation must exist. This can either be a legal or constructive obligation. The latter requires the company to be put into a position where there is a valid expectation on behalf of those affected by the company's decision that it will actually carry out its pledge. A mere intention to pay another party would not be sufficient. Thus, a provision for restructuring would require more than a board minute – it requires the company to make it public to its employees that it intends to make some of them redundant.

In addition to passing the definition of a liability, the company also has to ensure that both recognition criteria contained in Chapter 5 of the SOP are passed. That effectively means that there must be a probability of a transfer taking place, i.e. more than 50 per cent chance, and also that the provision can be reliably measured. This can often be achieved by working out the expected values from past experience.

Chapter 6 of the SOP is also incorporated in FRS 12 and it requires entities to value their provisions by working out their best estimate of the expenditure required to settle the obligation at the balance sheet date. If that cannot be achieved then the liability would need to be disclosed as a contingent liability in the notes.

(b) (i) *Genpower plc – Acceptability of current accounting policy*

Genpower has a legal obligation to clean up the environmental damage it has created in generating electricity from its nuclear power stations. Clearly it has a legal obligation to do so after the end of their effective life of ten years. The company estimated the costs of decommissioning the stations to be £180m and has accrued 10 per cent of that figure in its first year. Effectively it is trying to build up the provision slowly over the ten-year period.

Unfortunately that policy is not acceptable to FRS 12 which would argue that the company already has a full legal obligation at the start of the contract which must be provided in full at that date, i.e. 1 October 1999. However, FRS 12 recognises that the liability will not be discharged for ten years and thus the liability is overstated in present terms. It therefore requires the full provision to be discounted to present value so that the time value of money can be incorporated into the calculation. That figure is only £120m and that is the figure that should be included in the provisions at 1 October 1999. The debit entry is to regard the decommissioning as part of the original cost of building the power stations or as a negative residual value. It should therefore be added to the cost of the power stations.

Over the life of the power stations the discount will unwind and it will be necessary for companies to charge that unwinding to interest expense in the profit and loss account as well as increasing the value of the liability. The changes will look as follows:

			Original	*Revised*	
Profit and loss					
Fixed asset depreciation	(10% x £200m)		£20m		
	(10% x £320m)			£32m	
Provision for decommissioning			18m		
Unwinding of discount	(say £5m)			5m	
Balance sheet					
Tangible fixed assets					
Power station	(£200m) (£200m + £120m)	200m	200m	320m	
Accumulated depreciation	(£20m) (£20m + £12m)		(20m)	(20m)	(32m)
			£180m	£288m	
Provision for liabilities and charges					
Provision for decommissioning costs			£18m	£125m	

The treatment of the contamination costs is different since there is no legal obligation to clean up any contamination leaks unless they occur when the rods are in use. There was no contamination during the year ended 30 September 2000.

It could be argued, however, that there will definitely be a legal obligation in the future, based on past experience, that statistically there will be three leakages that will cost £90m over the ten-year period. That has been used by Rentokil Initial plc retain a provision for self-insurance on their balance sheet and it is commonly used in calculating provisions for warranties and return of goods sold for retailers. It may therefore be argued that there is a present obligation which can be reliably measured and that 10 per cent of £90m should be accrued this year.

Thus the charge for £9m (10 per cent x £90m) should remain in the profit and loss account and also as a provision for liabilities and charges on the balance sheet.

(b) (ii) No legislation

If there is no legal obligation, as there is no legislation against environmental damage, it could be argued that no liability should be created. However, there could instead be a constructive obligation. That could occur where a valid expectation is created by other parties that an entity will discharge its responsibilities. The company may well have published an environment policy statement that it will accept certain liabilities over and above current legislation. If it has this policy or has created a past record of normally cleaning up environmental damage then a provision should be created, The answer would be the same as (i) above.

If the company does not have a constructive obligation then no provision should be created. Instead the power stations should be recorded at cost of £200m and depreciation charged at 10 per cent, i.e. £20m, leaving a net book value of £180m.

9

Group Accounting

Solution 1 – Alpha plc

(a) Is Beta plc to be treated as a subsidiary under the Companies Act 1985?

The definition of a subsidiary has been changed with the implementation of the EC 7th Directive on group accounting. Underlying the philosophy behind the directive is the concept of reflecting economic substance/control within group accounting. The revised definition is more widely drawn to try and 'bring back into the net' certain 'subsidiaries' which previously were not legally defined as subsidiaries but which were very largely dependent upon a 'parent undertaking'.

The new definition is contained in Section 258, Paragraphs 2 and 4, which state that an undertaking is a parent of another if any of the following statements apply:

(1) It holds a majority of the *voting rights* in that undertaking. Alpha owns 50 per cent but not a majority.

(2) It is a member of the other undertaking and can appoint or remove a *majority* of its *board of directors*. No information is provided for Alpha.

(3) It has a right to exercise a *dominant influence* over the other undertaking either via provisions in the entity's articles/memorandum or via a *control contract*. No information is provided for Alpha.

(4) It is a member and controls, in agreement with others, a *majority* of the *voting rights* in the other undertaking. No information is provided for Alpha.

An undertaking is also a parent if it has a *participating interest* and:

(1) it actually exercises a *dominant influence*. Alpha appears to be in that situation as the friendly third party holds the rest of the shares in Beta plc, or

(2) both are managed on a *unified basis*. There is not sufficient information on Alpha to indicate fully unified operations rather than just unified management.

On balance the information appears to indicate that a subsidiary undertaking has been created, but confirmation would be required to ensure that the parent has in fact dominant influence over Beta plc.

(b) The effect of FRS 5

FRS 5 *Reporting the Substance of Transactions* requires companies to disclose all assets and liabilities which currently fail the legal definition. This is achieved by requiring a company to record transactions so that their commercial effect is fairly reflected.

For example, an asset is 'a resource controlled by an enterprise as a result of past events and from which future economic benefits are expected to flow to the enterprise'.

In terms of quasi-subsidiaries, control is defined as control via the medium of another enterprise, whereby effective control exists over and risks arise from the assets of another enterprise as if it were a subsidiary.

Quasi-subsidiaries should also be consolidated in the group accounts. Under company legislation they fail to meet the statutory definition of a subsidiary. Therefore the true and fair override must be applied to make the financial statements as relevant and reliable as possible, ensuring that they are consolidated.

(c) The need for a standard to define a subsidiary

There is a need for a general standard on group accounts but part of it should deal with an interpretation of the legal definition of a subsidiary. This is because, although the Companies Act 1989 did lay down the definition as in (a) above, it failed to clarify or expand some of the phrases adopted in the Act and has left it up to the profession to interpret them.

For example, phrases such as 'dominant influence', 'unified basis' and 'participating interest' need to be explained. The importance of this can be seen in the ASB's new standard on consolidated accounts (FRS 2). It could also be argued that it is a practical guide to help prevent directors deliberately setting up group structures in an attempt to avoid being caught up in the new expanded 'net' of subsidiaries.

Dominant influence is assumed to exist if there is effective control over an entity's financial and operating policies so as to gain benefits from its activities. The ASB statement makes it clear that the exercise of this influence includes both the power of veto as well as the active involvement by the 'parent' directors.

Unified basis is not regarded simply as representing unified management but assumes that the *whole* of the operations of the enterprise are completely integrated and managed as a single unit.

Participating interest means a long-term investment for the purpose of securing a contribution to an entity's activities by the exercise of control or influence. A 20 per cent holding is regarded as a presumption of participating interest.

FRS 2 is really an expansion/interpretation of the definitions contained in the Companies Act 1989, but it may not catch all the deliberate attempts by directors to circumvent the legal definition of a subsidiary. Therefore there is a need for additional guidance in FRS 5 to encompass any attempt at setting up quasi-subsidiary relationships outside the legal definition.

Solution 2 – Brandon Ltd

To: Finance director   Date
From: Chief accountant

Consolidation and related accounting policies

This memorandum details the following:

- The consolidated balance sheet (appendix 1) including the newly acquired subsidiary, Shepherd Ltd.
- The current method of accounting for goodwill and its effect on realised profits.
- A brief explanation of alternative policies available.
- The possible use of merger accounting.

(1) Goodwill

In preparing the consolidated balance sheet, goodwill has been accounted for in accordance with the new standard, FRS 10, which requires capitalisation, from 23 December 1998.

Goodwill has been calculated as the excess of the fair value of the purchase consideration over the fair value of the separable net assets acquired. Included in this is a contingent consideration of £95,000. This payment is dependent on certain profit targets being achieved, but it is expected to happen.

The brand names of Shepherd have been excluded from net assets since it is felt that they may not meet the 'separability' condition and cannot be sold independently from the rest of the business. There is also considerable doubt concerning a satisfactory basis of calculation.

Had the goodwill been written off there would be no effect on the realised profits of the group. This is because dividends are paid out of individual companies' profit and loss accounts and not from the consolidated accounts.

(2) *Alternative accounting policies*

Until FRS 10, there was wide variety of alternative policies available to account for goodwill:

(a) Capitalise goodwill and write it off through the profit and loss account over the asset's useful life. Thus £171,000 would be recorded this year as an intangible fixed asset and the amortisation would flow through the profit and loss account as an additional expense.

(b) Include brand names and any other intangible fixed assets acquired within the consolidated balance sheet, thereby reducing the goodwill figure. Only the brands of Shepherd may be included, as these are purchased. Those of Brandon must be excluded on the grounds that they are 'home grown'. There is no reliable active market for these brands. If the 'purchased' brands of Shepherd are included in the balance sheet then they should be written off through the profit and loss account over the brands' useful economic lives.

(c) Treat goodwill as a 'negative reserve', i.e. it is a debit on the other side of the balance sheet reducing shareholders' funds. Each year, over its estimated useful life, a transfer is made from this negative reserve to the profit and loss account. This is really a form of reserve accounting but it was acceptable to the secretary of the ASC at the time of SSAP 22's adoption and it has been applied in practice. However, it would no longer be acceptable under FRS 10, which requires capitalisation of goodwill as an asset.

(3) *The use of merger accounting*

If the consideration had been totally in shares, 1,045,000 shares of 10p each would have been issued, valued at £1 each. This is equal to the sum of contingent and actual cash paid. Since Brandon Ltd would be issuing these shares in exchange for 95 per cent of the share capital of Shepherd Ltd, the issue would qualify for merger relief under S131 Companies Act 1985. This can be achieved by either of the following methods:

(a) Valuing the shares at full value of £1,045,000 with the premium being credited to a merger reserve.

(b) Valuing the shares at nominal value of £104,500 (10p not £1) and not recognising a premium.

As a result of both (a) and (b) the £142,500 dividend received (£150,000 × 95%) will be regarded as realised because the underlying value of the investment will not have fallen below the carrying value of £104,500.

Merger relief is adopted mainly with the use of acquisition accounting.

The full adoption of merger accounting would not be possible because in substance this is clearly an acquisition and it fails to meet most of the criteria laid down in FRS 6 to determine a merger.

Appendix 1: Preparation of consolidated balance sheet as at 31 October 2001

Cost of control (95%)

	£'000		£'000
Investment in S	950	Share capital – S	190
Creditors – contingent consideration	95	Profit and loss a/c	570
		Revaluation reserve	114
		Goodwill – balance sheet	171
	1,045		1,045

Profit and loss account

	£'000		£'000
Minority interest (5% × 475)	24	Balance – B	1,800
Cost of control (95% × 600)	570	– S	475
Depreciation	1	Net current assets	143
Consolidated balance sheet	1,823		
	2,418		2,418

Minority interest (5%)

	£'000		£'000
Consolidated balance sheet	40	Share capital – S	10
		Revaluation reserve	6
		Profit and loss	24
	40		40

Revaluation reserve

	£'000		£'000
Cost of control (95%)	114	Balance – B	1,300
Minority interest (5% × 120)	6	Fixed assets	120
Fixed assets	50		
Consolidated balance sheet	1,250		
	1,420		1,420

Fixed assets

	£'000		£'000
Balance – B	2,150	Depreciation (2% × ¼ yr)	1
– S	625	Revaluation reserve	50
Revaluation reserve	120	Consolidated balance sheet	2,844
	2,895		2,895

Net current assets

	£'000		£'000
Balance – B	1,900	Cost of control	95
– S	50	Consolidated balance sheet	1,998
Dividend out of pre-acquisition profits (95% × 150)	143		
	2,093		2,093

Consolidated balance sheet as at 31 October 2001

	£'000
Intangible fixed assets	171
Tangible fixed assets	2,844
Net current assets	1,998
Long-term liabilities	(400)
	4,613
Share capital (B only)	1,000
Share premium (B only)	500
Revaluation reserve	1,250
Profit and loss account	1,823
	4,573
Minority interests	40
	4,613

Solution 3 – Scotty plc

(a) Calculation of fair value of Sulu Inc. as at 1 October 2000

	$'000		£'000
Net assets per Sulu Inc. 30.9.00 (note 2)	4,370		
Adjustments to reflect fair value			
Redundancy costs (note 2)	–		
Uniformity of accounting policies (note 5)	150		
Fair value of Sulu Inc.	4,520	$1.8/£1	2,511

Redundancy costs (note 2)

The costs are clearly defined and identified at acquisition and are confirmed by subsequent payments. Undoubtedly these would have been considered by Scotty plc in calculating the purchase price for Sulu Inc. However FRS 7 *Fair Values in Acquisition Accounting* would appear to preclude such a provision as it represents the acquiror's future intentions in controlling the new subsidiary. Therefore it should be recorded as a post-acquisition expense.

Investment in plant and machinery (note 3)

These are prospective acquisitions. If Sulu Inc. had invested in plant prior to the takeover, either cash/bank or creditors would also have been affected, thereby leaving net assets unaffected. It is merely a switch within the individual components of the same total net assets. No adjustment is therefore needed to fair value as at 1 October 2000.

Professional fees and directors' time and expenses (note 4)

These are costs incurred by Scotty plc in order to help the directors to decide whether or not to purchase Sulu Inc. As such they relate to the cost of the investment, not to the fair value of the net assets of Sulu Inc.

Only the professional fees have been included in the fair value of consideration as the directors' time and expenses are not evidenced by a market transaction and should be disregarded.

Stocks (note 5)

Part of the fair value exercise should be to ensure uniformity of accounting policies, and under SSAP 9 the LIFO method for stock valuation is not permitted. An adjustment has therefore been made to increase the net assets of Sulu Inc. at acquisition by $150,000.

(b) Calculation of goodwill in the consolidated balance sheet at 30 June 2001

	£'000	£'000
Fair value of consideration 1.10.00		
Ordinary shares (5m × 25p) at 30p market value		1,500
Cash – paid	750	
– deferred	200	
		950
		2,450
Acquisition costs : professional fees		30
Fair value of consideration		2,480
Fair value of net assets acquired 1.10.00		
£2,511,000 (from a) × 90% interest		2,260
Goodwill arising on consolidation 1.10.00		220

	£'000
Amortisation to 30.6.01 9/12 × 1/3 × 220 =	55
Net book value 30.6.01 (220 – 55) =	165

Note: Prior to FRS 10 *Goodwill and Intangible Assets* the company could adopt 'merger relief' under S131 Companies Act 1985/A141 CO 86. The excess of the fair value, i.e. the goodwill of £220,000, would have been offset against the share premium of 5m × 5p, i.e. £250,000. Now it must be capitalised.

(c) Earnings per share

Earnings per share are calculated on profits after extraordinary items and after taxation, minority interests and preference dividends, of £1,614,000 (£XX 2000), and shares issued and outstanding in the period of 51,250,000.

Workings

(1) Earnings

	Basic £'000	Diluted £'000
Group profit after taxation	1,614	1,614

(2) Number of shares

	Basic £'000	Diluted £'000
Balance at 1.7.00	47,500	47,500
Share exchange on acquisition		
1.10.00 (5,000 × 3/4)	3,750	3,750
Share options	–	1,083
(Assume share price 27p then		
discount is one-third, i.e. 9p/27p x 3,250)	51,250	52,333

(3) Earnings per share

Basic

$$\frac{1,614}{51,250} \times 100$$

$$= \quad 3.1\text{p}$$

Diluted

$$\frac{1,614}{52,333} \times 100$$

$$= \quad 3.1\text{p}$$

This *must* be disclosed under FRS 14, even if not material, or no difference between the figures. There is no requirement to publish a nil earnings per share under FRS 14 nor if the diluted EPS is antidilutive.

Solution 4 – Leo and Felix

(a) (i)   Acquisition accounting

Consolidated balance sheet as at 1 June 2001

	£'000
Fixed assets (24,600 + 9,750)	34,350
Net current assets (52,960 + 29,450)	82,410
Goodwill	15,010
	131,770
Ordinary shares (50,000 + 23,750)	73,750
Share premium (5,000 + 23,750)	28,750
Undistributed profits (Leo only)	2,560
	105,060
12% Debentures (20,000 + 5,000)	25,000
Minority interests	1,710
	131,770

Note: The assets of the subsidiary would normally be revalued to the fair value of assets acquired.

Workings

Cost of control

	£'000		£'000
Investment in Felix Ltd	47,500	Share capital	19,000
(23,750 x £2)		Share premium (95%)	5,700
		Undistributed profits (8,200 × 95%)	7,790
		Goodwill	15,010
	47,500		47,500

Minority interests (5%)

	£'000		£'000
Consolidated balance sheet	1,710	Share capital	1,000
		Share premium	300
		Undistributed profits	410
	1,710		1,710

(a) (ii) Merger accounting

Consolidated balance sheet as at 1 June 2001

		£'000
Fixed assets	(24,600 + 9,750)	34,350
Net current assets	(52,960 + 29,450)	82,410
		116,760
Share capital	(Leo only)	73,750
Share premium	(5,000 + 6,000 – 300 minority)	10,700
Undistributed profits	(2,560 + 8,200 – 410 minority – 4,750 capital adjustm't)	5,600
		90,050
12% Debentures		25,000
Minority interests		1,710
		116,760

Note: It is not necessary to revalue the subsidiary's assets to fair value.

Workings
Cost of control

	£'000		£'000
Investment in Felix Ltd	23,750	Share capital	19,000
(23,750 x £1)		Capital adjustment	4,750
	23,750		23,750

Minority interests (5%)

	£'000		£'000
Consolidated balance sheet	1,710	Share capital	1,000
		Share premium	300
		Undistributed profits	410
	1,710		1,710

(b) Methods of accounting for business combinations

PRIVATE AND CONFIDENTIAL

Mr J. S. Lemon   Todd, Andrew & Co.
Managing director   14 High St
Leo Ltd   London EC5 1JC
River St
Dubfast

Date

Dear Sir

Accounting for the acquisition of Felix Ltd

With reference to our conversation of 12 July 2001, I am writing to outline the effects of the two methods of accounting for the acquisition of Felix Ltd and to indicate the particular circumstances when each is appropriate.

Two distinct methods have evolved for dealing with business combinations: acquisition accounting and merger accounting. In order for the latter to be applied there should be a genuine 'pooling of interests' of the two companies. As such the combination is based largely on a share-for-share exchange basis. In fact, FRS 6 insists on a combination meeting five separate criteria:

(1) No party is portrayed as either acquirer or acquiree.

(2) All parties must participate in drawing up the new management structure.

(3) Both companies must be roughly the same size.

(4) The purchase price should not contain a material proportion of non-equity consideration.

(5) There should not be a substantial minority after the acquisition and any earn-out clauses would be prohibited.

In essence it is assumed that the substance of the combination represents a genuine pooling of interests.

Merger accounting is, however, mandatory in the above instances. Basically, it enables the combined financial statements to closely resemble the aggregate of the two separate companies. In addition, there is said to be no acquisition and therefore no need to 'freeze' the pre-acquisition profits of the acquired company in the balance sheet of the combined entity. The financial results of both companies are fully reflected in the consolidated accounts and corresponding figures are adjusted accordingly. Mergers are, however, expected to be rare in practice.

Acquisition accounting, on the other hand, assumes that there is a dominant party, i.e. a takeover. Therefore the fair value of the assets acquired should be recorded in the consolidated accounts. However, this is represented by share capital and reserves on the other side of the balance sheet which really represents paid-up capital which is not distributable. Group accounts will only include the parent's share of the subsidiary's post-acquisition profits.

In the particular case of Felix Ltd, 95 per cent of the shares have been acquired on a share-for-share exchange, therefore it is very possible that a genuine merger has occurred and merger accounting could apply. I would therefore advise that this method is adopted, provided that the true substance of the combination is in fact that of a merger.

The advantages can be seen by analysing the differing effects of the two methods:

(1) Pre-acquisition profits

These are not distributable under acquisition accounting. As a result, only £2.56m belonging to Leo Ltd may be included under distributable profits. With merger accounting the total profits from both companies are available for distribution, therefore £5.6m is available.

(2) Goodwill

Goodwill is inevitable in acquisition accounting. It represents the difference between the fair value of the consideration paid for the subsidiary and the fair value of its net assets. In the takeover of Felix Ltd, over £15m of goodwill was created which will have to be capitalised under FRS 10 and normally amortised through the consolidated profit and loss account over the period of its useful life.

Under merger accounting there is a difference between the nominal value of the investment and the net book value of assets merged. This amount of £4.75m has been written off against undistributed profits.

It is possible to obtain Court permission to write off goodwill against the share premium account, and in Great Britain and Northern Ireland it is possible to adopt Section 131/A 141 of the Companies Act 1985/(NI) Order 1986. Effectively, however, FRS 10 would override this if a true and fair position of the financial statements is to be disclosed.

(3) Share premium

Because the investment is recorded at nominal value under merger accounting, no share premium will emerge. However, under acquisition accounting, the excess over the nominal value of the shares issued in exchange will be credited to share premium.

Generally this account is of a quasi-capital nature. Apart from writing off preliminary expenses, discounts on debentures, premiums on redemption of shares, etc., any movement in the account is severely restricted. However, under the 'Merger relief' provisions described in (2) above it can be used to write off the goodwill created on an acquisition, provided that 90 per cent of the shares are acquired at acquisition. However, even this is now effectively prohibited by FRS 10.

(4) Revaluation of assets to fair value

With merger accounting it is not necessary to revalue either company's net assets to fair value. Under IAS 22 both companies can be revalued under the 'New Entity' approach but they can still adopt merger accounting.

In acquisition accounting, the net assets of the acquired company must be revalued to fair value, with consequent increased depreciation charges in the profit and loss accounts of subsequent years.

In summary, the company has to choose the method of accounting that represents the substance of the combination. If merger relief has been available under Section 131/A 141 then the £15.01m can be netted against a merger reserve of £23.75m created on the acquisition. In the past a number of companies have also investigated the possibility of creating reorganisation provisions and changing accounting policies to increase goodwill, thereby helping to boost post-acquisition profits. However the new FRS 7 now bans the creation of any provisions which represent an acquirer's future intentions, in the fair value exercise.

Merger accounting would appear to be the more attractive of the two options.

Yours sincerely
P.J. Todd

Solution 5 – Left plc and Right plc

(a) *Consolidated balance sheet as at 31 December 1999*

Acquisition accounting

	£	£
Fair value of purchase consideration		54m
(6 shares for 5 for 20m x £2.25 per share)		
Fair value of net assets acquired		
Fixed assets	43.5m	
Stocks	9.5m	
Other current assets	10.0m	
Current liabilities	(8.0m)	
Quoted debentures	(11.0m)	
		44m
Goodwill		10m

Cost of control

Purchase consideration	£54m	Share capital	£ 20m
		Share premium	5m
		Profit and loss account	14m
		Revaluation reserve (3.5 + 0.5 + 1.0)	5m
		Goodwill	10m
	£54m		£ 54m

Merger accounting

Cost of control

Purchase consideration	£24m	Share capital	£ 20m
		Profit and loss account	4m
	24m		24m

Consolidated balance sheet

	Acquisition	Merger	
Intangible fixed assets	£10.0m	£Nil	
Tangible fixed assets (60 + 40) (+ 3.5)	103.5m	100.0m	
Stocks (10 + 9) (+ 0.5)	19.5m	19.0m	
Other current assets (12 + 10)	22.0m	22.0m	
Current liabilities (9 + 8)	(17.0m)	(17.0m)	
Quoted debentures (15 + 12) (– 1.0)	(26.0m)	(27.0m)	
	112.0m	97.0m	
Equity share capital (30 + 24 new capital)	54.0m	54.0m	
Share premium (10 + 0) + (24m x £1.25)	40.0m	15.0m (10 + 5)	
Profit and loss account (18 + 0)	18.0m	28.0m	(18 + 14 – 4 adj.)
	112.0m	97.0m	

(b) Requirements of FRS 6 – Merger accounting

FRS 6 defines a merger as:

'A business combination that results in the creation of a new reporting entity formed from the combining parties, in which the shareholders of the combining entities come together in a partnership for the mutual sharing of risks and benefits of the combined entity, and in which no party to the combination in substance obtains control over any other, or is otherwise seen to be dominant, whether by virtue of the proportion of its shareholders' rights in the combined entity, the influence of its directors or otherwise.'

The definition has been drawn narrowly to reduce the number of reporting entities that could fall under its mantle. They should be rare combinations. On the other hand, the definition of an acquisition has been drawn to cover every 'business combination that is not a merger'.

The rationale behind the standard is that mergers should only result if, in substance, there is a genuine pooling of interests of the two parties. In effect, neither an acquirer nor an acquiree can be identified.

The definitions by themselves would not be sufficient and that is why FRS 6 introduces a number of additional criteria that need to be investigated before making a final decision in relation to the combination of Left and Right. The following should be considered:

(i) *The way the roles of each party to the combination are portrayed*
Does either party appear to be an acquirer or acquiree and is a new logo to be introduced containing both parties' former names? There is nothing in the facts provided that can give an opinion either way. More information is required in this regard.

(ii) *The involvement of both parties in selecting the new management team*
No information is available on this and therefore more information is required.

(iii) *The relative sizes of the parties to the combination*
Left holds 58,000/97,000 or 59.8 per cent and Right holds 39,000/97,000 or 40.2 per cent. This is fairly close as no one party is 50 per cent larger than the other. Thus merger accounting would be a possibility.

(iv) *Whether the shareholders of the combining entities receive any material consideration other than equity shares as part of the deal*
In this case the entire exchange was in the form of equity and thus again merger accounting is a possibility.

(v) Are there any earn-out clauses or material minority interests?
In neither of these situations is this the case so, again, merger accounting could be a possibility.

Overall, there is not enough information yet to make a final decision as to whether or not a combination is a merger or an acquisition. However, there are a number of favourable points in favour of merger accounting. The decision can only be taken after all five criteria have been investigated and the decision must be taken on the overall commercial reality or substance of the combination transaction.

There are major advantages in adopting merger accounting, which are:

(i) There is no goodwill created and thus no charge to profit and loss for the amortisation of that goodwill;

(ii) There is no share premium account created, which is generally regarded as a quasi-capital balance, not available for distribution;

(iii) There is no revaluation of the acquiree's net assets, resulting in future increased charges for depreciation;

(iv) None of the reserves of the merged entities need be frozen and both are still available for future distribution.

Solution 6 – Xtra plc

(a) (i) Acquisition accounting (FRS 7) or merger accounting (FRS 6)

FRS 6 *Acquisitions and Mergers* requires that, in order to determine whether or not a business combination meets the definition of a merger, it should be assessed against certain specified criteria. Failure to meet any of these criteria might indicate that the definition was not met and thus merger accounting could not be adopted for the combination. However, all five criteria must be viewed as a package and it is still up to the reporting accountant to take a subjective judgement as to whether or not, in substance, a genuine merger has resulted from the combination.

This entails considering the following five criteria:

Criterion 1

No party to the combination is portrayed as either acquirer or acquiree, either by its own board of management or by that of another party to the combination. FRS 6 elaborates on this by stating that where the terms of a share-for-share exchange indicate that one party has paid a premium over the market value of the shares, this is evidence that that party has taken the role of acquirer unless there is a clear explanation for this apparent premium other than being a premium paid to acquire control.

This is particularly relevant in the present situation where the value of the Xtra plc shares issued as consideration was £1,728,000 (1,440,000 × £1.2) to acquire Visual plc shares resulting in a premium of £288,000 plus cash of £172,800 (1,440,000 × 12p) plus cash.

This indicates, *prima facie*, that it was an acquisition. However, the exchange price was within the range (£1.10 – £1.35) of market prices for Visual plc during the previous year. This could well be a clear explanation for this apparent premium other than its being a premium paid to acquire control.

The circumstances surrounding the transaction also support the view that this is a merger. For example, the closure and redundancy programme applied to Xtra plc and not to Visual plc.

Criterion 2

All parties to the combination, as represented by the boards of directors or their appointees, participate in establishing the management structure for the combined entity and in selecting the management personnel, and such decisions are made on the basis of a consensus between the parties rather than by an exercise in voting.

The need for reapplication for posts and appearance before an interview panel indicates that there will be a consensus decision on appropriate personnel which would satisfy Criterion 2 even though the final result might be that the posts are largely filled by Xtra plc managers. Merger accounting would appear to be most relevant.

Criterion 3

The relative sizes of the combining parties are not so disparate that one party dominates the combined entity by virtue of its relative size.

This requires a consideration of the proportion of the equity of the combined entity attributable to the shareholders of each of the combining parties to test if one is more than 50 per cent larger than the other. This 50 per cent is, however, merely a rebuttable presumption. In this case, Xtra plc shareholders hold 2,000,000 shares and Visual plc 1,440,000 shares. This indicates that the criterion is satisfied even though the 1,440,000 shares are in consideration of 96 per cent of Visual plc's capital. Thus it would appear to be a merger.

Criterion 4

Under the terms of the combination or related arrangements, the consideration received by equity shareholders in relation to their shareholding comprises primarily equity shares in the combined entity; and any non-equity consideration, or equity shares carrying substantially reduced voting or distribution rights, represents an immaterial proportion of the fair value of the consideration received by the equity shareholders. Where one of the combining entities has, within the period of two years before the combination, acquired equity shares in another of the combining entities, the consideration for this acquisition should be taken into account in determining whether this criterion has been met.

This indicates that the cash payment of 12p per share should be taken into account. FRS 6 refers to the company legislation requirements for a transaction to be treated as a merger. This includes the provision that the fair value of any consideration other than the issue of equity shares given pursuant to the arrangement by the parent company did not exceed 10 per cent of the nominal value of the equity shares issued.

The cash payment represents 12 per cent of the nominal value of the equity shares issued and therefore the transaction should be accounted for as an acquisition.

Criterion 5

No equity shareholders of any of the combining entities retain any material interest in the future performance of only part of the combined entity. This criterion is concerned with situations where the allocation depended to any material extent on the post-combination performance of the business.

In this case the allocation is dependent on the eventual value of a specific liability as opposed to future operating performance. There are no earn-out clauses. This would probably indicate merger accounting.

Overall it is difficult to identify which is the most appropriate method but Criterion 4 would appear to make it very difficult to argue for merger accounting in this situation.

(a) (ii) Consolidated balance sheet – acquisition accounting

		Xtra plc £m	Visual plc £m	Consolidated £m	
Intangible fixed assets					
Negative goodwill	(W3)	–	–	(0.7968)	
Tangible fixed assets					
Land and buildings		1.20	1.30	2.5	
Fixtures, fittings and equipment		1.65	1.30	2.95	
Motor vehicles		0.86	0.30	1.16	
		3.71	2.90	6.61	
Current assets					
Stocks		0.60	0.20	0.80	
Debtors		0.49	0.16	0.65	
Cash	(W4)	0.15	0.34	0.3172	(0.49 – 0.1728)
		1.24	0.70	1.7672	
Creditors: amounts falling due within one year		(0.56)	(0.79)	(1.35)	
Net current assets		0.68	(0.09)	0.4172	
Total assets less total liabilities		4.39	2.81	6.2304	
Capital and reserves					
Ordinary shares of £1 each		2.00	1.50	3.44	(2.00 + 1.44)
Share premium	(W4)	–	–	0.288	
Revaluation reserve		0.49	0.31	0.49	(X only)
Profit and loss account		1.90	1.00	1.90	(X only)
		4.39	2.81	6.118	
Minority interest	(W5)			0.1124	
				6.2304	

Workings

1. Percentage holding   1,440,000/1,500,000 = 96%
2. Fair value of consideration: Shares   £ 1,728,000 (1,440,000 x £1.20 each)

    Cash   172,800 (1,440,000 x £0.12 each)

    £1,900,800

3. Fair value of net assets acquired:

	£m
Net assets (per question)	2.50
Land and buildings – revalued	0.44
Fixtures and fittings – revalued	0.12
Motor vehicles – devalued	(0.19)
Stock – devalued	(0.03)
Debtors – devalued	(0.03)
	2.81

X 96% = 2.6976m

Fair value of consideration	1.9008m
Negative goodwill	(0.7968)m

Negative goodwill should disclosed as a deduction from positive goodwill on the asset side of the balance sheet and should be subsequently credited to profit and loss over the period when the non-monetary assets acquired are sold or used up in the business.

4. Recording of investment in Visual plc

Dr	Investment in Visual plc		£1,900,800	
	Cr	Cash		£172,800
		Ordinary shares of £1 each		1,440,000
		Share premium		288,000

5. Minority interests: £2.81m net assets x 4% = £112,400

(b) (i) Acquisition of Audigram Ltd by Xtra

Calculation of goodwill

		£
Fair value of consideration (£1m x (0.9090 + 0.8264 + 0.7513)) (10% discount)		2,486,700
Direct cost – accountancy fees £60,000 + legal costs £40,000		100,000
		2,586,700
Fair value of net assets acquired		
Book value of assets acquired at 31 December 1997	2,200,000	
Revaluation of land and buildings	300,000	
	2,500,000	
90% acquired		2,250,000
Goodwill		336,700

Note: Provision for reorganisation and future operating losses must not be incorporated in the fair value exercise as they are not liabilities as at the date of acquisition. They are also specifically banned under FRS 7 *Fair Values in Acquisition Accounting*.

Under FRS 7, cash consideration is deferred and therefore the fair value should be discounted to present value at the rate at which an acquirer can obtain similar borrowings.

(ii) Accounting for deferred consideration

Deferred consideration should be disclosed in the acquiring company's balance sheet as the investment's cost at the discounted amount. The same amount will appear as a creditor for deferred consideration in creditors over/under one year.

In the profit and loss account the unwinding of the discount should be treated as a finance cost and charged as an interest expense in Xtra plc's profit and loss over the period of the liability.

Solution 7 – Growmoor plc

(a) (i) FRS 6 requires that to determine whether a business combination meets the definition of a merger, it should also be assessed against certain specified criteria:

> Merger: *A business combination that results in the creation of a new reporting entity formed from the combining parties, in which the shareholders of the combining entities come together in a partnership for the mutual sharing of the risks and benefits of the combined entity, and in which no party to the combination in substance obtains control over any other, or is otherwise seen to be dominant, whether by virtue of the proportion of its shareholders' rights in the combined entity, the influence of its directors or otherwise.*

Failure to broadly meet these criteria indicates that the definition was probably not met and thus that merger accounting is not to be used for the combination, as in substance the combination is an acquisition. This entails considering the following five criteria:

Criterion 1

No party to the combination is portrayed as either acquirer or acquiree, either by its own board or management or by that of another party in the combination.

Para. 61 of FRS 6 elaborates on this, stating that where the terms of a share-for-share exchange indicate that one party has paid a premium over the market value of the shares acquired, this is evidence that that party has taken the role of acquirer unless there is a clear explanation for this apparent premium other than its being a premium paid to acquire control.

This is relevant in the present situation where the value of the Growmoor plc shares issued as consideration was (1,500,000 × £1.20p=) £1,800,000 to acquire Smelt plc shares valued at £1,560,000, resulting in a premium of £240,000.

This indicates *prima facie* that it was an acquisition. However, the exchange price was within the range (£1.20–£1.50) of market prices for Smelt plc during the previous year. There could well be a clear explanation for this apparent premium other than its being a premium paid to acquire control.

The circumstances surrounding the transaction also support the view that this is a merger. For example, the closure and redundancy programme applied to Growmoor plc and not to Smelt plc.

Criterion 2

All parties to the combination, as represented by the boards of directors or their appointees, participate in establishing the management structure for the combined entity and in selecting the management personnel, and such decisions are made on the basis of a consensus between the parties.

The need for reapplication for posts and appearance before an interview panel indicates that there will be a consensus decision on appropriate personnel which would satisfy Criterion 2 even though the final result might be that the posts are largely filled by Growmoor plc managers.

Criterion 3

The relative sizes of the combining entities are not so disparate that one party dominates the combined entity by virtue of its relative size.

This requires a consideration of the proportion of the equity of the combined entity attributable to the shareholders of each of the combining parties to test if one is more than 50 per cent larger than the other. This 50 per cent is a rebuttable presumption. In this case, Growmoor plc shareholders hold 1,625,000 shares and Smelt plc 1,500,000 shares. This indicates that the criterion is satisfied even though the 1,500,000 shares are in consideration of only 80 per cent of Smelt plc's capital.

Criterion 4

Under the terms of the combination or related arrangements, the consideration received by equity shareholders in relation to their shareholding comprises primarily equity shares in the combined entity; and any non-equity consideration, or equity shares carrying substantially reduced voting or distribution rights, represents an immaterial proportion of the fair value of the consideration received by the equity shareholders. Where one of the combining entities has, within the period of two years before the combination, acquired equity shares in another of the combining entities, the consideration for this acquisition should be taken into account in determining whether this criterion has been met.

This indicates that the cash payment made on 15 June 1999 should be taken into account, being less than two years before the combination on 1 May 2001. Appendix 1 of FRS 6 refers to the Companies Act requirements for a transaction to be treated as a merger. This includes the provision that the fair value of any consideration other than the issue of equity shares given pursuant to the arrangement by the parent company did not exceed 10 per cent of the nominal value of the equity shares issued.

The transaction does not comply with this requirement and would be required to be treated as an acquisition.

Criterion 5

No equity shareholders of any of the combining entities retain any material interest in the future performance of only part of the combined entity.

This criterion is concerned with situations where the allocation depended to any material extent on the post-combination performance of the business. In the present case, the allocation is dependent on the determination of the eventual value of a specified liability as opposed to the future operating performance and the criterion is satisfied, i.e. there are no earn-out clauses in the agreement. On balance it would appear that the combination should be treated as an acquisition.

(ii) *Change of terms*

The Companies Act requirement is not met because the cash payment of £164,000 in 1999 is more than 10 per cent of the nominal value of the shares issued, which was £1,500,000.

The company has acquired 16 per cent of the shares of Smelt plc in 1999 and 80 per cent in 2001. The company could require the holders of the remaining 4 per cent to sell their shares on the same terms as those offered to the holder of the 80 per cent but, even if it did this, the new shares issued as consideration would be 1,575,000 and the Companies Act requirement would still not be satisfied with the cash payment of £164,000 being 10.4 per cent.

A further, and more common, possibility is that Growmoor plc could make a small bonus issue, say 1 for 10, prior to the exchange, thus increasing the nominal value of the equity given from £1,500,000 to £1,650,000. The cash payment of £164,000 is then reduced to less than 10 per cent of the nominal value.

(b)   The following reasons could be put forward for the approach taken by the ASB in formulating the FRS 7 requirements concerning provisions on acquisition:

The practice of companies creating provisions or accruals for future operating losses and/or reorganisation costs expected to be incurred as a result of an acquisition was abused. Companies created provisions which gave rise to a larger goodwill figure that could be written off immediately against share premium under S131 Companies Act 1985 and a provision against which expenses could be charged in subsequent accounting periods resulting in a higher profit figure. Directors on profit bonus schemes could therefore benefit personally if post-acquisition profits could be enhanced by the introduction of pre-acquisition provisions. In the post-acquisition period the effect of this was to prevent the accounts showing a true and fair view of the substance of commercial activities that had taken place in an accounting period.

(c) (i)   FRS 7, para 77, states that when settlement cash consideration is deferred, fair values are obtained by discounting to their present value the amounts expected to be payable in the future.

The appropriate discount rate is the rate at which the acquirer could obtain a similar borrowing, taking into account its credit standing and any security given.

For the Beaten Ltd acquisition the appropriate rate is 10 per cent, as stated in the question.

Treatment in the balance sheet of Growmoor plc as at 31 July 2001

The discounted deferred consideration payable is a form of debt instrument. It is this amount that will appear as the investment's cost in the acquiring company's balance sheet, i.e. £402,685. The same amount would appear as a creditor for the deferred consideration (100,000 × .9090 + 150,000 × .8264 + 250,000 × .7513). The liability would be split into £90,900 payable within one year and £311,785 payable in more than one year.

Treatment in the profit and loss account of Growmoor plc for the year ended 31 July 2001

Because the deferred consideration is a form of debt instrument, the difference of £97,315 between the discounted amount of the payments and the total cash amount (500,000 – 402,685) is treated as a finance cost to be charged as an interest expense in Growmoor's plc profit and loss account over the period the liability is outstanding so that the annual cost gives a constant rate on the liability's carrying amount. The finance cost charged in the accounts to 31 July 2001 is £3,335, representing one month's charge on £402,685 at 10 per cent finance charge.

(ii) *Goodwill calculation*

Goodwill is calculated as at the date of acquisition based on the discounted amount of the cash payments. This results in a negative goodwill figure of £282,315 (402,685 – 685,000).

Effect of deferred consideration

There is no adjustment to this figure on the stage payments of the consideration. Growmoor plc has obtained the benefit of deferring the payment of the consideration and the cost of the benefit is charged in the profit and loss account over the period of the deferral.

Effect of contingent consideration

The terms of the agreement are such that it is impossible to say whether and how much additional consideration will be paid and the appropriate treatment is to deal with the matter by disclosure rather than provision.

Enquiries would be needed to establish whether the service agreement with the directors of Beaten Ltd constitutes a payment for the business acquired or an expense for services. If the substance of the agreement is payment for the business acquired the payments would be accounted for as a part of the purchase consideration and, as they are quantified, they would be included within the goodwill calculation.

(iii) *Treatment of negative goodwill*

SSAP 22 required in para. 40 that any excess of the aggregate of fair values of the separable assets acquired over the fair value of the consideration given (negative goodwill) should be credited directly to reserves.

There have been a number of possible approaches which could be applied when accounting for negative goodwill.

One is the approach followed in the USA, which is to say that although the separable net assets are worth more than the value of the business as a whole they did not cost the acquirer that much and that accordingly the negative goodwill should be applied to reduce the separable assets to their cost to the acquiring company by proportionately writing down the value of the fixed assets of the acquired company, other than any marketable securities. However, this approach was considered in FRED 7, para. 53, and rejected on the grounds that a requirement to eliminate the negative consolidation difference by making an arbitrary allocation to reduce the otherwise determined fair values of non-monetary assets does not provide balance sheet information that is useful to those who wish to make assessments of the values of assets acquired in a business combination.

Another approach is to identify why the negative goodwill arose and to account for it based on that analysis. For example, in its Discussion Paper *Accounting for Goodwill* issued by the ASC in 1980, paras 11.2–11.4 state: 'negative goodwill may arise as a consequence of the expectations of future losses or reduced profits or alternatively may just represent a bargain purchase by the acquiror. The logical treatment of negative goodwill which is related to future losses would be to amortise the capital reserve over the expected period of such losses by crediting it to the profit and loss account as the provision is progressively realised over this period.'

In the present example the negative goodwill has arisen partly because there is an expectation of poor trading results with a loss of £100,000 which means that the business as a whole is at present worth less than is indicated by the values of the separable net assets.

Following on from FRED 7, FRS 10 *Goodwill and Intangible Assets* requires negative goodwill to be initially recorded as a negative asset (dangling credit) on the face of the balance sheet immediately below positive goodwill. It must then be transferred to the profit and loss account as the non-monetary assets acquired are sold or used up in subsequent years.

Solution 8 – Alps Ltd

To: The directors, Alps Ltd Group   Date

From: J. Smith, financial controller

Preparation of financial statements in accordance with the accounting standard, FRS 9 Associates and Joint Ventures

I have revised our latest draft group accounts to ensure that they comply with the latest standard FRS 9 (November 1997) and I can report as follows:

(1) Turnover

Both subsidiaries and the holding company should be included (Snow, Wind and Alps – see Appendix) but neither Cold nor Skis should have been in the turnover.

Skis is not an associated undertaking (see Appendix) as control of 17 per cent would be below the normal 20 per cent presumption in FRS 9 for significant influence. There could be evidence to rebut this but Mr Skis controls 55 per cent of the company, so it would seem unlikely that the company could exercise sufficient influence. Turnover from Skis should therefore be excluded.

(2) Depreciation

For the same reasons as (1) above, the depreciation of both Cold Ltd and Skis Ltd should be excluded.

(3) Profit before tax/tax

Once again Skis Ltd should be excluded because it is not an associated undertaking. However, 25 per cent of Cold's profit before tax and tax charges should be included. The information for the associates should be disclosed separately from the group companies.

(4) Minority interests

The calculations are correct. If a minority holds shares in an associate then that share should be reflected in the minority interest account.

(5) to (7) Retained profits

The retained profits for the year should be analysed between holding company, subsidiaries and associated undertaking, i.e. Alps £95,000, subsidiaries (£1,400) (9,800 – 11,200) and associated undertakings £2,000.

If Skis is not considered to be an associate, the dividend received/receivable should be included.

(8) Balance sheet – associated undertakings

The only associated undertaking is Cold Ltd, which should be valued as follows:

	£	
Share of net tangible assets	20,000	
Share of goodwill	30,000	} can be
Goodwill on acquisition	15,000	} combined
	65,000	

Skis Ltd should be included as an investment at cost.

(9) Loans

The loan from Cold Ltd (associate) should be separately disclosed. That to Skis Ltd should be included with other loans to companies outside the group.

I shall be available to discuss any of these issues over the next few days and shall ensure that corrective action is taken before the accounts are finalised.

Appendix

Group Structure of Alps Ltd

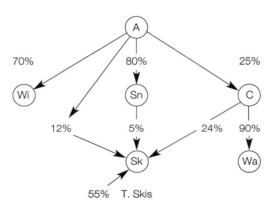

Wind Ltd

Clearly a subsidiary, requires full consolidation.

Snow Ltd

Clearly a subsidiary, requires full consolidation.

Cold Ltd

Presumed to be an 'associated undertaking' because more than 20 per cent of the shares are controlled. Evidence is required of significant influence by way of, perhaps, board representation and active involvement in strategic decision-making in the company.

It could be a subsidiary if there is evidence of 'dominant influence' by Alps Ltd, i.e. control over the operating and financial policies of Cold Ltd.

Warm Ltd

This is a subsidiary of Cold Ltd and therefore should be included with the group accounts of Cold Ltd. 25 per cent of that combined result will be included as an 'associated undertaking' of Alps Ltd.

Skis Ltd

For associated company status it is permissible to add the 12 per cent directly held by Alps plus 5 per cent via its subsidiary Snow. The 24 per cent held by an associate must be excluded. 17 per cent would not be classified as an associated undertaking under normal circumstances. Again, this can be rebutted if Alps is able to exercise significant influence over the affairs of Skis Ltd.

Solution 9 – X, Y and Z Group

(a) *Consolidated balance sheet of the X Group as at 31 March 1999*

		£m
Intangible fixed assets		
Goodwill (55 – 15 amortised)	(W1)	40
Tangible fixed assets (900 + 100 + 30 + 40 – 12 plp)	(W1)	1,058
Investment in associated undertaking	(W4)	47
		1,145
Net current assets (640 + 360 + 75 – 25% × 60)		1,060
		2,205
Creditors: amounts falling due after more than one year (200 + 150 + 15)		(365)
		1,840
Capital and reserves		
Share capital	(X only)	360
Share premium	(X only)	250
Reserves (1,086 – 15 goodwill amortised)	(W3)	1,071
		1,681
Minority interest	(W2)	159
		1,840

Workings

Group structure

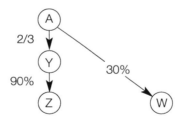

W1

Cost of control – Y (2/3)

	£m		£m
Investment in Y	320	Share capital (2/3 x 150)	100
Intangible assets – Y (2/3 x 30)	20	Share premium (2/3 x 120)	80
Stocks revalued (2/3 x 8 – 2)	4	Profit and loss – pre-acq. (2/3 x 120)	80
Bad debts (2/3 x 9)	6	Arbitration award (2/3 x 36)	24
		Tangible fixed assets (2/3 x 30)	20
		Goodwill (bal. fig.)	46
	350		350

Cost of control – Z (2/3 x 90% = 60%)

	£m		£m
Investment in Z (2/3 x 90)	60	Share capital (60% x 50)	30
Stocks revalued (60% x 5)	3	Share premium (60% x 10)	6
		Profit and loss – pre-acq. (60% x 20)	12
		Tangible fixed assets (60% x 10)	6
		Goodwill (bal. fig.)	9
	63		63

Total goodwill created on the two acquisitions is 46 + 9 = 55. Under FRS 10 this should be amortised over the asset's useful economic life of eleven years, i.e. £5m per annum.

The company wishes to reinstate the goodwill and therefore needs to record a prior year adjustment of £10m for the two years ending 31 March 1997 and 1998.

W2

Minority interests (1/3 Y, 40% Z)

	£m		£m
Investment in Z (1/3 x 90)	30	Share capital (1/3 x 150)	50
Inter-company stock profits (40% x 15)	6	(40% x 50)	20
Intangible assets (1/3 x 30)	10	Share premium (1/3 x 120)	40
Depreciation – Y (10% x 3 yrs x 10)	3	(40% x 10)	4
Depreciation – Z (10% x 3 yrs x 4)	1	Tangible fixed assets (1/3 x 30)	10
Share of losses in associated cos. (1/3 x 3)	1	(40% x 10)	4
CBS	159	Acc. reserves (1/3 x 210)	70
		(40% x 30)	12
	210		210

W3

Accumulated reserves

	£m		£m
Arbitration award (2/3 x 36)	24	Balance – X	1,050
Inter-company stock profits (60% x 15)	9	– Y	210
Cost of control – Y (2/3 x 120)	80	– Z	30
– Z (60% x 20)	12	Bad debts (2/3 x 9)	6
Minority interests – Y (1/3 x 210)	70	Stock (60% x 5)	3
– Z (40% x 30)	12	Stock (2/3 x 6)	4
Share of associated company losses (2/3 x 3)	2		
Depreciation on revalued assets (2/3 x 12)	8		
CBS	1,086		
	1,303		1,303

W4

Investment in W Ltd (30%)

	£m		£m
Investment in W	50	CBS	47
		Post-acq. losses (17 – 20 pre-acq.)	3
	50		50

Disclosure:

Share of net assets: 30% x £103m — 30.9

Goodwill 50 – (30% x 80 + 6 + 7) = 50 – 27.9 = 22.1 x 8/11 = 16.1

47.0

(b) Transitional provisions of FRS 10 Goodwill and Intangible Assets

Under FRS 10's transitional arrangements, reporting entities had a choice of two options on dealing with existing goodwill on previous acquisitions which were written off previously to reserves. The goodwill could be reinstated as in section (a). This requires a change in accounting policy and therefore a prior year reinstatement to opening reserves as well as restating the asset of goodwill on the balance sheet. The alternative approach would be to leave existing goodwill in the reserves and only apply the new standard from its date of inception. However, any goodwill in this instance must clearly be netted off against reserves. No dangling debit is now permitted.

Solution 10 – Archer plc

(a) Explanation of the difference between an associate and a joint venture

SSAP 1 *Accounting for Associated Companies* defined an associate as an entity in which the interest of the investor is for the long term and over which the investor is in a position to exercise a significant influence. FRS 9 *Associates and Joint Ventures*, which became effective for accounting periods ending on or after 23 June 1998, defines an associate as an entity in which the investor has a participating interest and over whose operating and financial policies the investor exercises a significant influence. To qualify as an associate, the investor must have a long-term interest and be actively involved and influential in the direction of its investee through its participation in policy decisions covering aspects of policy relevant to the investor, including strategic issues such as expansion/contraction of business, dividend policy, etc.

All investee's qualifying as associates under FRS 9 would have qualified under SSAP 1. However, an entity that may have originally qualified under SSAP 1 may not necessarily qualify under FRS 9. A long-term interest is not always a participating interest and being in a position to exercise significant influence does not always mean that this influence is actively exercised. The former SSAP 1 relied heavily on a 20 per cent shareholding as being of persuasive evidence that an associate relationship existed. Companies were accused of buying and selling sufficient shares to either deliberately fall below or above the 20 per cent limit.

Joint ventures must also be long-term arrangements in which no venturer alone can control the strategic issues of the reporting entity. Instead the relationship is that there is joint control and each major strategic decision requires the consent of each venturer. There is a veto which gives a degree of influence beyond that of a mere associate. The main determinant is the actual relationship in practice rather than the terms of the agreement. FRS 9 requires the use of the 'gross equity method' for recording the reporting entity's investments in joint ventures. It is similar to the equity method that is adopted for associates but the stronger influence requires additional information on the gross assets and liabilities underlying the net investment. In addition, on the face of the profit and loss account, the investing company's share of turnover of joint ventures is required to be disclosed as a memorandum.

(b) Archer Group

Consolidated profit and loss account for the year ended 31 December 1998

			£m	£m
Turnover	(3,000 + 200)			3,200
Cost of sales	(1,800 + 125)			(1,925)
Gross profit	(1,200 + 75)			1,275
Operating expenses	(500 + 25 + 12 goodwill amortised – 45 negative goodwill)			(492)
Operating profit				783
Share of associated profits	(30% x 640)		192	
	(Amortisation of goodwill W3)		(40)	
				152
				935
Interest payable	– group	(20 + 5)	(25)	
	– associate	(30% x 10)	(3)	(28)
Profit on ordinary activities before tax				907
Tax on ordinary activities	– group	(200 + 10)	(210)	
	– associate	(30% x 190)	(57)	
				(267)
Profit on ordinary activities after tax				640
Dividends paid and proposed				(180)
Retained profit for the group				460

Archer Group

Consolidated balance sheet as at 31 December 1998

			£m	£m
Fixed assets				
Intangible	– goodwill	(W1)	84	
	– negative goodwill	(W2)	(55)	
				29
Tangible	(2,200 + 40)			2,240
Investments	– investment in associated undertaking			
	(800 cost + (30% post-acq. retained profits 400 = 120			880
	– 40 goodwill amortised))			
				3,149
Current assets				
Stocks	(400 + 125)		525	
Debtors	(300 + 0)		300	
Bank and cash	(80 + 200)		280	
			1,105	
Creditors: amounts falling due within one year (480 + 30)			(510)	
				595
				3,744
Capital and reserves				
Ordinary shares of £1 each, fully paid up				1,200
Revaluation reserve				600
Profit and loss account	(1,700 – g'will 12 + neg. g'will 45 + Bow 35 (100%)			
	+ prior year adj. g'will 96 + share of assoc. 80)			1,944
				3,744

Workings

W1 *Reinstatement of goodwill*

	£m
Goodwill originally written off to reserves	120
Amortisation over 10 years	12 per annum
Prior year adjustment – 2 years	24
Current year charge	12
Net book value (120 – 24 –12)	84

W2 *Negative goodwill on acquisition of BOW Ltd*

	£m			£m
Fair value of purchase consideration		200	Release to profit and loss	
Fair value of assets acquired			Stock sold	125
Fixed assets	50		Depreciation (50 ÷ 5 yrs) =	10
Stock	250			135
		300		
Negative goodwill		(100)	135/300 x £m (100) = £45m released	
			Balance sheet £(100)m – £45m = £55m	

W3 *Purchase of ARROW Ltd (30%)*

	£m	£m		
Purchase consideration		800	Amortise £200m ÷ 5 years life =	£40m
Share capital	600		per annum	
Revaluation reserve	300			
Profit and loss account at acq.	1,100		Balance sheet £200m – £40m	= £160m
	2,000 x 30%	600	30% x £2,400m	= £720m
Goodwill		200		£880m

Solution 11 – Earth plc

(a) Consolidated profit and loss account for the year ended 31 December 1999

Consolidated	Earth	Wind	Adjustments	Water	
	£m	£m	£m	£m	£m
Turnover	460	250	(2)		708
Cost of sales	(180)	(70)	2		(248)
Inter-company stock profits		(0.1)			(0.1)
Gross profit	280	179.9			459.9
Net operating expenses (70 + 19 g'will amort.)	(89)	(30)			(119)
Operating profit	191	149.9			340.9
Share of associated undertaking's profit					
(180 x 30% = 54 – 5.9 g'will amort.)				48.1	48.1
Interest payable					
Group	(30)	(10)			(40)
Share of associated undertakings (10 x 30%)				(3)	(3)
Profit before taxation	161	139.9		45.1	346
Taxation	(50)	(40)	(30% x 50)	(15)	(105)
Profits after taxation	111	99.9		30.1	241
Minority interests		(19.98) 20%			(19.98)
Dividends proposed	(80)				(80)
Retained profit	31	79.92		30.1	141.02

(b) *Consolidated balance sheet as at 31 December 1999*

			£m	£m
Fixed assets				
Goodwill	(W1)			95
Tangible fixed assets	(W2)			840
Investments in associated undertaking	(W3)			209.1
				1,144.1
Current assets				
Stocks (240 + 180 – 0.1 inter-co. stock profits)			419.9	
Debtors (120 + 170 – 61 inter-co. balances)			229	
Bank and cash (480 + 10)			490	
			1,138.9	
Creditors: amounts falling due within one year (160 + 130 – 61 inter-co. balances)			(229)	
Net current assets				909.9
				2,054.0
Capital and reserves				
Ordinary shares of £1 each, fully paid up				600
Profit and loss account	(W4)			1,348.02
				1,948.02
Minority interests	(W5)			105.98
				2,054.00

Workings

W1 Cost of control (80%)

	£m		£m
Investment in Wind	550	Share capital	160
		Profit and loss (210 x 80%)	168
		Revaluation reserve	32
		Goodwill (bal. fig.)	190
	550		550

W2 Tangible fixed assets

	£m		£m
Earth	540	Profit and loss (depreciation)	
Wind	280	(£40 ÷ 10 years)	4
Revaluation reserve	40	Profit and loss (reserves)	
		(£40 ÷ 10 years x 4 years)	16
		CBS	840
	860		860

W3 Investment in associated undertaking (30% Water)

	£m		£m
Investment in Water	200	Profit and loss – goodwill	
Share of post-acquisition		Amortisation (£59 ÷ 10 yrs)	5.9
profits (30% x 360 – 310)	15	CBS	209.1
	215		215

Fair value of purchase consideration		200
Fair value of net assets acquired (160 + 310)	470 x 30%	141
Goodwill on acquisition		59

W4 Profit and loss account

	£m		£m
Cost of control	168	Earth	1,370
Minority interest (310 x 20%)	62	Wind	310
Inter-co. stock profits		Share of Water's post-acq. profits	15
(25/125 x 0.5 x 80%)	0.08		
Tangible fixed assets			
(20 depreciation x 80%)	16		
Goodwill amortised – Wind	95		
Goodwill amortised – Water	5.9		
CBS	1,348.02		
	1,695.00		1,695

W5 Minority interests (20% Wind)

	£m		£m
Inter-co. stock profits		Share capital	40
(25/125 x 0.5 x 20%)	0.02	Revaluation reserve	8
Tangible fixed assets		Profit and loss	62
(20 depreciation x 20%)	4		
CBS	105.98		
	110.00		110

W6 Revaluation reserve

	£m		£m
Cost of control (80%)	32	Tangible fixed assets	40
Minority interest (20%)	8		
	40		40

(c, d)

Internal memorandum

To: Finance director
From: Group financial controller
Date: 27 November 2000

Re: Accounting treatment adopted and disclosures to be made in respect of Water Ltd in the 1999 financial statements

Earth plc owns 30 per cent of the ordinary share capital of Water Ltd and therefore FRS 9 *Associates and Joint Ventures* is applicable. FRS 9 deals with the accounting treatment for associates, joint ventures and joint arrangements. It was published by the ASB in November 1997 and should be adopted by companies with accounting periods ending on or after 23 June 1998. The objective of the FRS is to reflect the effect on an investor's financial position and performance of its interests in associates and joint ventures as a result of its participating interest and significant influence in associates and of its long-term interest and joint control of its joint ventures.

Associate

An associate is defined as:

> 'An entity (other than a subsidiary) in which another entity (the investor) has a *participating interest* and over whose operating and financial policies the investor exercises a *significant influence.*'

Participating interest
This is generally presumed to represent a shareholding of more than 20 per cent that is held for the long term for the purpose of securing a contribution to the investor's activities by the exercise of control or influence arising from that interest. It must be beneficial and the benefits must be linked to the active exercise of significant influence over the investor's operating and financial policies. However, the 20 per cent rule is only presumptive and the key is the extent to which an entity actually actively gets involved in the decision-making of the investee.

Exercises a significant influence
The investor must be actively involved and influential in the investee's policies, particularly strategic issues such as:
• expansion/contraction of the business, changes in markets, etc.;
• dividend policy.

Note: Company legislation still has a rebuttable presumption that a 20 per cent holding is an associate and that both a participating interest and the exercise of significant influence exists. If a company feels that this should be rebutted that fact must be noted in the notes to the financial statements.

Accounting for associates

Consolidated accounts
Should adopt the equity method for all primary statements whereby the investment is initially recorded at cost, including any goodwill arising. Subsequently, the value is adjusted each period by the investor's share of the results of its investee less any amortisation of goodwill, share of relevant gains and losses and distributions to owners, i.e. dividends. The share of results is required to be recognised in the profit and loss account.

Investor's accounts
Should value the fixed asset investment at cost less amounts written off, or at valuation.

Consolidated profit and loss account
Share of associate's operating results should be included in the profit and loss account after group operating profits/losses. Any goodwill amortised should be included at this point. Share of exceptional items/interest should be disclosed separately from group accounts. All the investor's share in an associate should be included within the group totals although its share of tax should be separately noted.

Share of associate's turnover can be provided as a memorandum in the profit and loss but clearly distinguished from group turnover. Similarly, the investor's share of turnover should be clearly distinguished from group turnover.

Consolidated statement of total recognised gains and losses (STRGL)
The investor's share of total recognised gains and losses should be shown separately, if material, on the STRGL, or in a note referred to in the STRGL.

Consolidated balance sheet
The investor's share of net assets in the associate should be disclosed separately and any goodwill on acquisition less write-downs should be included, but disclosed separately.

Consolidated cash flow statements
Dividends received from associates should be included as a separate item below operating activities but before returns on investments and servicing of finance.

Disclosure
General – name, percentage of each class of share held, accounting period, indication of the nature of the business, material notes (e.g. contingencies and commitments) and balances due/to.

Additional – if certain thresholds are achieved (15 per cent and 25 per cent) based on share of gross assets, gross liabilities, turnover and three-year operating profit average.

Accounting for Air Ltd in the 2000 financial statements

FRS 9 *Associates and Joint Ventures* requires the investor's share of its joint venture's turnover to be disclosed in the consolidated profit and loss account – but not part of group turnover. Company legislation *only* permits group turnover exclusive of joint ventures. The disclosure should be as follows:

	£m
Turnover, including share of joint ventures (30 + (36 – 30 x 50%))	33
Less share of joint venture turnover	(3)
Group turnover	30
Cost of sales	(18)
Group operating profit	12
Share of operating profit of joint venture	3
Operating profit including share of joint venture	15

Note the elimination of inter-company sales and purchases of £30m. This must be deducted in arriving at the true amount of third-party turnover and profit.

Solution 12 – Baden plc

(A) (i) Distinguish between trade investment and associate

The main difference between an associate and an ordinary trade investment is that, in the latter case, the investor takes a passive role in the running of the business but in the former the shareholders do exercise considerable influence over the operating and financial policies of the investee. The associate normally implements accounting policies that are consistent with those of the investor. Under FRS 9 *Associates and Joint Ventures* the investor must actually exercise both a significant influence and have a participating interest so as to ensure that the investor secures a contribution to its activities by the exercise of control or influence.

FRS 9 states that a holding of 20 per cent or more of the voting rights suggests, but does not ensure, that the investor exercises significant influence. There is a presumption that the investor is involved in the strategic decisions made by the company. The FRS also suggests that the attitude towards the investee's dividend policy may indicate the status of the investment. In order to have associate status it would appear that the investor should have board representation in order for it to be able to participate in the decision-making process. The investor must be able not only to exercise influence but it should also be able to exercise it actively.

(A) (ii) Distinguish between a joint arrangement and a joint venture

A joint venture must be an entity whereas a joint arrangement is not. An entity is normally a limited company, partnership or incorporation association which has been set up to carry on a business or trade of its own. One example would be a number of oil companies that would be setting up a pipeline in the Alaskan tundra as a joint arrangement. This would be set up as it is too expensive and also environmentally unfriendly for a number of pipelines to be set up separately by each of the companies. All significant decisions are taken by all the participants.

However, a joint venture is where a separate entity has been set up and all parties require the consent of each other for any decision to be taken. Joint ventures are set up, however, for the purpose of making profits.

The accounting treatment of a joint arrangement is that the investor should record its own share of the joint venture's assets and liabilities and its incomes/expenses . However, in joint ventures, because they are legal entities they can only record the entity's share of profits/losses and gross assets/gross liabilities on the profit and loss account and balance sheet. It is illegal to record individual assets/liabilities on balance sheet as the entity has no control over the usage of such assets. Joint arrangements are, in effect, recorded as proportional consolidations.

(B) (i) How should the investment in Baden plc be treated in the consolidated balance sheet and profit and loss account?

The investment should be disclosed as a single line under FRS 9 as follows:

Calculation of goodwill

At 1 January 1997 – fair value of assets

	£m
Tangible fixed assets	30
Current assets	31
Creditors – within one year	(20)
Creditors – more than one year	(8)
	33
Shareholding 30% x £33m	9.9
Fair value of investment (note i)	14
Goodwill (bal fig.)	4.1

	£m
Disclosure in balance sheet	
Cost of investment	14
Post-acquisition profits 30% x (32 – 10 share capital plus 9 profit and loss reserve)	3.9
Goodwill written off (2 years x £1m per annum)	(2)
Additional depreciation charge (2 years x 20% x (30 fair value – 20 cost) x 30%	(1.2)
Investment in associate	14.7
Alternative disclosure	
Share of net assets (46 – share of stock profits 10)	36
Revaluation of tangible fixed assets	10
Additional depreciation (£10m x 20% = £2m x 2 years)	(4)
	42
Shareholding 30% x £42m	12.6
Share of goodwill (£4.1m less two years' amortisation £2m)	2.1
Investment in associate	14.7

The alternative disclosure is more correct since it does not disclose any element of profit as part of the investment.

Disclosure in the profit and loss account

	£m
Share of operating profit in associate	
(30% x £29m = £8.7m – goodwill 1 – inter-co. profit 3 – depreciation 0.6.m)	4.1
Exceptional item – associate (30% x £10m)	(3.0)
Interest payable – associate (30% x £4m)	(1.2)
Tax on profit on ordinary activities	
Associate (30% x £3m)	(0.9)

(B) *(ii) Show how the treatment of Baden plc changes if Baden were classified as an investment in joint venture*

Joint venture – gross equity method

Consolidated profit and loss

		£m
Turnover: Group and share of joint ventures		X + 53.1
(£212m gross less inter-company turnover £35m x 30%)		
Less share of joint venture turnover		(53.1)
Group turnover		X

Consolidated balance sheet

Share of gross assets		*21.3
Share of gross liabilities (30% x 12 + 10)		(6.6)
		14.7

* Computation of share of gross assets

			£m
Fixed assets	£37m + £10m revaluation – 4 additional depreciation	= 43 x 30% =	12.9
Stocks	£31m – 10 inter-company profit on stocks	= 21 x 30% =	6.3
			19.2m
Goodwill	£4.1m – amortised £2m		2.1m
			21.3m

10

Foreign Currency Translation

Solution 1 – Foreign currency translation

(a) *The difference between foreign currency conversion and translation*

Conversion

The process of conversion is adopted when an individual company needs to convert its exports/imports into sterling for its own financial statements. It is the actual exchange of one currency into another so that accounting statements are presented in a common currency. Exchange gains/losses will occur on conversion and will be credited/charged direct to the profit and loss account. Conversion will result in a real or realised gain/loss as the transaction to which it relates is complete.

Translation

The process of translation occurs when the assets, liabilities, income and expenses of an overseas branch or subsidiary are translated from a foreign currency into sterling prior to consolidation. This is necessary to enable the group financial statements to be recorded in the common currency of the dominant or parent organisation.

Translation does not result in a realised gain or loss until such time as the branch or subsidiary is disposed of.

(b) *Stated objectives of translation and any alternatives*

Paragraph 2 of SSAP 20 states the following objectives of foreign currency translation:

(1) The translation should produce results which are generally compatible with the effects of rate changes on a company's cash flows and equity.

(2) The translation should ensure that the financial statements present a true and fair view of the results of management actions.

(3) Consolidated accounts should reflect the financial results and relationships as measured in the foreign currency financial statements prior to translation.

Possible alternative objectives are as follows:

(1) Financial statements could be translated at the rates ruling at the transaction date, not at the closing rate. However, this is only permissible for conversion purposes and for use in the temporal method, i.e. when a subsidiary is a direct extension of the parent and is totally dependent on the parent company's currency.

(2) Ensure that the financial statements reflect commercial reality by adopting the actual rate of exchange ruling at the date of the transaction.

(c) Hyper-inflation – why adjust local currency financial statements first?

Where a foreign enterprise operates in a country with a very high rate of inflation the process of translation may not fairly present the financial position of that enterprise in a set of historical cost accounts (SSAP 20, Paragraph 26).

An example can illustrate the problem:

If inflation is 100 per cent per annum then a fixed asset purchased five years ago will be stated at a cost which is approximately only 6 per cent of its original value. This means that it becomes insignificant within the group accounts. One way around this in single companies has been the adoption of a modified version of historical cost accounting. A similar analogy would be to require annual revaluation of all foreign currency assets.

SSAP 20 therefore recommends that where hyper-inflation exists, foreign currency financial statements should first be 'revalued' locally. The process of translation can then take place. This is a combination of inflation and translation. This has been taken further by the Urgent Issues Task Force in Abstract No. 9. This states that in hyper-inflation situations (defined as 100 per cent inflation over three years) either the financial statements must be translated into a functional currency first or they must be prepared on a current price level basis prior to translation.

(d) Recording exchange gains and losses as movements on reserves

Reserve accounting is permitted for companies who invest in a foreign country and protect their currency exposure risk by financing the investment from foreign currency borrowings. The borrowings need not necessarily be in the same currency as the investment.

Exposure to exchange rate movements is therefore *hedged*.

In these situations the movement in borrowings is matched against the movement in the investments, and therefore economically no real gain or loss has been created. Thus under Paragraph 27 there are special provisions whereby the gain or loss on investments abroad are treated as monetary assets and not as non-monetary. The gain or loss is therefore recorded on the non-monetary investment and is available for offset against the gain or loss on borrowings. The offset is restricted to the lower of the two movements and only the difference is credited or written off to reserves.

Non-monetary assets are normally recorded at the exchange rate ruling at the date of transaction, and therefore any gain or loss on borrowings would go straight to the profit and loss account.

Solution 2 – SSAP 20

(a) The closing rate/net investment method

The closing rate method of translation assumes that a company which invests in an overseas entity is intending the investment to be long term and is interested mainly in dividend income and probably a long-term capital gain. The investor is not interested in the value of the individual assets and liabilities.

Overseas entities will often finance their operations in local currency loans, and generally they can be argued to be independent of the parent company.

The method assumes that the parent company records its investment in the foreign company at its net worth by translating the assets and liabilities in the balance sheet at the exchange rate ruling at the year end date. The profit and loss account can be translated at either the closing rate or at a weighted average rate if it is felt that this would show a fairer representation of the year's results. The particular policy adopted should be consistent from year to year.

(b) The temporal method

The temporal method should be adopted when a company invests in an overseas entity but the entity's affairs are so interlinked with the parent that it is really regarded as a direct extension of the parent's own activities. The entity is usually totally dependent on sterling as a currency and on the economic environment of the parent. The temporal method therefore attempts to record the investment in the foreign country as if the company were investing in specific assets and liabilities.

Monetary assets and liabilities are therefore translated at the exchange rate ruling at the end of the year, but non-monetary assets are translated at the exchange rate at their date of purchase. The profit and loss account should be translated at the rate when the transactions occurred, but in practice the average rate is adopted for ease of calculation.

(c) Using the temporal method

The temporal method should be adopted in preparing the consolidated financial statements when the relationship between the investor and the foreign entity is so close that the latter is a *direct extension* of the parent company.

Paragraph 23 of SSAP 20 sets out the factors to be considered:

(1) The extent to which the cash flows of the enterprise have a direct impact upon those of the investor.

(2) The extent to which the functions of the enterprise are directly dependent upon the investor.

(3) The currency in which the majority of the trading transactions are denominated, i.e. sterling.

(4) The major currency to which the operation is exposed in its financing structure, i.e. sterling.

Examples of situations where the temporal method may be adopted are stated in SSAP 20, Paragraph 24:

(1) When a foreign entity acts as a *selling agent* for the investor.

(2) When a foreign entity works as a *subcontractor* for the investor.

(3) When a foreign entity is *located overseas* for tax or exchange control purposes.

(d) Using the average rate for translating the profit and loss account

A holding company would adopt an average rate and not a closing rate for translating the profit and loss account because it better reflects the way in which profit accrues over the year, particularly if the exchange rates are volatile.

Over the last few years exchange rates have changed rapidly. This could have led to an artificially high or low exchange rate for the company at the year end which would fail to reflect a fair view of the performance for the year.

The company may have already adopted average rates in their monthly management accounts, and this would merely be an extension of that process.

Solution 3 – FC plc

(a) Journal entries for foreign currency transactions

(1) French supplier

	£	£
Dr Purchases	29,630	
Cr Creditors		29,630
Being the purchase of goods from France on 1 May 2001.		
(FF 280,000 @ FF9.45/£1)		
Dr Creditors	31,579	
Cr Bank		31,579
Being the payment for goods purchased from France on 1 August 2001.		
(FF300,000 @ FF9.50/£1)		
Dr Purchases	33,684	
Cr Creditors		33,684
Being the purchase of goods from France on 1 November 2001.		
(FF320,000 @ FF9.50/£1)		
Dr Creditors	674	
Cr Profit and loss (exchange gain)		674
Being the exchange gain on translation of creditors at the year end rate of exchange.		

Working
French supplier

	FF	£	£		FF	£	£
Bank	300,000	9.50	31,579	Balance b/d	50,000	9.60	5,208
Exchange gain			674	Purchases	280,000	9.45	29,630
Balance c/d	350,000	9.65	36,269	Purchases	320,000	9.50	33,684
	650,000		68,522		650,000		68,522

(2) Investment in Belgian customer

Non-monetary assets are normally recorded at the exchange rate ruling at the date of transaction, and the carrying value is left unchanged. An exception is hedging, when the acquisition of an asset is financed by a foreign currency loan to protect against fluctuations. In this case the value of the non-monetary asset is allowed to float according to the current exchange rate.

			£	£
2000	Dr Investments		56,250	
	Cr Bank			56,250
	Being the purchase of 8% investment in Belgian customer in 2000.			
	(BF3,600,000 @ BF64/£1)			
2000	Dr Bank		57,143	
	Cr Loan			57,143
	Being the creation of a loan to finance the Belgian customer.			
	(DM180,000 @ DM3.15/£1)			
1.1.01	Dr Investments		1,350	
	Cr Exchange gain			1,350
	Being an exchange gain for 2000 recorded in the financial statements.			
	(BF3,600,000 @ BF62.5/£1 = 57,600 – 56,250)			
1.1.01	Dr Exchange loss		549	
	Cr Loan			549
	Being exchange loss on loan.			
	(DM180,000 @ DM3.12/£1 = 57,692 – 57,143)			

		£	£
31.12.01	Dr Investments	2,300	
	(BF3,600,000 @ BF60.10/£1 = 59,900 – 57,600)		
	Cr Loan		1,324
	(DM180,000 @ DM3.05/£1 = 59,016 – 57,692)		
	Exchange gain		976
	Being exchange gain for the year.		

		£	£
31.12.01	Dr Debtors	632	
	Cr Income from fixed asset investments		632
	Being dividend received from the Belgian investment.		
	(BF38,000 @ BF60.10/£1)		

(3) Investment in Italian resort

	Lire ('000)	Lire/£1	£	
Property and fittings	520,000	2,130	244,131	Dr
Net current assets	106,000	2,130	49,765	Dr
			293,896	
Loan from Italian bank	400,000	2,130	187,793	Cr
Branch account			106,103	Cr
			293,896	

Translation of balances relating to Italian branch, at closing rate.

	£	£
Dr Bank	69,450	
Exchange loss	2,665	
Cr Branch current a/c		72,115
Being translation at average rate of remittances from foreign branch.		

	£	£
Dr Exchange loss	3,986	
Cr Branch current a/c		3,986
Being unrealised loss on translation of branch balance sheet.		

Working

Branch current account

	Lire ('000)	Lire/£1	£		Lire ('000)	Lire/£1	£
Balance b/f	204,000	2,050	99,512	Bank	150,000	2,080	72,115
Profit	172,000	2,080	82,692	Exchange loss			3,986
				Balance c/d	226,000	2,130	106,103
	376,000		182,204		376,000		182,204

(b) Balance sheet extracts as at 31.12.01

Fixed assets		2001	2000
Tangible assets	(a) (3) (520,000 ÷ 2,130/2,050)	244,131	253,658
Investments	(a) (2)	59,900	57,600
Current assets			
Prepayments and accrued income	(a) (2)	632	Unknown
Italian branch	(a) (3) (106,000 ÷ 2,130)/(84,000 ÷ 2,050)	49,765	40,976
Creditors: amounts falling due within one year			
Trade creditors	(a) (1) (350,000 ÷ 9.65)/ (50,000 ÷ 9.60)	36,269	5,208
Creditors: amounts falling due after one year			
	(a) (2)	59,016	57,692
	(a) (3) (400,000 ÷ 2,130/2,050)	187,793	195,122
		246,809	252,814

(c) The accounting treatment of the specific exchange differences

French supplier

This is a transactions problem, therefore translate all monetary assets and liabilities at the closing rate and non-monetary assets at the rate of exchange at their date of purchase or revaluation.

All exchange gains and losses must go through the profit and loss account (£674 for 2001 – SSAP 20, Paragraph 29).

Belgian investment

On hedging, the net exchange gain is taken direct to reserves (£976 for 2001 – SSAP 20, Paragraph 29).

Italian investment

Transactions (including remittances) should lead to exchange gains and losses being charged direct to profit and loss if they arise between the holding company and the subsidiary (£2,665 – SSAP 20, Paragraph 12).

Italian balance sheet

The loss on translation under the closing rate is unrealised and should be taken direct to reserves (£3,986 for 2001 – SSAP 20, Paragraph 19).

Solution 4 – Stunt Ltd

(a) Purchase of raw materials from USA

(i) $84,000/1.58 = £53,164.56

being the purchase of raw materials and trade creditors which should be recorded at a rate ruling at the transaction date at 1 December 1995.

(ii) $84,000/1.56 = £53,846.15 (trade creditor)

There is no change in the stock value of £53,164.56 since stock is a non-monetary item. An exchange loss arises on the retranslation of the monetary creditor and this equals £681.59 and should be expended to profit and loss (£53,846.15 – £53,164.56).

(iii) $84,000/1.60 = £52,500 (settlement of trade creditor)

The payment of £52,500 is less than the previous value and therefore an exchange gain of £1,346.15 is credited to profit and loss account (£53,846.15 – £52,500).

(iv) An exchange loss of £681.59 will be charged as a loss in the profit and loss account for the year ended 31 December 1995.

An exchange gain of £1,346.15 will be credited in the profit and loss account for the year ended 31 December 1996.

(b) French sales

The sales will be translated at the rate ruling on the date of the transaction (i.e. 1 December 1995)

FF600,000/10.8 = £55,555.56

At the year end (31 December 1995) the debtor, which is a monetary item, will be retranslated at the closing rate

FF600,000/9.6 = £62,500

This gives rise to an exchange gain of £6,944.44 which should be credited to profit and loss in the year ended 31 December 1995 (i.e. £62,500 – £55,555.56).

At the date of settlement at 31 January 1996

FF600,000/12.8 = £46,875

This gives an exchange loss of £15,625 which will be charged to the profit and loss account for the year ended 31 December 1996 (i.e. £82,500 – £46,875).

(c) Investment in Germany

(i) Foreign equity investments, which are financed by foreign borrowings, can adopt the hedging rules of SSAP 20 as long as the investment can either be sold or can generate sufficient future cash flows to repay borrowings. This enables any exchange gains/losses on the investment to be 'floated' and offset against the exchange gains/losses on the borrowings to the extent of the lower of the differences with any excess differences being charged/credited direct to reserves.

Investment: DM1,850,000/8.5	=	£217,647.05 initial investment
Borrowing: DM2,500,000/8.5	=	£294,117.64

(ii) Assuming no change in the investment and borrowing at the year end:

Investment: DM1,850,000/8.4	=	£220,238.09 (exchange gain of £2,591.04)
Borrowing: DM2,500,000/8.4	=	£297,619.04 (exchange loss of £3,501.40)

The two differences can be offset but the excess loss of £910.36 must be credited to reserves for the year ended 31 December 1995.

(d) Investment in Germany (continued)

(i) *Exchange gain/loss on settlement*

Repayment:	DM2,500,000/8.6	=	£290,697.67
As per (C)	DM2,500,000/8.4	=	£297,619.04
	Exchange gain		£6,921.37

(ii) *Value of the investment at 30 June 1996 and at 31 December 1996*

Investment	DM1,850,000/8.4	=	£220,238.09 (31 December 1995)
Investment	DM1,850,000/8.6	=	£215,116.27 (31 December 1996)
	Exchange loss		£5,121.82

Investment must be restated at the exchange rate at the date when the hedging borrowing is settled as subsequently all exchange gains/losses must be charged/credited to profit and loss. The investment must now be treated as a non-monetary asset.

(iii) *Accounting treatment of exchange gains and losses*

Exchange gain on borrowing	Cr	Reserves	£6,921.37
	Dr	Profit and loss	1,799.55
Exchange loss on investment	Dr	Reserves	£5,121.82

(e) *Accounting policies (extract)*

Accounting for foreign currencies

Transactions in foreign currencies are translated into pounds sterling at the rates ruling at the dates of the transactions.

Amounts receivable and payable in foreign currencies at the balance sheet date are translated at exchange rates ruling at the balance sheet date.

All translation differences are taken directly to the profit and loss account with the exception of where the company has borrowed foreign currencies to finance or provide a hedge against its foreign equity investments. In these circumstances the equity investments are translated each year at the closing rates of exchange and any difference taken to reserves are offset as a reserve movement by the exchange gain or loss on translating the foreign currency loans at the closing rates. Exchange gains and losses on the borrowings are offset only to the extent of the exchange differences arising on equity investments, any excess being charged/credited to reserves.

Solution 5 – Somco plc

Transaction A

		£	£
4.3.02	Dr Fixed assets (130,000 nidars ÷ 0.65)	200,000	
	Cr Creditors		200,000
25.8.02	Dr Creditors	200,000	
	Exchange loss – profit & loss	60,000	
	Cr Bank (130,000 nidars ÷ 0.50)		260,000

This is a normal trading transaction and should be written off as 'other operating expenses' in the profit and loss account.

Transaction B

		£	£
27.2.02	Dr Debtors (476,000 krams ÷ 7/£1)	68,000	
	Cr Sales		68,000
27.2.02	Dr Cost of sales	46,000	
	Cr Stock		46,000
25.5.02	Dr Bank (476,000 krams ÷ 6.7/£1)	71,045	
	Cr Debtors		68,000
	Exchange gain – profit & loss		3,045

This is a normal trading transaction and should be disclosed under the appropriate headings of sales, cost of sales, and gross profit. The exchange gain should be included under the heading 'other operating income' in the profit and loss account.

Transaction C

		£	£
2.9.02	Dr Debtors (53.376m sarils ÷ 2,224/£1)	24,000	
	Cr Sales		24,000
2.9.02	Dr Cost of sales	17,000	
	Cr Stock		17,000
31.12.02	Dr Exchange loss – profit and loss	277	
	Cr Debtors (53.376m ÷ 2,250/£1 = 23,723 – 24,000 = 277 loss)		277
7.2.03	Dr Bank (53.376m ÷ 2,306/£)	23,147	
	Cr Debtors		23,147
7.2.03	Dr Exchange loss – profit and loss	576	
	Cr Debtors (23,147 – 23,723)		576

This is a normal trading transaction and should be disclosed under the appropriate headings of sales, cost of sales, and gross profit. The debtor must be restated at the exchange rate at the year end as it is monetary in nature and the loss of £277 must be written off to the profit and loss account in 2002. The subsequent loss of £576 is caused by an event which occurred after the year end and is thus non-adjusting. It would only be disclosed in the notes if it is regarded to be material, and necessary to give the user a proper understanding of the financial statements.

Transaction D

		£	£
25.5.02	Dr Bank (426,000 rolads ÷ 1.5/£1)	284,000	
	Cr Loan		284,000
11.11.02	Dr Loan	284,000	
	Cr Bank (426,000 rolads ÷ 1.8/£1)		236,667
	Exchange gain		47,333

Although this is not a trading profit it should be written off in the profit and loss account under the heading 'other interest receivable and similar income'.

Transaction E

		£	£
9.11.01	Dr Investment (196,000 krams ÷ 7.3/£1)	26,849	
	Cr Loan (15,000 nidars ÷ 0.56/£1)		26,786
	Bank		63
31.12.01	Dr Investment (196,000 krams ÷ 6.9/£1 = 28,406 − 26,849 = 1,557)	1,557	
	C Exchange gain		1,557
	Dr Exchange loss	2,060	
	Cr Loan (15,000 nidars ÷ 0.52/£1 = 28,846 − 26,786 = 2,060)		2,060

The exchange loss of £2,060 can be offset against the exchange gain of £1,557. The excess loss of £503 must be charged to profit and loss under 'other interest payable and similar expenses'. The offset of £1,557 is carried out within the reserves (SSAP 20, Paragraph 51).

		£	£
31.12.02	Dr Exchange loss	2,273	
	Cr Investment (196,000 krams ÷ 7.5 = 26,133 − 28,406)		2,273
	Dr Loan (15,000 nidars ÷ 0.54 = 27,778 − 28,846)	1,068	
	Cr Exchange gain		1,068

The exchange loss of £2,273 on the loan is offset against the exchange gain in the reserves, but only to the extent of £1,068. The excess loss of £1,205 would be charged to the profit and loss account as in 2001.

Transaction F

Branch current account (head office)

		Rolads	R/£1	£			Rolads	R/£1	£
1.1.02	Balance b/d	638,600	1.6	399,125	2002	Bank	207,300	1.7	121,941
2002	Net profit	423,400	1.7	249,059		Exchange loss			98,893
					Dec.	Bal.c/d	854,700	2.0	427,350
		1,062,000		648,184			1,062,000		648,184

Composition of exchange losses

	£	£
Exchange loss on remittances		
207,300 ÷ 1.7/£1 average		121,941
207,300 actual		116,727
		5,214

Retranslation loss		£
Opening balance	638,600 Rs ÷ 1.6/£1	399,125
	638,600 Rs ÷ 2/£1	319,300
		79,825

Net profit restated			
	(423,400 – 207,300) 1.7/£1	127,118	
	(423,400 – 207,300) 2/£1	108,050	
			19,068
			98,893

The exchange loss of £5,214 is really a trading item and should be written off as an 'other operating expense'. The retranslation loss is unrealised and has no impact at present on cash flow. This loss should therefore be taken direct to reserves.

Solution 6 – Able Ltd

The translation method adopted (per SSAP 20) must depend on whether or not the New York branch is independent from the UK company. Normally the closing rate method is adopted unless the US branch is totally dependent on the UK. This would be indicated by most of the trading being in sterling, not in dollars. This is a judgemental issue, but it is assumed here that New York is sufficiently independent to be accounted for using the closing rate method.

Profit and loss account for New York for year ended 30 April 2001

All amounts are translated at the average rate of £1 = $1.74

	$	$	£	£
Sales		720,000		413,793
Opening stock	95,000		54,598	
Purchases	500,000		287,356	
	595,000		341,954	
Less closing stock	108,000		62,069	
		487,000		279,885
Gross profit		233,000		133,908
Local expenses	190,000		109,195	
Depreciation – showroom (4%)	20,000		11,494	
Depreciation – warehouse (4%)	12,000		6,897	
Loan interest (12% × 600,000)	72,000		41,379	
		294,000		168,965
Net loss for the year		(61,000)		(35,057)

Balance sheet of New York branch as at 30 April 2001

All amounts are translated at the closing rate of £1 = $1.70

	$	$	£	£
Fixed assets				
At cost	800,000		470,588	
Less accumulated depreciation	115,000		67,647	
		685,000		402,941

Balance sheet continued

	$	$	£	£
Current assets				
Stocks	108,000		63,529	
Debtors	70,000		41,177	
Cash	8,000		4,706	
	186,000		109,412	
Less current liabilities				
Local creditors	24,000		14,118	
Accruals – loan interest	60,000		35,294	
	84,000		49,412	
Net current assets		102,000		60,000
Total assets less current liabilities		787,000		462,941
Long-term loan		600,000		352,941
		187,000		110,000
Represented by				
Head office account		187,000		110,000

Workings

(1) Movement in head office account

	$		£
Opening balance 30 April 2000	230,000	1.58	145,570
Add loss for the year	(61,000)	1.74	(35,057)
Purchases	500,000	1.70	294,117
Remittances	(482,000)	1.70	(283,529)
Translation profit/loss (W2)	—		(11,101)
Closing balance 30 April 2001	187,000		110,000

(2) Profit/loss on translation

		$		£	£
Opening head office account					
Balance 30 April 2000	(op. rate)	230,000	1.58	145,570	
	(cl. rate)	230,000	1.70	135,294	
Loss					(10,276)
Translation of profit/loss for the year					
Net loss	(av. rate)	(61,000)	1.74	35,057	
	(cl. rate)	(61,000)	1.70	35,882	
					(825)
Total loss on translation					(11,101)

(3) Remittances

$			£
95,000	@	1.60	59,375
72,000	@	1.70	42,353
135,000	@	1.82	74,176
180,000	@	1.76	102,272
			278,176
Per head office account			283,529
Exchange loss			5,353

The exchange loss in the head office account should be treated as a movement in reserves.

Solution 7 – Farr Ltd

(a) *Closing rate method*

The closing rate method is used in the majority of cases to translate the financial statements of overseas subsidiaries into sterling prior to consolidation. This method recognises that an investor company regards its foreign subsidiaries as fully independent enterprises. Therefore their acquisitions are long-term investments in the net worth of those businesses as going concerns. The investor is not particularly interested in the individual assets and liabilities of those subsidiaries. In most cases the day-to-day operations of the subsidiaries are conducted in the currency of that subsidiary.

In a minority of situations, it is possible for the affairs of a subsidiary to be so interdependent with those of the investor that it is no longer appropriate to regard the foreign subsidiary as a separate entity. It is as if the investor has effectively 'jumped' over to the other country and is trading in its own right in that country. In this situation, where the subsidiary is a direct extension of the investor, the assets and liabilities should be treated as if they belonged directly to the investor and translated using the temporal method.

(b) *Consolidated balance sheet as at 31 December 2001*

	£'000
Intangible fixed assets	
Goodwill (W3)	720
Tangible fixed assets (900 + 1,210 + 600)	2,710
Net current assets (250 + 300 + 290)	840
Long-term loans	(2,350)
	1,920
Share capital	1,000
Reserves (W3)	920
	1,920

Statement of exchange differences

		Rocky Inc £'000		Baer GmbH £'000	Total £'000
Balance at 1 January 2001 (note 6)		(104)		29	(75)
Arising on opening net assets	(W1)	(134)	(W2)	46	(88)
Arising on profits for the year	(W1)	(17)	(W2)	5	(12)
		(255)		80	(175)

(c) *Alternative methods of accounting*

Non-monetary assets should be translated under SSAP 20 at the original rate at the transaction date. Monetary assets and liabilities are retranslated at each balance sheet exchange rate. Any exchange differences should be included in the profit and loss account. Farr has therefore included the exchange gain on the loan of £70,000 (W4) in the 2001 accounts.

The alternative accounting treatment is to *hedge*, a method which is available for foreign equity investments financed by foreign currency borrowings. This is achieved by denominating the investment at closing rate, i.e. allowing a non-monetary asset to be retranslated. The exchange gain or loss on the investment can be offset to the extent of the loss or gain on the borrowings. Any excess must be written off to the profit and loss account.

The impact on Farr Ltd's accounts would be to reduce the profits by £80,000, the offsetting process of £70,000 taking care of the remainder of the exchange loss.

(d) *The disposal of the investment in Baer GmbH*

The disposal of Baer GmbH would relate to a material segment, and under FRS 3 this is a closure of a significant part of the company's business and should be disclosed as an exceptional loss. No extraordinary item would be shown.

The trading results for the five months to 31 May 2002 should be separately disclosed as 'profit from discontinued operations' with suitable comparatives.

	£'000	£'000
Disclosure in parent company accounts		
Sale proceeds (note 7) DM4m @ 2.80 1.6.02		1,429
Cost		750
Exceptional loss		679
Disclosure in group accounts		
Sale proceeds (note 7) DM4m @ 2.80 1.6.02		1,429
Net assets at 31.12.01	890	
Retained profits to 31.5.02	163	
(DM480,000 @ 2.95)		1,053
Exceptional profit		376

Workings

(1) *Translation of Rocky Inc. balance sheet at 31 December 2001*

	$'000	Rate	£'000
Goodwill	975	1.5	650
Tangible fixed assets	1,815	1.5	1,210
Net current assets	450	1.5	300
Loan due to Farr Ltd	(1,875)	1.5	(1,250)
	1,365		910
Share capital (note 2)	525	1.05	500
Profit and loss account			
Current (note 8)	360	1.40	257
Prior years	480		*304
Exchange gains/(losses) (see below)	–		(151)
	1,365		910

	£'000
*Net assets at 31.12.00 (1,365 – 360 = 1,005 @ 1.25, note 9)	804
Less share capital	500
Reserves at 31.12.00	304

		£'000	£'000
Exchange differences			
Opening net assets – at opening rate	1,005 @ 1.25		804
– at closing rate	1,005 @ 1.50		670
			(134)
Profits for the year – at average rate	360 @ 1.40	257	
– at closing rate	360 @ 1.50	240	
			(17)
Exchange loss			(151)

(2) Translation of Baer GmbH at 31 December 2001

	DM'000	Rate	£'000
Tangible fixed assets	1,800	3.00	600
Net current assets	870	3.00	290
	2,670		890
Share capital (note 3)	1,020	3.40	300
Profit and loss account			
Current (note 8)	465	3.10	150
Prior year (note 3)	680	3.40	200
	505		*189
Exchange gains/(losses) (see below)	–		51
	2,670		890

	£'000
* Net assets at 31.12.00 (2,670 – 465 = 2,205 @ 3.20, note 9)	689
Less share capital and pre-acquisition reserves	500
	189

			£'000	£'000
Exchange differences				
Opening net assets	– at opening rate	2,205 @ 3.20		689
Opening net assets	– at closing rate	2,205 @ 3.00		735
				46
Profit for the year	– at average rate	465 @ 3.10	150	
	– at closing rate	465 @ 3.00	155	
				5
Exchange gain				51

(3) Consolidation workings

Cost of control

	£'000			£'000
Investment in Rocky Inc.	500	Share capital	– R	500
Investment in Baer	750	Share capital	– B	300
		Reserves	– B	200
		Goodwill		250
	1,250			1,250

Reserves

	£'000			£'000
Pre-acquisition profits – B	200	Balance	– F	300
Goodwill written off	180		– R	410
Consolidated balance sheet	920		– B	590
	1,300			1,300

Goodwill

	£'000		£'000
Balance – R	650	Reserves (20% × 900)	180
Cost of control	250	Consolidated balance sheet	720
	900		900

(4) Exchange differences on loan to finance Rocky Inc.

		£'000
Loan of $525,000 (note 2)	@ $1.50 31.12.01	350
$525,000	@ $1.25 31.12.00	420
Exchange gain		70
Investment of $525,000	@ $1.50 31.12.01	350
$525,000	@ $1.05 at acquisition	500
Exchange loss		150

Solution 8 – Howard plc

(a) Why the trade of Pau is more dependent on the economic environment of Howard plc

There are two methods of foreign currency translation – the temporal and the closing rate methods. The former must be adopted where an overseas entity is more dependent on the currency of the parent than in its own currency. Often it has been set up purely as a selling agency or sub-assembly operation. It is really a 'direct extension' of the parent's own business into that country. The foreign entity would be unlikely to survive without the parent company's support.

SSAP 20 sets out some criteria that should be investigated but these should all be looked at together before finally deciding on the most appropriate method to adopt. The factors that should be considered include:

(1) the currency in which most of the transactions are carried out, i.e. sterling or foreign currency;

(2) whether the overseas entity is buying and selling goods in its own right;

(3) whether the financing is mainly sterling and the extent to which the cash flows of the overseas entity have a direct impact on those of the parent company;

(4) the major currency to which the foreign operation is exposed in its financing structure, i.e. sterling.

(b) Preparation of consolidated profit and loss account and balance sheet using the method of translation for the year ended 31 January 2002

Consolidated profit and loss account of the Howard Group for the year ended 31 December 2002

		£
Turnover	(9,225 + 11,812.5)	21,037,500
Cost of sales	(6,027 + 7,725.375)	13,752,375
Gross profit	(3,198 + 4,087.125)	7,285,125
Distribution costs	(1,290 + 943.75)	2,233,750
Administrative expenses	(1,469 + 315)	1,784,000
Depreciation	(191 + 210)	401,000
Exchange loss		281,809

Profit on ordinary activities before tax		2,584,566
Tax	(195 + 946.25)	1,141,250
Profit on ordinary activities after tax		1,443,316
Minority interest	(40% of 1,390.316)	556,126
Profit for year attributable to ordinary shareholders		887,190
Dividend		183,000
Retained profit for year		704,190
Profit and loss at 1.1.2002		* 2,451,810
		3,156,000

* Howard plc (1,011 – 185 = 826) + Pau (60% × 2,709,684 = 1,625,810)

Consolidated balance sheet of the Howard Group as at 31 December 2002

		£'000	£'000
Fixed assets			
Intangible assets	(305 – 60% x 500 = 5 less amortised 40%)		3
Tangible assets	(1,765 + 3,850)		5,615
Current assets			
Stock	(2,245 + 490)	2,735	
Debtors	(615 + 250)	865	
Cash	(156 +1,350)	1,506	
		5,106	
Creditors falling due within 1 year			
Trade creditors	(2,245 + 625)	2,870	
Net current assets			2,236
			7,854
Creditors falling due after more than 1 year			
Loans	(1,230 + 1,240)		2,470
			5,384
Capital			600
Reserves (3,156 – 2 goodwill)			* 3,154
			3,754
Minority interest	(40% of 4,075)		1,630
			5,384

* Howard plc 1,011 + 60% × 3,575 = 3,156 – 2 goodwill amortised

Workings

1. Translation of Pau Ltd balance sheet as at 31 December 2002

	FF'000	Rate	£'000	
Tangible assets	38,500	10	3,850	historic
Stock	3,675	7.5	490	historic (3 mts. av.)
Debtors	1,750	7	250	closing
Cash	9,450	7	1,350	closing
Trade creditors	(4,375)	7	(625)	closing
Loan	(8,680)	7	(1,240)	closing
	40,320		4,075	
Share capital	3,500	10	350	historic
Profit and loss account				
Pre-acquisition	1,500	10	150	historic
Post-acquisition	35,320	bal.	3,575	bal. fig.
	40,320		4,075	

2. Translation of Pau Ltd profit and loss account for the year ended 31 December 2002

	Fr'000	Rate	£'000	
Turnover	94,500	8	11,812,500	average
Opening stock	4,760	10	476,000	historic
Purchases (bal. fig.)	61,915	8	7,739,375	average
Closing stock	(3,675)	7.5	(490,000)	historic
Cost of sales	63,000		7,725,375	
Gross profit	31,500		4,087,125	
Distribution costs	7,550	8	943,750	average
Administration expenses	2,520	8	315,000	average
Depreciation	2,100	10	210,000	historic
Exchange loss			281,809	
	19,330		2,336,566	
Tax	7,570	8	946,250	average
Profits after tax	11,760		1,390,316	
Dividends paid 30.6.02	4,200	8	525,000	
Retained profit for the year	7,560		865,316	
Profit and loss brought forward	27,760		2,709,684 (see W4)	
Profit and loss carried forward	35,320		3,575,000	

3. Exchange differences

			Kr'000	
Opening net monetary liabilities				
Fixed assets (closing 38,500 + depreciation for year 2,100)			40,600	
Opening stocks (given)				4,760
			45,360	
Less total net assets at start (40,320 closing – retained profit for year 7,560)			32,760	
			(12,600)	
(12,600) translated at 9.5 (opening rate)		£1,326,316		
(12,600) translated at 7 (closing rate)		1,800,000		
Exchange loss		(473,684)		
Transactions for the year				
Retained profit	7,560,000			
Depreciation	2,100,000			
Decrease in stock	1,085,000			
	10,745,000	@ 7 closing	1,535,000	
		@ 8 average	1,343,125	
Exchange gain		191,875		
Net exchange loss – profit and loss			(281,809)	

4. Opening balance sheet of Pau as at 31 December 2001

	£
Non-monetary assets (45,360 ÷ 10)	4,536,000
Net monetary liabilities (12,600 ÷ 9.5)	(1,326,316)
	3,209,684
Less share capital and pre-acquisition reserves	500,000
Opening post-acquisition reserves	2,709,684

(c) *Calculation of inter-company stock profits*

(i) Closing rate method

Dr	Profit and loss	4	
	Cr Stocks		4

Elimination of inter-company stock profits

Dr	Sales	14	
	Cr Purchases		14

Elimination of inter-group purchases and sales

Stocks are valued in the overseas subsidiary at closing rate, i.e. £14,000 ÷ 7.5 = 105,000Kr, then divided by 7 = £15,000; thus stocks will have to increase from original cost of £10,000 to £11,000 to reflect the exchange movement.

(ii) Temporal method

The same two journal entries would appear as above but no adjustment to the value of the stocks as they are retained at their historic rate in the books of the overseas subsidiary; thus stocks remain at £10,000.

11
Sundry Accounting Standards

Solution 1 – Brand accounting

Brands are a form of intangible asset. The issue of brands first came to prominence in financial accounting at the time of the Nestlé takeover of Rowntree. The directors of the victim company (Rowntree) tried to take defensive action against the predator (Nestlé) by writing to their shareholders to explain that many valuable brands developed by the company had not been incorporated in the balance sheet. This unsuccessful defence highlighted the importance that a company should attach to its brands.

The first attempt to incorporate brands into the financial statements was Grand Metropolitan plc's decision to record brand names on its balance sheet. The decision arose out of the accounting requirements of SSAP 22. Under this standard, goodwill on acquisition had to be written off immediately against reserves or else capitalised and subsequently amortised over the economic life of the goodwill. The former option led to an understatement of a company's net assets and adversely affected gearing. On the other hand, the amortisation option resulted in lower reported profits for several years and thus a reduction in the vital measure of earnings per share. As a result acquisition companies examined very closely the precise wording in SSAP 22 (Paragraph 30): the amount attributed to purchased goodwill should not include any value for *separable intangibles*. The amount of these, if material, should have been included under the appropriate heading within intangible assets in the balance sheet. This was further amplified by Paragraph 13: separable net assets may include identifiable intangibles such as those specifically mentioned in the balance sheet formats, i.e. concessions, patents, licences, trademarks and similar rights and assets; other examples include publishing rights, franchise rights and customer lists. The inclusion of acquired brands therefore did not contravene SSAP 22 but strictly complied with it.

Some of the arguments raised in favour of brand inclusion were:

(1) Recording the true worth of assets in the balance sheet
In the retail and service sector valuable assets are not currently recorded in the balance sheet. Their inclusion would result in a truer and fairer picture of the value of the net assets in the balance sheet and gearing ratios would be more realistic. Revealing their true value should reduce the opportunities for a predator to gain control of those assets at a bargain price due to shareholder ignorance of the true value of their investment.

(2) Valuing brands on the balance sheet avoids the need to amortise goodwill
Many retail companies argue that brands do not depreciate in value and it is therefore essential to separate them from depreciating goodwill. In the same way that nearly 25 per cent of properties are no longer depreciated in practice, if the company maintains the value of a brand by high expenditure on marketing then no depreciation or amortisation is necessary. Companies such as Interbrand Inc (brand valuers) argue that brands such as Guinness, Cadbury's Flake, etc. have been in existence for many years and their value is in fact appreciating rather than depreciating.

(3) Valuing brands on the balance sheet avoids the need to write off goodwill to reserves
By applying Paragraphs 13 and 30 of SSAP 22, goodwill could be called by another name, i.e. a brand. This reduced the amount of goodwill calculated on acquisition that needed to be written off directly to reserves.

(4) Inclusion of brand names increases the revaluation reserve and also shareholders' funds
Incorporating the asset in the balance sheet will result in an equivalent reserve. Shareholders' funds will increase and the debt/equity or gearing ratios will be reduced. The company will therefore appear to be more creditworthy and this may make further financing available to these companies. The banks, however, may already have discounted this factor in their lending policy.

One important advantage is that reduced gearing may allow the company to reduce the effects of a stock exchange rule that transactions worth more than 25 per cent of shareholders' funds require prior shareholder approval.

The arguments given against the inclusion of brands on the balance sheet were:

(1) The inclusion of brands contradicts the principle of traditional historical cost accounting
The inclusion of brand names at their realisable value is strictly against traditional historical cost accounting and is really a partial move towards value-based accounting. The profession has yet to move in this direction but in ED 51 it had taken the decision that even revaluations of fixed assets are against historical cost conventions. With recent reports such as the ICAS's *Making Corporate Reports Valuable* and the joint ICAS/ICAEW *The Way Forward*, a long-term objective will probably be to develop a value-based system. The final draft of the Statement of Principles has unfortunately not moved along this long-term route, and permits both options, i.e. historic cost and revaluation.

(2) The difficulty of measuring and valuing brands
There is a wide variety of measurement techniques in practice, e.g. the Interbrand multi-disciplinary approach, discounted cash flow, cost writeback, capitalisation of royalties, market value, etc. There is no absolutely acceptable method of valuation at present. Also under historical cost accounting it can be argued that only acquired brands should be incorporated as there is a definite transaction. Homegrown brands, however, are subjectively valued using one of the above methods but are not confirmed by a market transaction.

(3) Problems in deciding on the period of useful life and depreciation
It can be argued that brands have a useful life. ED 52 suggested that brands are really synonymous with goodwill and the accounting treatment should be the same. This has been largely confirmed by FRS 10, which requires identical accounting for intangible assets and goodwill. The determination of the useful life of a brand is, however, as difficult as that for goodwill.

(4) Problems in deciding whether a permanent diminution has taken place
FRS 11 advises that any sudden impairment of a tangible fixed asset should be charged against pre-tax profits. However, it is particularly difficult in the case of a brand name. For example, should a food manufacturer which finds one of its brands to be contaminated regard this as due to operational difficulties or as temporary devaluation caused by external factors? The former should be charged against reserves while the latter should be written off through the profit and loss account. FRS 11 requires that any impairment, whether temporary or not, be written off, either to reserves or profit and loss, depending on the specific circumstances.

On balance it would appear that the arguments in favour of brand accounting are quite strong. Therefore brands should be treated as assets in the balance sheet despite the London Business School's report *Accounting for Brands*, which discourages their inclusion.

Solution 2 – Sour plc

(a) Three reasons why Cream plc changed its accounting policy to recognise acquired brands

(1) To ensure that valuable brands are included in the balance sheet
Brands first came to the attention of the accountant at the time of the Nestlé takeover of Rowntree in 1988. In a defence document to their shareholders, the directors of Rowntree pleaded with them not to sell their shares to Nestlé as they felt that the price of 890p failed to

reflect the true value of the brands which the company had developed over the years but which were not recorded on their balance sheet. The defence failed but it warned other directors that a valuable asset was going unrecorded in the balance sheet and that without it companies were vulnerable to an unwanted takeover bid.

Obviously the inclusion of brands will enhance the value of the company's net assets and give greater strength to the company's balance sheet. Subsequently companies such as RHM have included even homegrown brands in the balance sheet as a successful defence against a hostile bidder, in this case Goodman Fielder Wattie.

Under FRS 10, as long as a fair value can be attributed to purchased brands at the date of acquisition, it may be capitalised.

(2) To improve the gearing ratio of the company and obtain additional external funding
The inclusion of acquired brands as assets will enable reserves to be increased and thus gearing reduced. If, on acquisition, Cream plc could describe part of the difference between purchase price and net assets as brands and not as goodwill then the write-off of goodwill to reserves would be reduced and this would lead to a lower gearing ratio.

In Cream plc's case the gearing can be calculated as follows:

Brands included

Loans   1,577.5 ÷ 7,200 net assets × 100   = 21.9%

Brands excluded

Loans   1,577.5 ÷ (7,200 − 3,437.5 acquired brands) × 100   = 41.9%

This reduced gearing makes it much easier to borrow additional funds.

(3) To avoid problems of goodwill write-off to reserves
Companies in the service sector which have been particularly acquisitive have found the write-off to reserves under SSAP 22 to be so high as to result in negative reserves. This can be unacceptable to the banking fraternity and makes the payment of dividends practically, if not legally, impossible.

It is common for goodwill to represent over 50 per cent of the purchase price in a takeover. It contains all the favourable advantages such as location, human skills and, of course, brands acquired. Under SSAP 22 if an asset, tangible or intangible, can be separately identified and sold in its own right, then it should be recorded separately on the balance sheet. Companies such as Grand Metropolitan plc and Guinness plc have recorded their valuable acquired brands on the balance sheet for this reason. To date, these brands have not been amortised by the companies, therefore earnings per share is not affected. FRS 10 will retain the ability to include purchased brands on the balance sheet, provided that they can be valued at fair value at acquisition.

Cream plc have included brands in the balance sheet at cost of £3,437,500. If this had represented goodwill, reserves would have been reduced by £3,437,500 to £2,395,000 or else it would have been amortised to the profit and loss account. If a ten-year life was assumed this would lead to a reduction in earnings of £343,750 per annum which would affect the earnings per share and price/earnings ratio of Cream plc. Unfortunately, under FRS 10, brands will have to be capitalised and written off over a useful economic life of twenty years or less. This would seem to be a likely scenario for Cream plc.

(b) The accounting problems

(1) The inclusion of an asset
In order for an asset to be incorporated in the balance sheet it is essential that two recognition criteria should be met and that the rules in FRS 5 *Reporting the Substance of Transactions* and FRS 10 *Goodwill and Intangible Assets* should be complied with.

In terms of the recognition tests brands can only be recorded in the balance sheet if their value or cost can be reliably measured and if they are likely to result in the creation of future economic benefits. FRS 10 refers specifically to intangible assets such as brands and argues that they are synonymous with goodwill. Therefore, if the acquired brands are capitalised they should be amortised over the useful economic life of the brand in the same way as goodwill, over a normal maximum of twenty years or, in rare circumstances, they may be written off over a longer period – or even not amortised at all. In the latter case they must be reviewed for any impairment in their value.

It is therefore essential that a proper external valuation has been carried out on the acquired brands to confirm the value of £3,437,500.

(2) To improve gearing

As has been seen earlier the inclusion of a brand as an intangible asset not only increases the net assets of the business but also increases its reserves, with a consequent fall in gearing. However, once FRS 10 is implemented and its accounting policy brought into line with that for goodwill, then the asset will eventually be amortised through the profit and loss account over its useful economic life.

At present brands are not being amortised, therefore Cream plc's policy of leaving a permanent asset in the balance sheet may only be a temporary reprieve. There are problems in defining the useful economic life and most companies who have incorporated brands on their balance sheet have refused to amortise them. They argue that the company has committed itself to expend monies on maintaining the asset via substantial advertising and market research expenditure. The same argument has been adopted by companies who have refused to depreciate their properties. They argue that the buildings are not falling in value because expenditure on maintaining and refurbishing them to a high standard ensures that they do not physically depreciate, i.e. the maintenance expenditure has replaced the depreciation.

These arguments are acceptable but the value of brands must be continually proved by carrying out an annual impairment review of assets.

(3) Avoiding write-off of goodwill to reserves

The recognition of brands to avoid immediate write-off to reserves does not pose any particular problems for the company because the inclusion of brands either as separate assets or as goodwill in the balance sheet is in line with standard accounting practice.

The only real problem is the requirement to ultimately amortise the asset over its useful economic life. This will, if pursued by the ASB, lead to a reduction in earnings per share and possible adverse effects on the P/E ratio and the company's share prices.

Solution 3 – Short plc

Internal memorandum

To: Assistant management accountant
From: Management accountant
Re: Accounting treatment of finance costs of preference share issue
Date: 20 June 2001

(a) The finance costs to be allocated to the profit and loss account should be governed by the rules in FRS 4 *Capital Instruments*. In particular, FRS 4 requires the difference between the total payments during the life of a capital instrument and the net proceeds received initially, to be recorded as finance costs in the profit and loss account.

The finance costs should be allocated to profit and loss so as to ensure that the total finance cost of any preference shares issued are allocated on a constant rate on the outstanding amount over the life of the instrument. This will require the adoption of a sum of the digits or actuarial approach for allocation. A straight-line method would not be acceptable. The preference shares will increase by the finance cost each year and be reduced by any dividends paid or payable.

The finance cost should be reported in the profit and loss account as part of the finance cost or interest payable and recorded after operating profit.

The preference shares are legally part of capital and reserves but it has the nature of debt and thus FRS 4 insists that it still be included within capital and reserves but, in addition, it must be recorded separately as non-equity on the balance sheet – to indicate that it has priority over ordinary share capital in relation to both repayment and dividend receipt.

The charge to profit and loss account needs to be backed up by a detailed 'interest payable' note which details out the break-up of the charge to profit and loss.

(b) Calculation of the finance cost for five years ended 30 September 1998

Total payments		£
Dividends payable 4% x £10m x 5 years		2,000,000
Repayment 10m shares at £1.35		13,500,000
		15,500,000
Less net proceeds received		
Gross proceeds	£10,000,000	
Less finance costs	100,000	
		9,900,000
Total finance costs		5,600,000

	Opening carrying amount £m	Finance costs (10%) £m	Net liability £m	Cash flow £m	Closing carrying amount £m
1994	9,900	990	10,890	(400)	10,490
1995	10,490	1,049	11,539	(400)	11,139
1996	11,139	1,114	12,253	(400)	11,853
1997	11,853	1,184	13,037	(400)	12,637
1998	12,637	1,263	13,900	(13,900)	–
		5,600			

The effective cost of preference shares was given as 10 per cent. Under the sum of the digits approach the finance cost would be 5(5 + 1) /2 = 15, i.e. 1/15, 2/15, 3/15, 4/15 and 5/15 each year for the next five years (373, 747, 1120, 1494 and 1866).

(c) Balance sheet of Short plc as at 1 October 1998

Capital and reserves	£m	
Ordinary shares of £1 each, fully paid up	100	
Share premium account	25.8	} 135.8
Capital redemption reserve (0 + 10)	10	
Profit and loss account (59.7 – 10)	49.7	
	185.5	
Net assets (199 – 13.5)	185.5	

On redemption of the preference shares these must be replaced by either a new issue of shares or a transfer out of distributable reserves into a 'locked-up' capital redemption reserve (nominal value).

The double entries were as follows:

		£m	£m
Dr	Redeemable preference share capital	13.5	
Cr	Bank		13.5

being the repayment of preference shares at a premium of £1.35 per share

		£m	£m
Dr	Profit and loss account	10	
Cr	Capital redemption reserve		10

being the transfer from distributable reserves to maintain capital

Solution 4 – Fledgeling Ltd

(a) Convertible debt – FRS 4

Total payments		
Redemption value	£300,000	
Annual interest		
£6,820 x 5 years	34,100	
£18,000 x 4 years	72,000	
£17,250 x 1 year	17,250	
	423,350	
Less net proceeds on issue	200,000	
Total finance cost	223,350	

Allocation of total finance cost

Year end	Opening balance	Profit and loss (8.9%)	Cash paid	Closing balance
£	£	£	£	£
31.12.1996	200,000	17,800	(6,820)	210,980
31.12.1997	210,980	18,777	(6,820)	222,937
31.12.1998	222,937	19,841	(6,820)	235,958
31.12.1999	235,958	21,000	(6,820)	250,138
31.12.2000	250,138	22,262	(6,820)	265,580
31.12.2001	265,580	23,367	(18,000)	271,217
31.12.2002	271,217	24,138	(18,000)	277,355
31.12.2003	277,355	24,685	(18,000)	284,040
31.12.2004	284,040	25,280	(18,000)	291,320
31.12.2005	291,320	25,930 rounded	(317,250)	Nil
		223,080		

Under FRS 4 the total finance cost must be allocated on a basis which provides a constant rate of return on the outstanding amount. This has been achieved by applying the effective interest rate of 8.9 per cent rather than the actual interest charged in the period. It should be noted that the premium of £100,000 payable at end of the period is treated as part of the total finance cost.

(b) Redeemable convertible preference shares – FRS 4

(i) Under FRS 12 *Provisions, Contingent Liabilities and Contingent Assets*, the parent company has a possible obligation to repay the redeemable preference shares in its subsidiary, Nest Ltd. As such, this should be disclosed as a contingent liability note in the notes to the financial statements. The note should disclose the nature of the contingent event, the uncertainties expected to effect its ultimate outcome, an estimate of its financial effect and particulars of any security offered.

(ii) *Total payments*

Redemption value	20,000 shares at 8%	£160,000
Annual dividends	5 years at 8% x £20,000	8,000
		168,000
Net proceeds	20,000 shares at £5 each	100,000
Total finance costs		68,000

Allocation of total cost of preference shares

Year ended	Opening balance	Profit and loss (9.85%)	Cash paid	Closing balance
31.12.1996	£100,000	£9,850	£(1,600)	£108,250
31.12.1997	108,250	10,663	(1,600)	117,313
31.12.1998	117,313	11,555	(1,600)	127,268
31.12.1999	127,268	12,536	(1,600)	138,204
31.12.2000	138,204	13,613	(1,600)	150,217
31.12.2001	150,217			

This is £9,783 short so the effective rate should be higher than 9.85 per cent. However, this is the rate given in the question. As an alternative the sum of the digits approach could be adopted. This would result in 5/15 being charged in the first year, 4/15 in the second year, etc.

Year ended	Opening balance	Profit and loss	Cash paid	Closing balance
31.12.1996	£100,000	£4,553 (1/15)	(1,600)	£102,953
31.12.1997	102,953	9,067 (2/15)	(1,600)	110,420
31.12.1998	110,420	13,600 (3/15)	(1,600)	122,420
31.12.1999	122,420	18,133 (4/15)	(1,600)	138,953
31.12.2000	138,953	22,647 (5/15)	(1,600)	160,000
31.12.2001	160,000			

(c) *Factoring agreement – FRS 5*

(i) *Disclosure on the balance sheet*

Current assets (extract)
Debtors

Gross trade debtors	£500,000	
Less provision for bad debts 4%	3,800	
		£496,200
Less non-returnable proceeds	405,000	
		£91,200

Note: This is a linked presentation situation.

Creditors: amounts falling due within one year (£4,500 + £9,000)   £13,500

Workings

1. Bad debt provision

Gross debts	£500,000
Less non-recourse finance (£450,000 x 90%)	405,000
	95,000
Bad debt provision (4%)	£3,800

2. Credit protection fee   £450,000 x 1% = £4,500

3. Accrued interest charge

| Given | £9,000 |

(ii) The disclosure required in the notes to the financial statements

The terms of the agreement.

The gross amount of factored debts outstanding at the year end.

Statement by the directors that the company is not required to support any losses nor is there any intent to do so.

Statement that the factoring company has agreed in writing that it will seek repayment of the finance only from the debts factored and it will have no recourse to any other assets of the company.

Solution 5 – Brigade plc

(a)(i) *Zero-coupon bond*

In accordance with FRS 4 the bond should be stated as a liability at the amount of the net proceeds received. The FRS requires the difference between the amount received on issue and the amount repaid on maturity to be accrued over the term of the bond and charged to the profit and loss account accordingly.

(ii) The rate of interest inherent in the bond is $£907,908/£500,000 = 1.816 = 22\%$ (from table).

Year	Opening bal.	P&L a/c	Paid	Closing bal.
	£	£(22%)	£	£
31.12.2001	(£500,000)	£110,000	–	610,000
31.12.2002	(£610,000)	£134,200	–	744,200
31.12.2003	(£744,200)	£163,708	907,908	Nil

(b) *Long-term work in progress*

Adjustments to draft accounts	Dr	Cr
	£	£
Sales		1,350,000
Cost of sales	1,420,000	
Provision for future losses – expense	200,000	
Provision for loss on contact		200,000
Debtor	150,000	
	1,770,000	1,550,000
Bank (1,420 costs incurred less 1,200 payments received)		220,000
	1,770,000	1,770,000

Note 1

	£'000	£'000
Contract price		3,000
Costs to date	1,420	
Estimated cost to completion	1,350	
		(2,770)
Estimated total profit on completion		230
Additional costs		(500)
Expected loss		(270)

Work in progress

	£'000			£'000
Total costs incurred	1,420	Cost of sales		1,420

Contract profit and loss

	£'000			£'000
Cost of sales	1,420	Sales (45% × 3,000)		1,350
Provision for losses	200			

Debtor

	£'000			£'000
Sales	1,350	Bank		1,200
		Balance c/d		150
	1,350			1,350

Provision for losses

	£'000			£'000
		Profit and loss		200

Solution 6 – UK plc

(a) *Reconciliation of US to UK GAAP*

	$m
Profit of US Inc computed according to American GAAP	25
(1) Premium on acquisition add back amortisation	1
(2) Development costs – share charged against profit	(4)
(3) Stock valuation – reduction in cost of sales under FIFO	7
Profit of US Inc to be incorporated into UK plc group accounts	29

- SSAP 22 recommends that goodwill should preferably be written off to reserves at the point of acquisition, so that under UK rules there would be no intangible assets of $20m to amortise over a projected life of 20 years. The UK plc balance sheet, however, would disclose general reserves reduced by the $20m written off. *Note*: Under FRS 10, goodwill now has to be capitalised and subsequently amortised similarly to USA.

- SSAP 13 allows development costs to be capitalised and spread over the life of the development, whereas in the USA a more conservative rule prevails and such costs are written off against profits when they are incurred. If the development meets the rules set out in SSAP 13 that:

    - it is a clearly defined project with separately identifiable expenditure;
    - there is reasonable certainty of technical feasibility and commercial viability;
    - profits from the development cover the costs; and the company has sufficient resources to complete the development;

  the costs can be deferred. The project is expected to last five years and therefore UK profits would be reduced by $20m ÷ 5 yrs = $4m amortisation of development costs.

- SSAP 9 states the LIFO stock valuation does not satisfy its general principle of providing a fair approximation of the expenditure actually incurred and the Inland Revenue does not normally accept LIFO-based accounts. The figures suggest that stocks have increased in quantity and cost per unit so that using cost of sales based on more recent prices (LIFO) the profit would be $7m lower than that with a cost of sales based on the lower price paid for earlier batches of materials, etc. (FIFO).

(b) The suggestion that all countries should abandon domestic accounting standards to follow international standards is an attractive idea, but not really a practical one. Some countries would not wish to give up local differences stemming from local law, e.g. the coded system versus the common law system, and others for political reasons would not wish to submit to rules which they see as alien to their culture. It is difficult to frame an agreed set of International Standards because of such differences. Often, to gain agreement, compromise and the adoption of alternative methods, within the Standard, reduce the rigour and usefulness of International Standards. International Standards will, however, be helpful to multi-national companies and the shareholders who finance such companies via stock exchanges in different countries. If common standards are adopted then the financial statements would produce the same financial results between the various countries, thus making it easier for users to understand and interpret them.

International accounting standards are becoming increasingly important and are being incorporated relatively quickly into UK accounting standards for the following reasons:

(1) Karl van Hulle, the Commissioner in the EU responsible for accounting, decided to back the IASC rather than encourage the development of European accounting standards, and the EU (in June 2000) agreed that all members apply IAS to listed companies by 2005.

(2) The loose federation of stock exchanges (IOSCO) agreed that, provided that the IASC can produce approximately 40 'hard core' standards that are acceptable internationally, then it will adopt those for all major listings on the world stock exchanges. These have now basically been completed by the IASC.

(3) The French and German governments decided to back the IASC.

(4) A new international board (IASB) was set up in April 2001 with technical experts and with the involvement of FASB from USA.

Solution 7 – Related party transactions

(a) (i) Importance of disclosure of related party transactions

Related party relationships exist where there are close relationships which could result in some of these parties being more highly favoured than those dealing with the company at full arm's length. It is therefore important that reporting entities be as open as possible in their dealings with these parties. It is similar to the analogy of an audit not only being independent but also being seen to be as independent as possible of the client. There is an assumption that, in related party situations, transactions may not be recorded at full arm's length. These relationships can have a significant effect on the financial position and operating results of the company and can lead to transactions that would not normally be undertaken. Even if there are no transactions between the related parties it is still possible for the operating results and financial position of a company to be affected by the relationship.

However, in the absence of contrary information, it is assumed that the financial statements of an entity reflect transactions carried out on an arm's-length basis and that the entity has independent discretionary power over its actions and pursues its activities independently. If these assumptions are not justified because of related party transactions, then disclosure of this fact should be made. Even if transactions are at arm's length, the disclosure of related party transactions is useful because it is likely that future transactions may be affected by such relationships. The main issues in determining such disclosures are the identification of related parties, the types of transactions and the information to be disclosed.

The topic was brought to the attention and forefront of the ASB when the Maxwell affair broke and the sudden realisation of a close relationship between a director and the company's pension fund in the Mirror Group.

(ii) Should small companies obtain exemption from FRS 8?

The disclosure of related party information is more important to the user of small company financial statements than large entities. The relationship is likely to be more significant due to the disproportionate influence that a director/owner, etc., might have over the business. A director/owner has considerable influence and users should be made aware of any material transactions that might affect them.

Of course, it is possible that the costs of providing such information could outweigh the benefits of reporting it. However, this point of view is difficult to evaluate but the value is very likely to be more material in the context of a small company. The FRSSE, developed specifically for smaller entities, requires disclosure of material transactions with related parties including the disclosure of personal guarantees given by directors in respect of any borrowings made by the reporting entity.

The Companies Acts were regarded as insufficient in giving adequate disclosure in that they concentrated on providing information re directors but were limited with regard to other parties. The FRSSE and FRS 8 were therefore published to broaden out the required disclosure and require a comprehensive set of overall regulations in the area.

(b) (i) Are the following events related party disclosures under FRS 8?

FRS 8 gives express exemption from disclosure of the normal financing arrangements between a company and its bankers. However, in this case the merchant bank holds 25 per cent of the shares in the entity and could possibly be classed as an associated relationship. If this were the case then all material transactions would need to be disclosed between the two parties. In addition the merchant bank would appear to exercise significant influence over the entity as it has a member of its own on the board of directors of AB. However, the 25 per cent holding and membership on the board would not be sufficient to ensure an associated relationship. The bank must also take an active part in the operating and financial policies of the other entity. It could be, for example, that the other 75 per cent of the shares are held by another party and thus clearly the bank has little influence. Also, merchant banks often do not regard their investments in other companies as associates but merely investments. FRS 9 *Associates and Joint Ventures* says that if the business of the investor is to provide capital to the entity accompanied by advice and guidance then the holding should be accounted for as an investment rather than an associate.

If the relationship is deemed to be an associate then the company would need to disclose all material transactions and that would include disclosure of all management fees, interest, dividends, etc., as well as details of the terms of the loan.

(ii)

One of the main exemptions permitted by FRS 8 is the elimination of all inter-group transactions and balances on consolidation. The transactions that need to be disclosed will be limited to those that were incurred when X was not part of the group (i.e. between 1 July 1999 and 31 October 1999) but not those that occurred prior to 1 July 2000. There is no related party relationship between RP and Z as it is simply a business transaction unless there has been a subordinating of interests when entering into the transaction due to influence or control.

(iii)

Pension schemes for the benefit of the employees of the reporting entity are related parties of the entity. The requirements of FRS 8 were largely introduced to quell the discomfort felt after the Mirror Group pension scheme fell insolvent at the time of the Maxwell affair. However, FRS 8 expressly exempts the contributions paid from disclosure but it does insist on disclosure of other transactions with the group. The transfers of fixed assets of £10m and the recharge of administrative costs of £3m must be disclosed, but not the £16m of contributions paid.

The investment managers of the pension scheme are employees and would not normally be regarded as a related party of the reporting company. However, a related party relationship would exist if it can be demonstrated that the investment manager could influence the operating and financial policies of the reporting entity through his/her position of non-executive director of the company. Directors are deemed to be related parties under FRS 8 and, although the management fees of £25,000 may not be material from the reporting entity's perspective, FRS 8 insists that materiality (in the case of individuals) should be considered in the context of individual directors as well and, if material, should be disclosed. It would certainly be the case that £25,000 would be significant in this context and the fee should therefore be disclosed.

Solution 8 – Tweed Ltd

(a) *Related party disclosures – FRS 8*

FRS 8 *Related Party Disclosures* specifically does not require any disclosure of the relationship and transactions between a company and other parties simply as a result of their role as providers of finance in the normal course of business even though they may be able to influence the company's decision-making process. A similar exemption also applies to transactions with utility companies, government departments and their sponsored bodies as well as other parties such as major customers and suppliers on which the company might be economically dependent.

A major customer would not be treated as a related party merely because the importance of retaining its business had a significant effect on the company's decision making, nor would a lending bank be treated as a related party merely because the terms of the loan enabled the bank to restrict the company's borrowing or investing facilities. However, if there are any other transactions outside normal activity then all material transactions should be disclosable.

Is a venture capitalist a related party? It has a 30 per cent interest and could be said to have an associated relationship. However, in order to have this relationship, the venture capitalist must have a significant influence over the operating and financial policies of the entity. Rarely do venture capitalists have this relationship as their business is to provide seed corn capital and professional advice but they tend to leave the major operating decisions to the major players. It is more like a trade investment than an associate relationship.

FRS 8 does make the presumption that a person owning or able to control over 20 per cent or more of a company's voting rights is a related party. In many circumstances an investor with a 30 per cent stake and a director on the board would be expected to have the level of influence over the company's financial and operating policies that would make it a related party. If this were the case the company would have to disclose all material transactions with the venture capitalist. Disclosable transactions may include the management fees paid, interest charged and the amount and terms of the loan due to the venture capitalist. Only if it could be demonstrated that the venture capitalist does not have an influence over the company would FRS 8 not apply.

(b) *Accounting for government grants – SSAP 4*

The principle underlying SSAP 4 *Accounting for Government Grants* is that grants should be released to profit and loss on the basis that best matches the grants with the related expenditure to which they are intended to contribute. SSAP 4 allows matching to be achieved either by deducting the grant from cost or by crediting the grant to a separate capital grants reserve. However, legal advice would suggest that the latter approach only would be acceptable under company legislation. The effect on the profit and loss is the same, regardless of the method adopted, but the deferred credit approach does result in a grossing up of the balance sheet.

If the grant had been netted against cost, there is a danger that no provision for impairment in value would be created as the net carrying value would be less than the asset's recoverable amount, and the profit and loss account would continue to be charged with depreciation on net cost. However, this hides the fact that it could result in an unacceptable transfer from a non-distributable to a distributable reserve.

Buildings: 1990-1996	7 years	Cost £800,000
	Useful economic life to date	
	7 years out of total life of 25 years	
	Depreciation 7/25 x £800,000	£ 224,000
		Net book value £576,000
Grant: 1990-1996	£800,000 x 40%	£320,000
	Release to profit and loss 7/25 x £800,000	£89,600
		Carrying value £230,400

(c) Accounting for a defined benefit scheme – SSAP 24

Under SSAP 24 *Accounting for Pension Costs*, surpluses and deficits must be spread over the estimated remaining useful economic life of the employees in the scheme. All surpluses/deficits thus recorded must be incorporated in the profit and loss account.

The accounting treatment is different from the funding since the actuaries may well decide to make up the deficits by accelerating the annual funding contribution rate or by paying up lump sums.

| Year | Funding | Profit and loss account | | | Balance sheet |
		Normal	Deficit	Total	prepayment
	£	£	£	£	£
1997	176,000	176,400	–	176,400	Nil
1998	266,400	176,400	30,000	206,400	60,000
1999	266,400	176,400	30,000	206,400	120,000
2000	266,400	176,400	30,000	206,400	180,000
2001	176,400	176,400	30,000	206,400	150,000
to 2006	176,400	176,400	30,000	206,400	Nil (2006)

Payroll of £1.8m x 9.8% regular contribution equals £176,400 per annum.

Increased temporary contributions for three years from 1998 to 2000 equals £1.8m x 14.8%, i.e. £266,400.

Deficit £270,000/9 years = £30,000 additional charge per annum.

(d) Management buyout – deliberate suppression of creditors

This is not a transaction of the current year and represents a fundamental error of the previous management team. If the directors had been aware of this deliberate suppression the accounts would never had been signed off nor would the auditors have provided the company with a clean audit report.

It must be treated as a prior year adjustment and therefore adjustment against opening reserves. It should not be charged in arriving at this year's profit performance. The prior year adjustment should also be reported as a recognised gain/loss as part of the statement of total recognised gains and losses.

Solution 9 – AX plc – disclosure under FRS 13 and fair values

(a) (i) Concerns about current accounting practice

Since the beginning of the 1980s the growth and complexity of financial instruments that are available to companies has expanded greatly, particularly in their ability to totally transform and manage the risks that companies face. However, the accounting standards have failed to keep pace with these developments and in many cases they are not even recorded on balance sheet, despite the fact that they could represent many millions of unrecorded debt. The concerns were brought to the forefront of standard-setters' attention with the collapse of Barings Bank and the fact that it was a dealer in Singapore (Nick Leeson) who had the ability to achieve this without it being obvious to anyone in control of the organisation.

The problem lies with the existing historic cost basis. Companies measure their financial assets at amortised cost even though there are reliable, quoted market prices and the fact that the assets are readily saleable in most instances.

At the present time all unrealised gains and losses arising from changes in the value of many financial instruments are often ignored. Unrealised losses are recognised if the financial instruments are valued on the basis of the lower of their cost or market value but ignored if they are hedged. They could therefore be overlooked. It also means that companies can choose when they want to recognise profits on financial instruments, so as to smooth profits. This applies equally to derivative and non-derivative products.

There are also problems with hedge accounting, mainly because it relies on management intent, and thus their recording will differ as management intent changes. In these situations circumstances can change very quickly in the financial markets and the resultant effect on a company's derivatives can quickly transform the risk profile of a company. The present accounting framework does not adequately make this movement in financial position and risk transparent to the users of financial instruments.

(a) (ii) *Disclosure is not sufficient*

Disclosure of the risk is an essential first step in making users aware of the inherent difficulties in companies adopting derivative products. However, it is not the full solution. The primary statements – both profit and loss and balance sheet – must fairly present the true cost of using the instruments and their associated fair values in those statements. Notes are not a substitute for fair reporting as readers very rarely go into the depth of the notes and they expect the primary statements to provide a clear view of the performance of the entity as well as its financial position.

The ASB has commenced by issuing FRS 13 *Derivatives and Other Financial Instruments: Disclosure* as a first step in the process. It requires entities to disclose, in narrative form, the risks that the company faces and the strategies that it has adopted to deal with those risks. As a supplement, reporting entities should also disclose back-up numerical data on those main risks, showing details of financial assets and liabilities, their currencies, whether fixed or floating, etc.

The next stage is to introduce recognition and measurement rules so that these derivatives are brought on to balance sheet and their related unrealised gains and losses recorded in the performance statements – probably in the statement of total recognised gains and losses (STRGL). At present there is still no consensus on how to measure these instruments but it is likely that current values will eventually be reported. The recognition and measurement standard will incorporate all types of financial instruments, not just derivatives.

(b) (i) *Discuss three ways in which gains and losses on financial instruments might be recorded in the financial statements*

There are four possible ways to measure gains and losses on financial instruments:

(i)   All gains and losses should be reported in the profit and loss account;

(ii)   Certain gains and losses should be disclosed in the profit and loss account, while others should be in the STRGL;

(iii)   Some gains and losses could be assets in the assets/liabilities or as part of shareholders' funds and subsequently recycled through the profit and loss account, once realised;

(iv) Some gains and losses could be held temporarily in equity via the STRGL and then subsequently recycled to the profit and loss account once they are realised.

(i)   All gains/losses in the profit and loss account
All gains and losses represent performance for the year. If all changes in value are recorded in the profit and loss then it should help to restrict abuses and manipulation of performance that has occurred in the past. Currently there are difficulties in deciding which gains/losses should go into the STRGL and the profit and loss and it has led to some arbitrary allocations between the two statements.

(ii) Certain gains/losses in the STRGL and some in the profit and loss account
Different types of gains and losses are reported separately. Those which are unrealised and long term would be recorded in the STRGL whereas those which are short term and realised should be reported in the profit and loss account. This would protect the profit and loss from volatile movements and is the approach recommended by FRED 22 to deal with actuarial deficits/surpluses (STRGL) and normal pension contributions (profit and loss). However, this requires the derivation of strict principles in choosing which statement the gains/losses should be reported, otherwise there will be little comparability across reporting entities.

(iii) Gains and losses deferred until realised and then recycled through the profit and loss account
The gains/losses would be difficult to meet the definition of assets/liabilities. However, the alternative of recording the gains/losses as part of shareholders' funds would amount to reserve accounting that was banned many years ago with the publication of SSAP 6 and its successor FRS 3. There would also be difficulties in deciding when realisation takes place and this leads to manipulation of profits.

(iv) Gains and losses are first recorded in the STRGL and then recycled to profit and loss
This is similar to (iii) above. All gains and losses would be recorded in the year they occur but would later be recorded again as a realised gain/loss. This amounts to double counting of gains/losses. Under this approach the STRGL is a 'holding tank' but this conflicts with FRS 3 which regards both the profit and loss and the STRGL as separate but complementary performance statements. Both must be read together in order to get a full picture of performance.

(b) (ii) Fair value reporting – AX plc

	1999 £'000	2000 £'000	2001 £'000
Historic cost – interest 5%	1,500	1,500	1,500
Adjustment to fair value	–	267	(288)
Effective interest	1,500	1,767 (6% x £29.45m)	1,212 (4% x £30.29m)
(Gain)/loss on change in fair value	(550)	571	–
Net charge to profit	950	2,338	1,212

Fair value of debenture at 30 November 1999
Interest £1.5m x discount rate of 6% = £ 1.42m
Capital and interest 30.11.2001
(£31.5m x 6%)   = £28.03m
                                 £29.45m
Capital at nominal value   £30.00m
Gain on fair valuation   £0.55m

Fair value of debenture at 30 November 2000
Capital and interest 30.11.2001
(£31.5m x 4%)   = £30.29m
Fair value (£29.45 + 0.267m)   29.72m
Loss on fair valuation   (0.57m)

Solution 1 – Tram Ltd

(a) *Profit on disposal of property – FRS 3 and FRS 15*

Under FRS 3 *Reporting Financial Performance* the profit/(loss) on disposal should be accounted for by reference to the net carrying amount of the asset. Any past revaluation surplus or deficit in the revaluation reserve should be dealt with as a reserve transfer and not taken through the profit and loss account. This is re-emphasised in FRS 15 *Tangible Fixed Assets*.

Profit on disposal	Net sale proceeds	£16m
	Balance sheet net assets	15m
	Profit on disposal	1m

Disclosure
Assuming material, £1m profit should be disclosed separately on the face of the profit and loss account, after operating profit but before interest payable and disclosed as a 'super-exceptional' item.

Sufficient information should be disclosed to enable a reader to be in a position to make their own judgement as to how each item should be treated in the financial statements and to make any adjustments to EPS for their own purposes. The company may, if desired, compute an alternative EPS based on pre-exceptional items but this must be reconciled to the official FRS 14 *Earnings Per Share* version.

(b) *Deferred taxation – SSAP 15 and FRS 19*

The £2m tax is out of proportion to the £1m gain since a percentage of the tax relates to the gains previously recorded in the revaluation reserve. Therefore it is reasonable to apportion the tax on the gain on a rational basis between gain recognised in the profit and loss account and the balance on reserves. The tax attributable to the surplus on revaluation reserve should be disclosed in the statement of total recognised gains and losses.

Under FRS 16 *Current Tax* and the proposed FRS 19 *Deferred Taxation* the tax charge/credit must follow the accounting gain/loss.

Splitting the tax in the same proportion to the gains:

Profit and loss	1/9 + 1 x £2m	=	£200,000
STRGL	9/9 + 1 x £2m	=	£1,800,000 (via revaluation reserves)

(c) *Research and development – SSAP 13*

(i) SSAP 13 *Accounting for Research and Development* requires the cost of fixed assets acquired or constructed to provide facilities for research and development to be capitalised and subsequently written off over the asset's useful life. The cost of constructing the warehousing and testing facility should be capitalised and written off over its useful economic life, as outlined in SSAP 13.

In this case the cost should be depreciated over four years. At 31.12.1996 the balance sheet would show the following:

Fixed assets	£
Buildings	90,000
Accumulated depreciation	22,500
Net book value	67,500

(ii) SSAP 13 requires development expenditure to be written off in the year it is incurred, except in those specific circumstances when it may be carried forward as an asset and subsequently matched against future revenue. In this case there appears to be:

– clearly defined project;
– separately definable expenditure;
– reasonable certainty of the outcome of the project; and
– assumed sufficient working capital to finance the project.

The £275,000 on project High Speed may be deferred and written off against profits.

		£
1996	10/50 x £275,000	55,000
1997	20/50 x £275,000	110,000
1998	20/50 x £275,000	110,000
		275,000

The 1996 balance sheet would show £220,000 (i.e. £275,000 – 55,000) as an item under the heading 'deferred development expenditure'. An alternative approach would be to spread the development costs of £275,000 evenly over the life of the three years of the project, i.e. c.£92,000 per annum.

(iii) Expenditure on general research of £85,000 should be written off in the profit and loss account in the period incurred in accordance with SSAP 13.

The 1996 profit and loss account would show the following charges:

	£
Depreciation	22,500
Development costs	55,000
General research	85,000
	162,500

(d) *Calculation of the fair value on the acquisition of Line Ltd*

	Book value £'000	Revaluation surpluses/deficits £'000	Provisions created £'000	Policy changes £'000	Fair value £'000
Fixed assets					
Tangible	440	55 (1)			495
Investments	55	14 (2)			69
Current assets					
Stocks	110		(14) (3)	(6) (3)	90
Debtors	197				197
Bank	33				33
	340				320
Creditors under 1 year					
Bank	42				42
Trade creditors	83				83
Other creditors	28				28
Accruals	14				14
	167				167
Net current assets	173				153
Total assets less current liabilities	668				717
Creditors over 1 year					
Loans	83				83
Deferred tax	124			28 (5)	152
Other	28			220 (4)	248
	235				483
Net assets	433				234
Fair value of consideration		£ 275,000 x 1.08			297
Goodwill					63

FRS 10 *Goodwill and Intangible Assets* now insists that goodwill be capitalised as an intangible asset and subsequently amortised over its estimated useful economic life which should not normally exceed twenty years.

Solution 2 – Low Paints

(a) *Advise Mr Low on accuracy of the earnings per share calculation*

Under FRS 14 *Earnings Per Share*, the calculation of earnings per share (EPS) should be based on earnings attributable to the ordinary shareholders divided by the weighted average number of shares that were outstanding during the year.

The numerator is based on the reported earnings in the profit and loss. According to information provided by the directors, the earnings for the year ended 31 October 2001 was £4.8m. However, those earnings were not calculated in accordance with standard accounting practice as governed by the SSAPs and FRSs promulgated by the Accounting Standards Board (ASB).

The issues recalculation of earnings are as follows:

(1) *Capital grant*
Under SSAP 4 *Accounting Treatment of Government Grants*, capital grants should be credited to a separate capital grants reserve and be released to income over the same period as the depreciation of the fixed asset. Only 10 per cent of the £5m should have been recorded as

income and thus £4.5m of grant needs to be deducted from income and transferred to a capital grants reserve on the balance sheet.

(2) Issue costs
Under FRS 4 *Capital Instruments*, issue costs are regarded as part of the cost of issuing the shares and should not be charged to profit and loss. Under the Companies Act they may initially be charged against the share premium account. The directors have erroneously charged the cash element of the fee to profit and loss. This should be reversed. The whole £300,000 must be charged to share premium.

The issue of 100,000 ordinary shares at a premium of 20 per cent should have gone respectively to share capital and share premium and not to profit and loss account. They represent capital contributions, not gains. A journal entry needs to debit profit and loss and credit the other two accounts appropriately.

Overall a net increase in reported profit of £60,000 should result.

(3) Finance lease
When SSAP 21 *Accounting for Leases and Hire Purchase Contracts* is linked with FRS 5 *Reporting the Substance of Transactions*, the commercial reality of a transaction must be reflected in the financial statements. Although legally the company sold a property at a profit, that property will have to be repurchased as Low Paints has signed an unconditional agreement to do so in four years' time. The reality is that this is a loan, not a sale, and thus the profit of £0.5m should be removed from the profit and loss account.

As the property will remain on balance sheet, an additional charge for depreciation will be required of £200,000 (£4m ÷ 20 years). As a loan is also now to be recorded, a charge for notional interest should be provided for the interest implicit in the lease. Normally this should be charged on a constant rate of return on the outstanding amount but, for simplicity, a straight-line charge of £250,000 has been made (£5.5m – £4.5m ÷ 4 years). Overall that results in a net fall of £950,000 in profits.

As a result of these changes I estimate that the reported profits should be reported at a loss of £590,000, not a profit of £4.8m. There is therefore no case for paying out any bonuses as clearly the earnings per share does not exceed the agreed 'normal' earnings per share of 50p.

Workings – earnings

	£'000
Profit as originally reported	4,800
Capital grant adjustment (£5m – 0.5m)	(4,500)
Issue cost and share issue adjusted	60
Lease adjustment	(950)
Revised loss	(590)

In addition to the errors recorded in the calculation of earnings, the company has not recorded the weighted average number of shares correctly either. Although the rights issue took place after the year end and therefore is post-balance sheet, FRS 14 requires EPS to be adjusted for the bonus element in the post-balance sheet issue. It is calculated as the fair value of shares cum rights divided by the theoretical ex-rights price. The fair value of the shares is £2 each and a 1:4 rights issue would result in a theoretical ex-rights price of £1.92 (4 shares × £2 = £8 + 1 share × £1.60 = £1.60 and total of £9.60 ÷ 5 shares). The bonus element is therefore £2/£1.92.

Workings – shares

Ordinary shares pre-rights	6,000,000
Public issue (4m – 3m sold by Mr Low) x 10/12 year	916,667
Bonus issue 6,916,667 x £2/£1.92	7,204,861

Overall the EPS should be amended and now be recorded as a loss per share of (8.2p). This is calculated as follows:

Workings – EPS

Earnings as adjusted	(590,000)
Ordinary shares	7,204,861
Earnings per share	(8.2p)

(b) Ethical issues on calculation of EPS

Financial directors are under pressure to enhance EPS as far as possible as analysts regard it as a key measure of performance. In addition, many bonus schemes are related to that ratio. Directors should apply the accounting standards correctly but should not overstep the mark and act in a fraudulent manner.

Managers have a duty to guard, preserve and enhance the value of the enterprise for the good of all touched by it, including employees, the general public and government.

A market can only be free if competition is fair and that requires that all users are considered within the overall social and ethical environment. In my opinion the directors have not acted fraudulently but they did appear not to understand or follow the accounting standards. They should be advised that it is their legal responsibility to prepare the financial statements in accordance with the standards and that they could be brought to the attention of the Financial Reporting Review Panel (FRRP). They have the power to take them to Court and, if necessary, be jailed for failure to comply.

Solution 3 – Temperate plc

(1) Plant and equipment

	£	
Cost 1 May 2000	25,000	
Residual value	1,000	
Depreciation	24,000	÷ 4 years = £6,000 per annum
Capital grant amortisation	6,000	÷ 4 years = £(1,500) per annum

FRS 15

The gross cost less the residual value of the asset should be charged to the profit and loss account over its useful life of four years. The straight-line method of depreciation has been adopted and the charge should be £6,000 per annum.

The gross cost less accumulated depreciation of the plant must be shown in the balance sheet together with all other fixed assets at their book value at the end of the year.

SSAP 4

Capital grants are amortised to the profit and loss account over the useful life of the related assets. There is therefore a credit of £1,500 to each year's profit and loss account.

The grant is initially credited to a deferred capital grants reserve account, and each year £1,500 will be released to the profit and loss account. The balance of grants not released is shown separately in the balance sheet as 'Deferred income', not included in shareholders' funds.

The revenue grant of £500 for skilled employees must be credited to the profit and loss account over the period in which the expenditure is incurred, i.e. it must be matched.

In addition the accounting policy for government grants should be disclosed.

FRS 12

The government grant is a contingent liability in that if the conditions are not fulfilled in the contract, part of the grant may have to be repaid. This requires a note to the balance sheet to disclose the possible financial consequences.

(2) Research and development expenditure

Project A

The project has not yet reached the stage of successfully developing a cure for baldness and would probably meet the criteria for applied research (per SSAP 13). As such, its costs should be written off immediately to the profit and loss account. It could lead to an enhancement of the company's future profitability but the relationship is very tenuous. The amount written off should be disclosed in the notes to the financial statements as part of research and development written off to profit and loss as incurred.

Project B

The project has reached the stage where the company is confident that an improved formula product will be on sale from May 2002. The project is 'development' under SSAP 13.

The company has the choice of either writing off the expenditure immediately or deferring it as an intangible asset. It will then be amortised to the profit and loss account over the life cycle of the product or over a time period equal to the asset's useful life. In order for the asset to be recognised certain conditions must be met:

- the project must be clearly defined;
- the expenditure must be separately identifiable;
- it must be possible to assess the outcome with reasonable certainty in terms of both commercial viability and technical feasibility;
- the future revenue must cover future development and related production costs;
- sufficient funds must be available to complete the project.

In the balance sheet, the movement in the deferred asset should be disclosed in the notes and the asset must be recorded separately, outside current assets.

Project C

This project is not research and development but it is work carried out for a third party which will be reimbursed in full. As such, it is defined as work in progress and should be included as a current asset in the balance sheet.

For all of these projects the statement of accounting policies should include one on research and development.

(3) Investment properties

Under SSAP 19 (paragraph 11) investment properties should be included in the balance sheet at their open-market value. Any changes therein should not be taken to the profit and loss account but should instead be disclosed as a movement in an investment property revaluation reserve (IPRR).

However, under paragraph 13, if the reserve is insufficient to cover the deficit then any excess deficit must be charged directly to the profit and loss account.

Thus the increase in value of £5,000 for investment property no. 1 should be credited to the IPRR and the asset value increased in the balance sheet. The reduction in value of £35,000 for investment property no. 2 will initially be used to write off the previous surplus in the IPRR for that asset to the extent of £25,000. The remaining loss of £10,000 can still be offset against the balance on the revaluation reserve relating to other investment properties, and there is £45,000 available for this purpose.

The investment properties will now be valued at £320,000, not £350,000, and the IPRR will stand at £35,000 not £65,000.

The warehouse has fallen in value by £20,000, and this permanent diminution exceeds the balance of £18,000 on the fixed asset revaluation reserve (FARR). At present, £18,000 could be offset first against the £20,000 and only the excess of £2,000 written off to the profit and loss account. However, FRS 15 requires all of the £20,000 to be written off to profit and loss, if caused by economic factors, and in addition a reserve transfer is required to remove the £18,000 revaluation reserve to revenue reserves. This would also accord with FRS 3 when the £18,000 would also have to be recorded as part of the note of historical cost profits and losses, as it is realised.

The company will have to disclose the gross value of the fixed assets in the accounts (at value or cost); the accumulated depreciation written off; the market value of the investment properties and the movements of both the IPRR and the FARR.

(4) Bad debts

(a) Major customer – £200,000 (10 per cent of turnover)

Under the provisions of FRS 3, this would probably be classified as an exceptional item since it is clearly material and bad debts are normal activities of the business. However, its size is so large and abnormal that it should be disclosed separately if the financial statements are to disclose a true and fair view.

The debt would not fit the definition of extraordinary items which are outside ordinary activities and are argued to occur infrequently and have a high degree of abnormality. Therefore the debt should be written off above the line in calculating the company's earnings per share.

(b) Expropriation of the company's assets in Zenda – £100,000

This would clearly have been classified as an extraordinary item under SSAP 6 since it arose from an event outside the ordinary activities of the business. Expropriation of assets is not a normal event for the company, and the size of £100,000 is material. However FRS 3 would now require an exceptional treatment since the new definition of ordinary activities incorporates political changes.

As such, £100,000 should be written off to profit and loss and included in calculating the company's earnings per share. A separate note will be required to explain the details of exceptional items.

(5) Stock valuation

The valuation of stock is governed by SSAP 9 which defines cost as that expenditure incurred in the normal course of business to bring the stock to its present location and condition. The expenditure includes both material and conversion costs. The latter includes direct labour, production overheads and other overheads. The absorption of overheads has to be calculated according to a normal level of activity, thereby excluding abnormal fluctuations in activity. Costs are then compared with net realisable value and the lower figure is adopted to value the stock.

In this case normal activity would be 80,000 units of production per annum. The machine breakdown is ignored. Administration overheads are not included because they are not necessary to bring the stock to its present location or condition. Production overheads would be charged at £3.75 per unit (£300,000 ÷ 80,000 units). Therefore total unit costs would be £11.75 (£8 + £3.75) and the stock would be valued at cost of £58,750 (5,000 units × £11.75). No information is available on net realisable values but they will be assumed to be higher than £11.75 per unit.

As a result, administration costs of £100,000 and under-absorbed production overheads of £75,000 (20,000 units production below normal × £3.75) will be written off to the profit and loss account.

Solution 4 – Helene plc

The Financial Director
Helene plc
394 Dart Road
Edinlon E45 6YT

A.N. Adviser
Advisor & Co
Steep Hill
Edinlon E34 7FT

Date

Dear Sir

Helene plc – accounting principles year end 31 December 2001

With reference to your letter of 10 July, I have now completed my investigation into the three specific accounting areas of the company that you requested me to consider:

(1) Deferred taxation.

(2) Valuation of investments in subsidiaries.

(3) Acquisition of a freehold property.

I have considered each of these in terms of the accounting principles involved, the possible alternative courses of action available and a recommendation as to how to apply the accounting standards to ensure that the company maximises its net assets and earnings per share (EPS) in the short term.

(1) Deferred taxation

(a) Accounting principles

The purpose of deferred taxation is to ensure that the tax charge in the financial statements is matched to the accounting profit earned, regardless of the date of payment of the tax. It is provided by accountants under FRS 19 when timing differences emerge between taxable profit (as defined by the Inland Revenue) and accounting profit (as defined by UK Generally Accepted Accounting Principles). These differences do not alter the total tax paid, merely the timing of the payment of the tax. In Helene's case the difference is caused by the Inland Revenue granting accelerated capital allowances but disallowing the depreciation charged in the financial statements. The capital allowances (CAs) claimed have been greater than depreciation charged and thus taxable profit has been lower than accounting profit. This will, however, reverse in future years when depreciation starts to exceed CAs. Thus tax saved in the early years is compensated by increased tax in later years. The saving is therefore only temporary and in order to ensure that the overall tax charge matches with the accounting profit, an additional deferred tax charge needs to be created.

(b) Alternative courses of action

Under SSAP 15 there was no requirement to provide for all timing differences. The full provision basis has been the policy for Helene. Instead, SSAP 15 permitted companies to employ a partial provision approach and to simply provide for the amount of tax that was likely to be paid in the foreseeable future (three to four years). The full provision, however, had to be entered into the accounts as a contingent liability note to the balance sheet. From January 2002, under FRS 19, a full provision is required although if the time lags are material, the balance may be discounted to provide a more realistic value for the liability.

(c) The impact on net assets and EPS

By applying the rationale of SSAP 15 and only providing for those timing differences that are likely to crystallise in the foreseeable future, the company had an opportunity in the past to improve its net assets by releasing some of the full provision to reserves. In addition, it was probable that the current year's deferred tax charge could have been reduced, thereby helping to boost earnings per share. This would still be possible if the company adopts the discounting option, under FRS 19. It must be remembered, however, that the unwinding of discount in future years will reduce earnings per share.

If discounting were adopted, this will result in a prior year adjustment (PYA) under FRS 3 as it would represent a change in accounting policy. Reserves and comparisons would therefore have to be restated. In addition, the PYA should be included at the foot of the statement of total recognised gains and losses.

(2) Valuation of investments in subsidiaries

(a) Accounting principles
Parent company books

The investments in subsidiaries should be valued at cost less any impairment in the value of the investment. The main accounting principle is therefore applied in the decision as to whether or not an investment should be written down.

In Helene's case, the net assets of subsidiary A are only £0.5 million but the cost of investment is £2.4 million. There would appear to be an impairment in value. Thought should be given to the amount of write-down. However, as the parent controls the subsidiary it may be that the fall in asset values has been a deliberate policy by the parent and does not affect the value of the investment.

Group accounts

In the group accounts the difference between the cost of the investment and the fair value of the net assets acquired has been calculated as goodwill. The company has decided to capitalise goodwill for company A and subsequently amortise it over a period of five years. Thus a decision must be taken as to whether the five remaining years are a fair write-off period. If it is felt that the asset has been impaired in value, FRS 10 requires an immediate write-down to its net recoverable amount.

(b) Alternative courses of action
Parent company

Under SSAP 22, the parent could have left company A at its present cost and not written it down, using the argument that this is only a temporary fall in the value of the investment and not a permanent fall. FRS 10, however, requires a write-down whether or not the impairment is permanent or temporary. Companies B and C should clearly be left at their existing value or cost.

Group accounts

A write-down of goodwill to its recoverable amount will have the effect of reducing the EPS in the year of write-down but it will lead to higher EPS in the future because amortisation will be lower in future.

As regards net assets, they will be reduced by the amount of write-down but this will occur eventually anyway over a period of five years. To maximise net assets at present, no write-off should be recommended.

(c) The impact on net assets and EPS

Maximisation of EPS will be achieved if the company continues with the present policy and writes off goodwill over the next five years. Similarly, net assets are maximised if the company adopts that policy and does not immediately write down the goodwill.

(3) Acquisition of freehold property

(a) Accounting principles

Currently the asset is leased on an operating lease basis and rent is charged directly to the profit and loss account at £325,000 per annum. If the asset is acquired at £5 million and financed by a bank loan repayable in five equal annual instalments, then an asset and a liability are created with no effect on overall net assets. The asset would then be depreciated over its useful economic life.

Interest at 12 per cent on the loan will replace the rental charge in the profit and loss account as per working 1.

(b) Alternative courses of action

The company could perhaps argue that the total interest charges should be spread evenly over the life of the asset, giving a better matching of cost to asset usage. As a result, the profit and loss account will be charged considerably less in years 1 and 2 compared with the actual interest charge but this would reverse in years 3 to 5. However, under FRS 4 *Capital Instruments*, the finance cost should bear a constant rate to the outstanding amount. As this declines each year, so should the finance cost.

The policy of depreciation can vary depending on the method adopted. Also, if a considerable portion of the property is land it can be left on the balance sheet at cost and no depreciation is required. Under the recent Financial Reporting Review Panel's decision on the Forte accounts, if the company spends a considerable amount on refurbishment and maintenance, so that the property cannot in fact depreciate, or so that any depreciation charge would be insignificant, then a case can also be made for non-depreciation of buildings. However, under FRS 15 *Tangible Fixed Assets*, the buildings would need to be reviewed annually for any impairment.

(c) The impact on net assets and EPS

If the company argues that no depreciation is necessary on the property then obviously both EPS and net assets are given a boost. However, the increased interest charge, even if a straight-line approach is adopted, will lead to a reduction in EPS for five years. In addition, the asset and loan will have to be created but there should be no effect on overall net assets. Furthermore, net assets will not change on the repayment of the loan. However, under FRS 15 tangible fixed assets, the buildings would need to be reviewed annually for any impairment.

Working 1

	Rental charge	Interest charge 12% *	Interest straight line
	£'000	£'000	£'000
Year 1	325	600	360
2	325	480	360
3	325	360	360
4	325	240	360
5	325	120	360
	1,625	1,800	1,800

	£
* 12% × £5,000,000	600,000
12% × £4,000,000	480,000
12% × £3,000,000	360,000
12% × £2,000,000	240,000
12% × £1,000,000	120,000
	1,800,000

Solution 5 – Northbrook plc

(a) *Issues to be considered*

Deferred consideration – £250,000

Key issues to consider are as follows:

(1) Fair value of consideration

This cash payment in two years' time is certain and therefore should be included as part of the fair value of consideration. It should be provided in the accounts.

(2) Possible discounting to net present value

As the consideration is not due for two years there is a strong case for discounting the £250,000 to its net present value. A weighted average discount rate would be appropriate.

Contingent consideration – £500,000

If part of the purchase consideration is contingent on the occurrence or non-occurrence of one or more uncertain future events, it is necessary to consider whether the future event is probable or possible.

Under FRS 12 *Provisions, Contingent Liabilities and Contingent Assets*, if it is probable that the £500,000 will be due, i.e. profits before tax of Irving Ltd for the three years will exceed £1,250,000, then the £500,000 should be provided as part of the fair value exercise. On the other hand, if it is no more than possible that the consideration will be paid then it should merely be disclosed in the notes as a contingent liability.

	Likely future profits £
2002 (329,000 + 10%)	362,000
2003 (+ 10%)	398,000
2004 (+ 10%)	438,000
	1,198,000

As this is less than the £1,250,000 required to earn the £500,000 payment it seems to fall under the possible category.

Since the £500,000 is clearly material the following facts should be disclosed in a note:

- The nature of the event.
- The uncertainties surrounding the event.
- An estimate of the financial effect of the event or a statement to the effect that it is not practicable to make such an estimate.

(b) *Consolidated balance sheet as at 30 September 2001*

	£'000	£'000
Fixed assets		
Intangible assets – goodwill	385	
Tangible assets (4,512 + 1,777 + 1,250(J3) – 723(J3))	6,816	
		7,201
Current assets		
Stocks (1,891 + 829 – 750 (J4))	1,970	
Debtors (1,077 + 600 + 300(J2) + 947(J4) – 20(J7))	2,904	
Cash (57 + 500)	557	
	5,431	
Creditors: amounts falling due within one year		
(1,519 + 1,371 + 360(J3) + 375(J5))	(3,625)	
Net current assets		1,806
Total assets less current liabilities		9,007
Creditors: amounts falling due after more than one year		
(250(J1) + 305(J3))		(555)
		8,452
Capital and reserves		
Called-up share capital		1,000
Reserves		7,064
		8,064
Minority interests		388
		8,452

Journal entries – Northbrook plc

			£'000	£'000
(1)	Dr	Investment in Irving Ltd	250	
	Cr	Creditors		250

Being the deferred consideration due on the acquisition of Irving Ltd, due on 1 June 2003.

			£'000	£'000
(2)	Dr	Debtors	300	
	Cr	Investment in Irving Ltd		236
		Reserves		64

Being 80% of the final dividend of £375,000 due from Irving Ltd in respect of the year ended 30 September 2001 split between that paid out of pre-acquisition profits and that which is post acquisition (see working 1)

			£'000	£'000
(3)	Dr	Tangible fixed assets	1,250	
		Reserves (balancing figure)	138	
	Cr	Current liabilities		360
		Long-term liability		305
		Accumulated depreciation		723

Being the capitalisation of a finance lease to bring the accounting policy into line with SSAP 21. No prior year adjustment has been made and the £138,000 alteration has been debited to reserves (see working 2).

			£'000	£'000
(4)	Dr	Cost of sales	750	
	Cr	Sales £1.2m × £750,000/£950,000		947
	Dr	Debtors	947	
	Cr	Stock		750

Being the recording of turnover and related cost of sales in relation to the long-term contract, in accordance with the revised version of SSAP 9.

(5)	Dr	Reserves – pre-acquisition	295	
		– post-acquisition	80	
	Cr	Creditors		375

Being the final dividend proposed by Irving Ltd for the year ended 30 September 2001.

(6)	Dr	Reserves – pre-acquisition	225	
	Cr	Provision for reorganisation costs		225

Being costs required to reorganise the business of Irving Ltd at the date of acquisition.

(This is no longer permitted by FRS 7 and has been excluded from the final solution)

(7)	Dr	Reserves – post-acquisition	20	
	Cr	Provision for bad debts		20

Being additional provision required for the year.

Workings

(1) Dividends ex Irving Ltd

	Northbrook £'000		Irving £'000
Final dividend			375
Held by Northbrook (80%)	300		
Lower of post-acquisition (1.6.01 – 30.9.01)			
1/3 = 100		1/3 = 125	
or note (2) post-acq. profits 100 – 20 bad debt × 80%	64	or 100 × 80%	80
Pre-acquisition	236		295

(2) Finance leases

	£'000
Original cost 1.10.98	1,250
Total repayments	1,800
Finance charges	550

	Opening balance £'000	Paid £'000	Liability £'000	Finance charge £'000	Closing balance £'000	
30.9.99	1,250	360	890	220	1,110	40% Sum of the
30.9.00	1,110	360	750	165	915	30% digits
30.9.01	915	360	555	110	665	20% (assuming
30.9.02	665	360	305	55	360	10% rentals paid
1.10.02	360	360				in advance)

Creditor at 30.9.01	£'000
Current	360
Long-term 360 – 55	305
	665

	£'000
Depreciation 25% reducing balance (3 years) 313 + 234 + 176 =	723
Net book value 30.9.99	527
	1,250

Effect on reserves of capitalising the finance lease	£'000
Finance charges 1999 to 2001 (220 + 165 + 110)	495
Depreciation 1999 to 2001 (313 + 234 + 176)	723
	1,218
Previous charge to profit and loss – repayments	1,080
	138

(3) Consolidated workings

Cost of control (80%)

	£'000		£'000
Investment in subsidiary	1,950	Share capital – I	200
Investment in Irving Ltd (J1)	250	Dividend ex pre-acq. profits (J2)	236
		Reserves	1,352
		Goodwill	412
	2,200		2,200

Reserves

	£'000		£'000
Minority interest		Balance – N	6,968
(20% × (2,085 – 375 – 20))	338	– I	2,085
Proposed dividend		Dividend post-acq. ex Irving (J2)	64
(Pre 295 + 80 (J5))	375	Sales ex long-term contract (J4)	947
Capitalisation of fin.lease (J3)	138		
Cost of sales ex long-term contract (J4)	750		
Provision for bad debts (J6)	20		
Cost of control			
((2,085 – 100 – 295) × 80%)	1,352		
Goodwill amortisation	27		
Consolidated balance sheet	7,064		
	10,064		10,064

Minority interests (20%)

	£'000		£'000
Consolidated balance sheet	388	Share capital – I	50
		Reserves	338
	388		388

Goodwill

	£'000		£'000
Cost of control	412	Reserves (1/3 yr × 1/5 × 412)	27
		Consolidated balance sheet	385
	412		412

Solution 6 – Sheerwater Ltd

(a) Profit and loss extract for years ended 30 June

		2001	2002	2003	2004	2005
		£	£	£	£	£
Turnover	(W3)	20,000	20,000	20,000	20,000	20,000
Cost of sales	(W3)	20,000	16,000	16,000	14,000	14,000
Gross profit		–	4,000	4,000	6,000	6,000
Pension cost	(W1)	9,500	10,750	10,750	10,750	10,750
Depreciation	(W2)	25,000	25,000	25,000	25,000	25,000
Interest payable	(W2)	23,283	19,912	15,861	10,993	4,951
Profit on disposal of fixed asset	(W4)	68,750	–	–	–	–

(b) Balance sheet extract as at 30 June

		2001	2002	2003	2004	2005
		£	£	£	£	£
Tangible fixed assets						
Leased asset at cost	(W2)	125,000	125,000	125,000	125,000	125,000
Accumulated depreciation		25,000	50,000	75,000	100,000	125,000
		100,000	75,000	50,000	25,000	–
Current assets						
Stocks and WIP	(W3)	5,000	14,000	8,000	4,000	–
Debtors	(W3)	20,000	20,000	20,000	20,000	20,000
Prepayments	(W1)	–	1,250	2,500	1,250	–
Creditors: amounts falling due within one year	(W5)	20,088	24,139	29,007	35,049	–
Creditors: amounts falling due after more than one year	(W5)	88,195	64,056	35,049	–	–

(c) Notes to the accounts – extract

Note 1 Accounting policies

(1) Pension costs

The company operates a defined benefit final pay scheme for its employees. The scheme is reviewed triennially by XYZ and actuaries, and the date of the latest review was 30 June 2001. Pension contributions are held in an externally administered fund. The accounting policy adopted in accordance with SSAP 24 is to spread the pension cost evenly to the profit and loss account over the average service lifetime of the employees in the scheme.

(2) Finance leases

Assets acquired under a finance lease are included as fixed assets in the financial statements in accordance with SSAP 21. They are included at cost less depreciation over their useful economic lives. Interest payable is disclosed in the profit and loss account including the interest element within the leasing payments.

(3) Stocks and work in progress

Sales and cost of sales are recognised during the course of a long-term contract on a partial completion basis. Stocks are valued at the lower of cost and net realisable value.

(4) Disposal of a previously revalued fixed asset

The profit on disposal has been calculated as the difference between the sales proceeds and the carrying value in the balance sheet. Any previous surplus is included in arriving at the profit and is transferred to the profit and loss account from the revaluation reserve.

Workings

(1) Pension costs

	£
Regular cost 9.5% × £100,000	9,500
Variation £5,000 ÷ 4 years	1,250 (2002 to 2005)
	10,750

		SSAP 24			FRS 17		
	Funded	*P & L*	*Prepayment*	*Funded*	*Provision*	*P & L*	*STRGL*
	£	£	£	£	£	£	£
2001	9,500	9,500	–	9,500	(5,000)	9,500	(5000)
2002	12,000	10,750	1,250	12,000	(2,500)	9,500	–
2003	12,000	10,750	2,500	12,000	nil	9,500	–
2004	9,500	10,750	1,250	9,500	nil	9,500	–
2005	9,500	10,750	–	9,500	nil	9,500	–

P.S. Under FRS 17 *Retirement Benefits*, the deficit would be charged to the reserves immediately and would also appear as a recognised loss in the statement of total recognised gains and losses. The standard will apply from June 2003.

(2) Leased asset – per SSAP 21

	£	
Total rentals 10 × £20,000	200,000	in arrears
Fair value of the asset	125,000	
Finance charge	75,000	

Year beginning	*Opening balance*	*Half-year interest*	*Paid*	*Half-year balance*	*Half-year interest*	*Paid*	*Interest to P&L*
	£	£	£	£	£	£	£
1.7.00	125,000	12,025	20,000	117,025	11,258	20,000	23,283
30.6.01	108,283	10,417	20,000	98,700	9,495	20,000	19,912
30.6.02	88,195	8,484	20,000	76,679	7,377	20,000	15,861
30.6.03	64,056	6,162	20,000	50,218	4,831	20,000	10,993
30.6.04	35,049	3,372	20,000	18,421	1,772	20,000	5,144
30.6.05	193	(193)					(193)
		40,267	100,000		34,733	100,000	75,000

Depreciation based on a straight-line approach should be calculated to spread the £125,000 over the lower of the total lease term and estimated useful life (both five years) = £25,000 per annum.

(3) Long-term work in progress – per SSAP 9

Contract cost

		£			£
2001	Costs incurred	25,000	2001	Cost of sales*	20,000
				Balance c/d	5,000
		25,000			25,000
2002	Balance b/d	5,000	2002	Cost of sales	16,000
	Costs incurred	25,000		Balance c/d	14,000
		30,000			30,000
2003	Balance b/d	14,000	2003	Cost of sales	16,000
	Costs incurred	10,000		Balance c/d	8,000
		24,000			24,000
2004	Balance b/d	8,000	2004	Cost of sales	14,000
	Costs incurred	10,000		Balance c/d	4,000
		18,000			18,000
2005	Balance b/d	4,000	2005	Cost of sales	14,000
	Costs incurred	10,000			
		14,000			14,000

* No profit to be taken

Contract profit and loss

		£			£
2001	Cost of sales	20,000	2001	Value of work done (turnover)	20,000
2002	Cost of sales	16,000	2002	Value of work done	20,000
2003	Cost of sales	16,000	2003	Value of work done	20,000
2004	Cost of sales	14,000	2004	Value of work done	20,000
2005	Cost of sales	14,000	2005	Value of work done	20,000

Contract debtor

		£			£
2001	Value of work done	20,000	2002	Bank	20,000
2002	Value of work done	20,000		Balance c/d	20,000
		40,000			40,000
2002	Balance b/d	20,000	2003	Bank	20,000
2003	Value of work done	20,000		Balance c/d	20,000
		40,000			40,000
2003	Balance b/d	20,000	2004	Bank	20,000
2004	Value of work done	20,000		Balance c/d	20,000
		40,000			40,000
2004	Balance b/d	20,000	2005	Bank	20,000
2005	Value of work done	20,000		Balance c/d	20,000
		40,000			40,000

(4) Gain/disposal of revalued asset

	£	£
Proceeds on disposal of an asset 1.7.00		200,000
Revalued book value 1.7.00		
Cost 1.7.97	100,000	
Depreciation 10% × 2 yrs to 30.6.99	20,000	
	80,000	
Revalued	70,000	
	150,000	
Depreciation 1 yr × 1/8 to 30.6.00	18,750	
		131,250
Profit on disposal		68,750
Reversal of surplus on revaluation reserve		70,000
		138,750

Note: Per FRS 3 and FRS 15 only £68,750 should be credited to the profit and loss account and the £70,000 should be a reserve transfer from revaluation reserve to the profit and loss account.

(5) Creditors – leased asset

Amounts falling due within one year

		£
2001	£40,000 – £19,912	20,088
2002	£40,000 – £15,861	24,139
2003	£40,000 – £10,993	29,007
2004	£40,000 – £4,951	35,049

Amounts falling due after more than one year

		£
2001	£120,000 – £31,805	88,195
2002	£ 80,000 – £15,944	64,056
2003	£ 40,000 – £ 4,951	35,049

Solution 7 – Sofa Ltd

Profit and loss account for the year ended 31 December 1998

	£'000	£'000
Turnover		140,000
Cost of sales (W1)		(69,620)
Gross profit		70,380
Distribution costs (W1)	26,472	
Administration expenses (W1)	17,648	
		44,120
Operating profit		26,260
Interest payable and similar charges (14,250 + 500 (W6))		(14,750)
Profit on ordinary activities before tax		11,510
Tax on ordinary activities (W4)		(5,860)
Profit on ordinary activities after tax		5,650
Dividends		
Preference dividends (W5)	545.455	
Ordinary dividends (750 + (W3) 750)	1,500	
		2,045.455
Retained profit for the year		3,604.545
Retained profit as at 1.1.1998	10,250	
Prior year adjustment	(120)	
Retained profit as at 1.01.1998		10,130
Retained profit as at 31.12.1998		13,734.545

Balance sheet as at 31 December 1998

	£'000	£'000
Tangible fixed assets (W2)		12,440
Current assets		
Stocks (3,000 + 500 (W6))	3,500	
Debtors (61,750 – 7,500 (W6) + 1,100)	55,350	
Cash at bank (400 + 7,000 (W6) + 5,500 (W5) – 250 (W5))	12,650	
	71,500	
Creditors: amounts falling due within one year		
(40,000 + 750 (W3) + 5,800 (W4) + 500 (W6) + 1,000)	(48,050)	
Net current assets		23,450
		35,890
Provisions for liabilities and charges (W4)		(360)
		35,530
Capital and reserves		
Called-up share capital (15,000 + 5,000)		20,000
Share premium (1,000 + 500 (W5)		1,500
Capital redemption reserve (0 + 295.455 (W5))		295.455
Profit and loss account		13,734.545
		35,530

Workings

W1 Cost allocation

	Cost of sales	Distribution	Administration	Total		
	£'000	£	£	£		
Employee costs	17,100	10,260	6,840	34,200	(5:3:2)	Note 1
Overheads	26,000	15,600	10,400	52,000	(5:3:2)	Note 1
Depreciation – property						
(2,000/50 years)	20	12	8	40	(5:3:2)	Note 2
Depreciation – plant						
(15% x 2,600)	195	117	78	390	(5:3:2)	Note 2
Depreciation – motor vehicles						
(20% x 6,800)	680	408	272	1,360	(5:3:2)	Note 2
Depreciation – fixtures						
(10% x 2,500)	125	75	50	250	(5:3:2)	Note 2
Purchases	25,500			25,500		
Opening stocks	3,000			3,000		
Closing stocks	(3,000)			(3,000)		
	69,620	26,472	17,648	113,740		

W2 Tangible Fixed Assets

	Freehold land	Freehold property	Plant & machinery	Motor vehicles	Fixtures & fittings	Total	
Cost	£'000	£	£	£	£	£	
At 1.1.1998	2,500	2,000	4,000	6,800	2,500	17,800	
Accumulated depreciation							
At 1.1.1998	–	–	1,400	1,360	440	3,200	Note 2
Charge for the year	–	40	390	1,360	250	2,040	
Prior year adjustment	–	120*	–	–	–	120	
	–	160	1,790	2,720	690	5,360	
Net book value at 31.12.1998	2,500	1,840	2,210	4,080	1,810	12,440	

* Should be treated, from 2001 on, as a change in estimate

W3 Dividends

15m shares x 5p = £750,000   Note 4

W4 Taxation

Corporation tax	5,800,000	Dr Profit and loss account, Cr Balance sheet	Note 5
Deferred tax	60,000	(£1.2m x 30%) = £360,000 B/S – £300,000 OB	
	5,860,000		

W5 Redeemable preference shares – FRS 4

				£	
Total payments	– annual dividend	(10 years x 5% x 5m shares)		2,500,000	
	– redemption	(5m shares x £1.20)		6,000,000	
				8,500,000	Note 6
Net proceeds received	– gross	(5m shares x £1.15)	5,750,000		
	– issue costs		(250,000)		
				5,500,000	
Total finance costs				3,000,000	

$$\frac{N(n + 1)}{2} = \frac{10(10 + 1)}{2} = 55$$

Year	Opening balance		Finance cost	Payments	Closing balance
1998	5.5m	10/55 x 3m	545,455	(250,000)	5,795,455
1999	5,795,455	9/55 x 3m	490,909	(250,000)	6,036,364
2000	6,036,364	8/55 x 3m	436,364	(250,000)	6,222,728

W6   Reporting substance – FRS 5

Consignment stocks   Rights and rewards with SOFA Ltd

(Can sell or transfer to another distributor, it cannot be forced to return the furniture)

Dr	Stocks	500,000	
Cr	Creditors		500,000

Factoring of debt   No recourse, therefore debtors are extinguished as risks are now with the finance company

Dr	Bank	7,000,000	
	Finance costs	500,000	
Cr	Debtors		7,500,000

Solution 8 – XYZ plc

To: Assistant accountant
From: Management accountant   Date
Subject: Accounting treatments proposed for items (a) to (d)

(a) This is a material contract at 'arm's length' in which our managing director has a significant interest. As such, it may be a transaction falling under the disclosure rules of FRS 8 *Related Party Disclosures*. The important factor in deciding whether the two parties are related is the substance of their relationship. Further enquiries need to be made to decide whether XYZ plc can influence the financial and operating policies of LMN Ltd, which is unlikely on the facts disclosed so far. If, however, one of the parties to a transaction is subject to control (LMN), and the other to influence (XYZ), from the same source (managing director), then this transaction should be treated as a related party matter. A director is a 'deemed' related party under FRS 8 and therefore these transactions would probably appear to meet the FRS definition. Much depends on the commercial substance of the transaction, which may raise the presumption that the parties are related (unless there is evidence to the contrary) if key management of the two businesses are related and can act in concert to influence the reporting entity. If LMN is just a customer of XYZ, this is not a related party transaction, but if there is a possibility that transactions may not be at 'arm's length' in the future, readers of the accounts should be put on their guard that this normal assumption may not always hold true. Disclosure should be a note detailing names, relationship, amount, the transaction, and amounts due at the year end, and details of any provision for bad debts or bad debts written off as well as a written narrative about any unusual aspects of the transaction.

(b) GHI Ltd sold goods to XYZ plc for a profit of £10 million. This inter-group trading should be cancelled out on consolidation since it is not part of group turnover sold outside the group, nor is it part of group cost of sales. The profit element in the stock of XYZ should be deducted from the group stock, and normally from the group reserves, by debiting group reserves and crediting group stock. However, 20 per cent of the profit belongs to the minority interest in GHI. Thus, only 80 per cent of the profit should be debited to group reserves and 20 per cent debited to minority interest. Under FRS 2 *Accounting For Subsidiary Undertakings* the 20 per cent profit attributable to minority interests should be recorded as follows:

	Debit	Credit
	£m	£m
Consolidated reserves	8	
Minority interests	2	
Stock		10

(c) There is certainly ample precedent for valuing brands and bringing them onto the balance sheet, and the accounting entries suggested would be quite correct. RHM plc incorporated their homegrown brands 'Mr Kiplings Cakes' and 'Hovis' bread on to their balance sheet several years ago for £640m. However, before the brand can be treated in this way, XYZ must establish that it is an asset with a reliable valuation, and that the item can be separated from the normal goodwill of the business. For a brand to be an asset it is expected to be more than just a trade name, but to stem from a number of factors associated with the product which suggests an income stream continuing into the future (FRS 5). It is often difficult to identify the earnings of a single branded product, and even more difficult to justify estimates of future earnings. Items such as market share, competition and market conditions are very difficult to predict, and the calculation of a present value for the income stream would need to be carefully substantiated if the auditors are to accept the figures.

However FRS 10 *Goodwill and Intangible Assets* now insists that before homegrown intangibles are capitalised there must be a clearly defined market value for those assets and they must be sold in an active market.

(d) *Prima facie* a profit of £6 million has been made by this transaction and this should be disclosed as an exceptional item in the profit and loss account. FRS 3 states that the profit or loss on disposal of an asset should be accounted for in the profit and loss account for the period in which the disposal occurs, as the difference between the net sale proceeds and the net carrying amount of the asset, whether historical cost or a valuation. The revaluation gain was recognised in previous years and thus cannot be shown as part of the profit for this year. Otherwise the gain would be incorporated twice within the performance statements. This gain has, however, now been realised, which confirms the gain recorded by the revaluation, and it should be transferred from revaluation to disposable reserves since it is now available for distribution as a dividend. The transfer is disclosed in the reconciliation of movements in shareholders' funds.

Solution 9 – Wood Group plc

Group structure

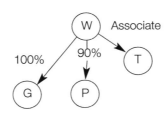

(a) **Wood Group plc – group profit and loss account for the year ended 31 October 2001**

	£'000	£'000
Turnover		
Continuing operations:		
ongoing	108,535	
acquisitions	16,045	
	124,580	
Discontinued operations	30,800	
		155,380
Cost of sales		(123,762)
Gross profit		31,618
Distribution costs	(12,290)	
Administrative expenses	(12,028)	
		(24,318)
		7,300
Other operating income		500
Income from interests in associated undertakings		2,040
Operating profit		
Continuing operations:		
ongoing	9,348	
acquisitions	905	
Discontinued operations	(413)	
		9,840
Continuing operations:		
Profit on disposal of tangible fixed assets	913	
Loss on disposal of investments	(255)	
	658	
Discontinued operations:		
Loss on sale of operations	(1,779)	
		(1,121)
Subtotal carried over…		8,719

Subtotal brought over...		8,719
Income from investments	928	
Interest payable	(806)	
		122
Profit on ordinary activities before taxation		8,841
Tax on profit on ordinary activities		
(2,666 + 510 associates)		(3,176)
Profit on ordinary activities after tax		5,665
Minority interests		
Equity		(221)
Non-equity ((600,000 × 5% = 30,000) × 20%)		(6)
Profit attributable to members of the parent company		5,438
Dividends		
Finance cost of non-equity shares (460,000* × $^4/_{10}$)		(184)
Retained profit for the year		5,254

*	Payments: 2m + (4 yrs × 7% × 2m dividends)	2.56m
	Net proceeds: 2.2m – 0.1m issue costs	2.10m
		0.46m

Wood Group plc – group balance sheet at 31 October 2001

	£'000	£'000
Fixed assets		
Intangible assets		1,503
Tangible assets		23,163
Investments: Associated undertakings	2,103	
Other trade	1,643	
		3,746
		28,412
Current assets		
Stock		19,071
Debtors		14,964
Cash at bank and in hand		6,440
		40,475
Creditors: amounts falling due within		
one year (working 1)		18,149
Net current assets		22,326
Total assets less current liabilities		50,738
Creditors: amounts falling due after more than		
one year (working 2)		(7,174)
Provision for liabilities and charges		(1,219)
Accruals and deferred income		
Deferred government grants		(1,511)
		40,834
Minority interests (working 3)		
Equity	330	
Non-equity	126	
		(456)
		40,378

Capital and reserves

Called-up share capital	11,200	
Share premium account (3,670 – 405 issue costs)	3,265	
Revaluation reserve	677	
Other reserves (184 – 140)	44	
Profit and loss account (working 4)	25,192	
Shareholders' funds	40,378	
Equity	38,234	
Non-equity	2,144	(Working 5)
	40,378	

Workings

(1) **Creditors: amounts falling due within one year**

	£'000
Bank overdraft	1,211
Instalments on finance leases	554
Trade creditors	13,935
Corporation tax	2,309
Proposed dividend – preference share	140
	18,149

(2) **Amounts falling due after more than one year**

	£'000
Loans repayable 1.1.05	6,542
Instalments on finance leases	632
	7,174

(3) **Minority interest**

	£'000
Preference dividend (5% × 600,000 × 20%)	6
Preference shares (20% × 600,000)	120
Non-equity interest	126
Equity interest (balancing figure)	330
	456

(4) **Profit/loss account**

	£'000
Balance per question	25,376
Finance costs on preference shares (0.46m × $^4/_{10}$)	(184)
	25,192

(5) **Shareholders' funds**

	£'000
Non-equity funds	
Preference capital	2,000
Other reserves (184 – 140 pref. div.)	44
Share premium (200 – 100 issue costs)	100
	2,144

Equity funds

Ordinary shares	9,200
Share premium	3,165
Revaluation reserve	677
Profit and loss	25,192
	38,234

(b) Information to be disclosed in the group financial statements re the acquisition of Good plc. These are contained in FRS 6 as follows:

    (i)   Names of the combining parties

    (ii) Number and class of shares issued together with other consideration

    (iii) Method of business combination – i.e. merger or acquisition accounting

    (iv) Fair value table disclosing details of book value of net assets acquired, adjustments and fair values, including goodwill

    (v) Significant changes to accounting policies to achieve uniformity.

As well as FRS 6, FRS 1 requires details of the effects on the cash flow statement by separately disclosing the cash consideration from the net cash balances taken over on acquisition.

Under FRS 3 the post-acquisition results of an acquisition are recorded separate from, but part of, continuing operations.